AF352473

In His Voice

In His Voice

<hr>

Maurice Blanchot's Affair with the Neuter

DAVID APPELBAUM

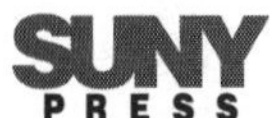

Published by
STATE UNIVERSITY OF NEW YORK PRESS
Albany

© 2016 State University of New York

For information, contact
State University of New York Press
www.sunypress.edu

Production, Laurie D. Searl
Marketing, Michael Campochiaro

Library of Congress Cataloging-in-Publication Data

Appelbaum, David.
    In his voice : Maurice Blanchot's affair with the neuter / David Appelbaum.
        pages cm
    Includes bibliographical references and index.
    ISBN 978-1-4384-5979-0 (hardcover : alk. paper)
    ISBN 978-1-4384-5981-3 (e-book)
    1. Whole and parts (Philosophy)   2. Perspective (Philosophy)
3. Nothing (Philosophy)   4. Blanchot, Maurice.   I. Title.

BD396.A67 2016.
843'.912—dc23   2015012445

10 9 8 7 6 5 4 3 2 1

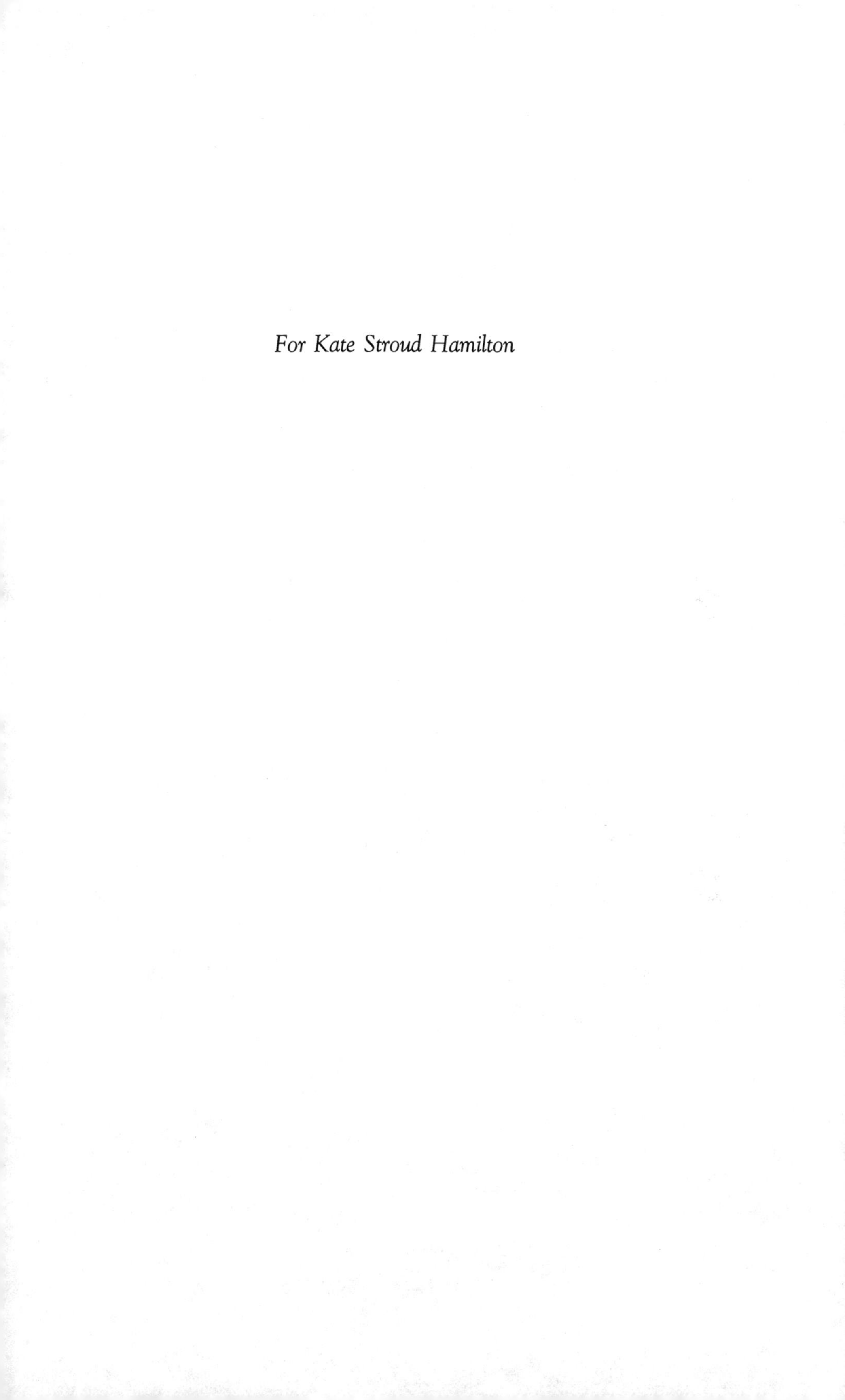

For Kate Stroud Hamilton

Ah this blind voice, and these moments of held breath when all listen wildly, and the voice that begins to fumble again, without knowing what it's looking for and again the tiny silence and the listening again, for what, no one knows, a sign of life perhaps, that must be it, a sign of life escaping someone, and bound to be denied if it came, that's it surely, if only all that could stop, there'd be peace, no, too good to be believed, the listening would go on, for the voice to begin again, for a sign of life, for some one to betray himself, or for something else, anything, what else can there be but signs of life . . .

—Beckett, The Unnamable

Contents

Preface

In His Voice: Maurice Blanchot's Affair with the Neuter has a twofold aim. The first is to deepen a post-phenomenological investigation of authorial voice, the voice that appears on the scene of writing. The second is to utilize as frame and resource Maurice Blanchot's discoveries vis-à-vis voice. They represent crossings or chiasma between his thinking and my own. His prolonged fascination reveals, in its principal insight, that the writer's voice in a literary work lacks a direct presentation and has one given in response to a second voice—the other's voice or the otherwise than voice. Only with this responsiveness does the singularity of authorial voice make its appearance.

Blanchot conceives of the alterity as a murmurous null point of vocalization. It is the sirens' song, with allusion to Homer, or the cacophonous resonance of unadorned being, the *il y a* of Levinas, a motile chaos that precedes subjectivity, consciousness, and the properly human. Normally suppressed in the name of linguistical efficacy and worldly reality, its irrepressibility is the quilting point of literature since Romanticism. Writers such as Hölderlin, Rilke, Kafka, Mallarmé, René Char, and Beckett lead Blanchot to speak of the authorial voice that embodies otherness as *the neuter*. The neuter voice, avoiding the repressive tendencies both of everyday language and philosophical discourse, reveals a menace to our appropriation of being and the order of things. Confronting it as reader, one falls under an exigency quite different from that of worldly comportment.

In accordance with current views, voice itself also has a twofold nature. It declares, yielding statements about the world, and it performs, presenting enactments of what it has power to do. To secure its signature, authorial voice is faced with a paradoxical task in relation to the alterity that speaks through and constitutes it. Since no statement of what lies beyond meaning is possible, it relies on performance to do the trick. Thus, the "logic" of how to present a performance of inscription is never far from my concern. By the same token, naked criticism, analysis, and explication of Blanchot's texts are less useful and more peripheral facets of the current study. Instead, it would debut an exemplary performance of the scene of writing, who, where, and what takes place—with Maurice Blanchot as designated writer.

Abbreviations

Maurice Blanchot

AO   *Awaiting Oblivion*. Tr. John Gregg (Lincoln, University of Nebraska Press, 1997)

F   *Friendship*. Tr. Elizabeth Rottenberg (Stanford, Stanford University Press, 1997)

FP   *Faux Pas*. Tr. Charlotte Mandell (Stanford: Stanford University Press, 2001)

I   *The Instant of My Death* (with *Demeure: Fiction and Testimony* by Jacques Derrida). Tr. Elizabeth Rottenberg (Stanford, Stanford University Press, 2000)

IC   *The Infinite Conversation*. Tr. Susan Hanson (Minneapolis, University of Minnesota Press, 1993)

LM   *The Last Man*. Tr. Lydia Davis (New York: Columbia University Press, 1987)

SL   *The Space of Literature*. Tr. Ann Smock (Lincoln, University of Nebraska Press, 1982)

The Station Hill Blanchot Reader. Ed. George Quasha, Tr. Paul Auster, Lydia Davis, and Robert Lamberton (Barrytown, NY, Station Hill Press, 1998): This anthology includes translations of *Thomas the Obscure* (TO), *Death Sentence* (DS), *The Madness of the Day* (MD), *When the Time Comes* (WTC), and *The One Who Was Standing Apart from Me* (TOW).

SNB   *The Step Not Beyond.* Tr. Lycette Nelson (Albany, SUNY Press, 1982)

UC   *The Unavowable Community.* Tr. Pierre Joris (Barrytown, NY, Station Hill Press, 1988)

WD   *The Writing of the Disaster.* Tr. Ann Smock (Lincoln, University of Nebraska Press, 1986)

WF   *The Work of Fire.* Tr. Charlotte Mandell (Stanford, Stanford University Press, 1995)

Jacques Derrida

A   *Aporias.* Tr. Thomas Dutoit (Stanford: Stanford University Press, 1993)

AL   *Acts of Literature.* Ed. Derek Attridge (New York: Routledge, 2002)

D   *Dissemination.* Tr. Barbara Johnson (Chicago: University of Chicago Press, 1981)

DE   *Demeure: Fiction and Testimony* (with *The Instant of My Death*, by Maurice Blanchot). Tr. Elizabeth Rottenberg (Stanford: Stanford University Press, 2000)

EO   *The Ear of the Other: Otobiography, Transference, Translation.* Tr. Peggy Kamuf (Lincoln: University of Nebraska Press, 1988)

G   *Glas.* Tr. John P. Leavey Jr. and Richard Rand (Lincoln: University of Nebraska Press, 1986)

GD   *The Gift of Death.* Tr. David Wills (Chicago: University of Chicago Press, 1995)

MB   *Memoirs of the Blind.* Tr. Pascale-Anne Brault and Michael Naas (Chicago: University of Chicago Press, 1993)

P   *Parages.* Tr. Tom Conley, James Hulbert, John P. Leavey, and Avital Ronell (Stanford: Stanford University Press, 2011)

PM   *Paper Machine.* Tr. Rachel Bowlby (Stanford: Stanford University Press, 2005)

SM   *Specters of Marx: The State of the Debt, the Work of Mourning, and the New International.* Tr. Peggy Kamuf (New York: Routledge, 1994)

SP   *Speech on Phenomena and Other Essays on Husserl's Theory of Signs.* Tr. David B. Allison (Evanston: Northwestern University Press, 1973)

WM   *The Work of Mourning.* Tr. Pascale-Anne Brault and Michael Naas (Chicago: University of Chicago Press, 2001)

Emmanuel Levinas

EE   *Existence and Existents.* Tr. Alfonso Lingis (Pittsburgh: Duquesne University Press, 2001)

EN   *Entre Nous.* Tr. Michael B. Smith and Barbara Harshav (New York: Columbia University Press, 1998)

OB   *Otherwise than Being: or, Beyond Essence.* Tr. Alphonso Lingis (Pittsburgh: Duquesne University Press, 1998)

OG   *Of God Who Comes to Mind.* Tr. Bettina Bergo (Stanford: Stanford University Press, 1998)

PN   *Proper Names.* Tr. Michael B. Smith (Stanford: Stanford University Press, 1996)

TI   *Totality and Infinity: An Essay on Exteriority.* Tr. Alphonso Lingis (Pittsburgh: Duquesne University Press, 1961)

Martin Heidegger

BT   *Being and Time.* Tr. Joan Stambaugh (Albany: SUNY Press, 2010)

OWL   *On the Way to Language.* Tr. Peter D. Hertz (New York: Harper and Row, 1971)

PLT   *Poetry, Language, Thought.* Tr. Albert Hofstadter (New York: Harper and Row, 1971)

Others

AC   Leclaire, Serge, *A Child Is Being Killed.* Tr. Marie-Claude Hays (Stanford: Stanford University Press, 1998)

IE   Bataille, Georges, *Inner Experience.* Tr. Stuart Kendall (Albany: SUNY Press, 2014)

MB   Foucault, Michel, *Maurice Blanchot: The Thought from Outside.* In *Foucault/Blanchot.* Tr. Jeffrey Mehlman and Brian Massumi (New York: Zone Books, 1990)

TIC   Nancy, Jean-Luc, *The Inoperative Community.* Tr. Peter Connor, Lisa Barbus, Michael Holland, and Simona Sawhney (Minneapolis: University of Minnesota Press, 1991)

Introduction

The present study offers a close reading of Maurice Blanchot's texts. It keeps in mind his counsel to read lightly and without recourse to a critical mind that burrows down for "the crux of the matter." "Close" is measured in degrees of proximity, a perilous word since Blanchot takes it to mean "touching not presence, but rather difference" (AO 60). Different moods or attunements help keep closeness at arm's length, like annoyingly close, threateningly close, tantalizingly close. I mean close as interior to the work signed by Blanchot, and, therefore, near to heart, dear, a privileged invest-ment, an expense.

Lightness dictates a pursuit of traces of the signing as they appear—perhaps aimlessly. This sounds like Heidegger's lingering over thought since philosophy doesn't have to get anywhere, since there is no ready-made des-tination. In Blanchot's work is Heidegger's ghost, and Blanchot's confron-tation with the repeated phantomization positions his thinking. Reading Blanchot is reading the concatenation attracted to the epochal event of *Being and Time*.

The material is based on a single, probably unverifiable, premise: that the origin of Blanchot's writing—the traumatic impetus that animates its complex—is found in two short *recits*: "A Primal Scene?" and *The Instant of My Death*.[1] Together they comprise fewer than six pages and (in my mind) frame unique autobiographical (autothanatalogical) material. Two distinct encounters with an ineffable thing whose effects "changed his life" and levied a demand: to produce work that regards language in a new way and to take "inner experience" as the sole authority in matters of intelligence. Both lessons come from his mentor and friend Georges Bataille, who wrote, "Opening myself to inner experience, I have placed all value, all authority in it."[2] Each *recit* narrates a formational incident in the emergence of Blanchot's voice. "A Primal Scene?"—with or without the question mark—makes reference to Freud's contention that a child's witness of the parents' sex act traumatically marks her for life. Blanchot's scene is of a boy's vision that pierces the everyday screen to see the abyss over which a human life dangles. *The Instant of My Death* describes the stain left on his life in the course of facing a firing squad (like Dostoyevsky), in Blanchot's case a Nazi unit. It marks its survivor by annulling the place that death reserves for him, the erasure of erasure.

In keeping with the book's intent, a moment arrives when writing actualizes what the voice would put in writing, inscribing and entombing it in the crypt of language. The proximity of the two—writing voice and inscription—defines a fold or invagination that contains a host of questions centered on the event of authorship and the authorial voice. There the exterior gives voice to a counterlife that can powerfully affect what is written. The gift and its economy of exchange motivate this book's research.

Many of the same themes have been treated by exceptional minds such as Foucault, Deleuze, Cixous, Kristeva, Levinas, and Jacques Derrida. Their voices infiltrate the text as it offers a performance of voice, understood as a multiple. Recitations from their works form a choral background that sustains the life of their signatures. The text yields a work of mourning insofar as memory of their thought traces matters presently at hand.

The supplementary theme that concerns me is the thing called Narcissus. There is the myth retold by Ovid, a late myth, and there is Freud and all he wrought. In the background are Lacan and Merleau-Ponty and Derrida and Levinas. Others could be added: Nancy, Lacoue-Labarthe, Louis Lavelle. This could be a text on primary narcissism, desire, and subjectivity. A notion of being, now current, has at the core a *conatus essendi*, an always already desiring. The discussion recurs to how the primary theme of voice is affected by "narcissistic proclivities."

The five chapters are intended not as partitions of a field but repetitions of the same specular science of the voice. Each pertains to an aspect of its peculiar and originary iteration of, perhaps, the primal word. They are:

1. Narcissus

2. The Mirror

3. Death as instance

4. Echo

5. Voice *eo ipso*

I

Narcissus

·•·———·•·

In Search of a Method

To follow the haunt of Maurice Blanchot, the stage whisper of his voice—
in citation, implied citation, unto the silent citation as when before God,
prayerfully (as the present writing)—the important thing is the work: a
movement toward conversation. To trace the ghost is not yet dialogue
but invocation of the signature that lurks, singularly and universally, of
Blanchot, the companion who stands apart from me. Duplicity is doubled:
it isn't certain that there is only one.

These things the whisper might have conveyed. But the vocalization
comes through a mask, a per-sona, and that belongs to Derrida. His inaugural study of mimetics unveils the voice that philosophy mimes by use of
language ("meaning is use"), together with an entire field of mimetography
disseminated across thought of all kinds, in particular, that which follows.
Accordingly, to understand Blanchot's voice through a performance of ventriloquism seems apt. How else to study voice than to try the other's on, lip
synch it, impersonate and take it to be a character role? Blanchot's voice
needs to be provoked into writing the text, if only as imposture, mockery,
or travesty of same. It would then call attention to a manner of vociferation
that the author's living laryngeal vocality was unable to provide. Besides,
repetition trumps one-time-only presentation. The rerun shows defects and
excesses in a splendor that the premiere masks. Besides, if live voice is
understood *nachtraglich*, then the written voice is anterior.

In a mimetic text, production, co-production, or giving production
to outsourcing is accomplished through citations, borrowings, remixes, recitations, *recits* of other texts, texts where the writing has been leavened

by reading—in every tense—in a looking-glass exchange which is epochal (*epoche*, arrest or suspension.) The intertextuality of the document attests to the fact that no text can exist in isolation: the "all in the all." As if in a Leibnizean universe, each monadic text contains holographically a replica of every textual monad. However the metaphysics, mimetics cares about reuse of material. The miming force relates directly to itself in repeats and doubles that return by detour to the place where, circling around to itself once again, it catches up with the selfsame circulation. Said otherwise, impoverishment of writing is contagious and afflicts choice of theme, vocabulary, style, and reading—an echo can only repeat the already said. Reading plays a lead role in the mimed event: not mere reading skills—a quick spell-check or test for grammaticality—but the more significant fact that reading changes the meaning. A text is susceptible to an exterior intelligence that penetrates its interior and becomes interior to it. Reader is companion to writer and the two are bound in a complex and ambivalent bond.

Why a mimetic text? First, it imitates voices of other texts. It recites in their voice. Second, it concerns the image and the imaginary that dissimulates absence. The image belongs to an earlier *episteme* when resemblance ruled over representation and the sign. The image is essentially a resemblance. Resemblance is self-reflexive. Resemblance in this case has to resemble itself. The text presents a prolonged absorption into the imaginary, exhumed in a series of inscriptions made to give it voice.

One branch of mimetics, of special interest to the present study, is ventriloquism. This is to speak the part of the dumb one who then puts it in writing, inscribing words as though spoken; the counterfactual will bear deep scrutiny. There is a sending or throwing of voice to another who appears to speak it. The thrown voice voices for the double, voices the double in grasping what the voice would be like—an imagination. But thrown voice is an imitation of a mute one to which the voice is thrown; it imitates its own imagination of that one, an imagining of the imagination which it resembles. One could say: it is imitation of an image and how it intransitively impersonates. It imitates the imaged voice when it voices phonetically and syntactically. It must follow rules of each.

The thrown voice, therefore, is always a second and not an original. The original voice is one's everyday version when one ventriloquates. The thrown voice lacks originality, is of derivative status, if any, and always already is a copy—in fact, a copy of a copy, low down in Plato's canonical ordering: a simulacrum. The original voice, following Levinas, must be capable of sincerity, voicing without deception. Here, voice is lure, transgressive by nature.

The text, in addition, is polyvocal, both in a logical and a progressive sense. It moves from a restricted mime of a single voice—Blanchot's—and working with material received, spreads wings of self-consciousness and opens to voices that contest in advance the very inquiry they are in the midst of performing. To enter the general economy of mimetics goes some distance toward the presentation of a verbal text, in Levinas's sense of the word.[1]

The Alchemical Dream: Narcissism Is Being Killed

That forgetfulness exists: this remains to be proved.

—Nietzsche

If there were a protocol for murder, it would be possible to embrace the transgressive point of view offered by the neuter. It first would be necessary to access the outside, engage the *pas au-delà*, and move beyond dazzling, dialectizable thought. Murder then would be a ritual one, sacrificial in nature, in which an absolute prohibition would have been suspended. In effect, death of a commitment to logocentrism that dwells within the house of being would have been accomplished. The entity would be "the child within," the child-Narcissus, whose desire constitutes (in a god-like way) the entirety of being-in-the-world and motivates the agon of affirmation and negation.[2]

The protocol is not difficult to state. It belongs to a lucidity preserved by a subterranean history, an arcana: "Putrefaction precedes the generation of every new form in existence."[3] The killing of kid-Narcissus proceeds by marrying him to his beloved image, the figure reflected to his fascinated gaze with the same lustral magnetism that emanates from his eyes. The blissful union is preserved by sealing the two, image and living presence, together and separate from the founded world. As they unite, a new mode, a new voice, is born—that of the neuter itself, the *ipse* (does it have one?), risen from the cloistered condition. Child-Narcissus and his beloved merge, image and animate being, to yield the hybrid half-breed: the neuter. That which arises from the tomb, the secret encryption, has never before appeared; its utter novelty is radical such that it cannot be *as such*. Its appearance is a gap, a hiatus, in the otherwise smooth function of *Sinngebung*, the meaning-making mechanism that produces the world. Killing the child engenders the adult capable of living neither passively nor actively but outside life altogether.

The story is of dying (not death), but with an irony—the coupling joins the living to the non-living. The marriage insures that death is impossible. "You can't kill a dead man." In the death sought by Serge Leclaire, it is necessary again and again to kill the child-Narcissus in order to produce the voice.[4] The achievement is never accomplished because of the extraordinary insistence that exercises power over the not yet as well as the to come—and is joined to the most ancient and immemorial. The murder both no longer takes place and has never yet. In death's failure, Narcissus must exist dying the agony of an unfruitful (unconsummated) union with the beloved image, while the limpid pool changes with the seasons and the ages and epochs of humankind. The child-Narcissus must accept eternal dying, surviving the very sacrifice that inaugurates the creative advance of voice. He, like the compulsive, is free only to repeat the protocol, the confinement within the hermetically sealed space; the failure to emerge as an alterity marks him as a "being without being," an eternal thing. The accomplishment, moreover, falls short of what death would have wrought and institutes an illegible cipher in the non-place between living and dead, presence and absence. His unnatural attraction—to the inanimate and nonorganic, a mere play of light upon a surface—marks the child-Narcissus as unable to catch up with death, or alternatively, prone to overshoot it. The inconstancy that belongs to the *mi-lieu* is why he is so cherished. His figure, "unnatural" desire, is a portal to the step not beyond, *pas au-delà*.

The failure—like Orpheus's—should not be determinative since he—unlike Orpheus—is granted more than one chance to comply with protocol. Like Orpheus, though for different reasons, the undertaking is doomed from the onset. Orpheus's could not be won because he sought the impossible: to bring to daylight's dialectic a silhouette of nocturnal opacity. He wanted to replace the obscure object of his love with the known and knowable and to uphold the work of song, *poiesis*, to the world. But Eurydice was not graspable as a shade, image of life that is non-living, and hence Orpheus's glance backward—transgressing the law he had signed and to which he had been assigned—was a reflex, unavoidable as a blink in sudden light, bound to the contradictory terms of the arrangement with Hades. With Narcissus, it is different. The beloved image, it is true, does not belong to the world of the living any more than the dead Eurydice did. But with Narcissus, no law forbids repetition and in fact, repetition is his law. To end the death of the image, to bring life to it through the magic of an embodied embrace, he begins a vigil at the pool's edge. Leaning ever more closely without decreasing the separateness, never de-distancing (*Ent-fernung*), he weds his gaze to that of the other's, is sequestrated within the interweaving, and would be eventually recast in the neuter, neither himself nor the reflection, nor strictly speaking a mix of both.[5]

In the account is a displacement of the narrative. Tradition in Ovid has it that the child Narcissus is unable to narrow the separation between himself and the mirrored image. His intense longing for union is matched by that in the gaze that returns his. Put the other way, that gaze, the image looking back to the source of sight, the living being, gains an independence and sees Narcissus like itself, inert and immobilized by a surfeit of feeling. It is the excess that expresses the lack that must be other than copy, repetition, or simulation. The image owns a "superior" viewpoint that recognizes life as the event of recalcitrance. Life gets in the way of death, thwarts its arrival, finds its measure in death's nonarrival, and embraces the *conatus* that signs death away, relegates it to impossibility, and heeds the eternal drum of dying whose percussion will never have fallen silent. The image knows life as event, a fastness that withstands figuration, image, narrative, that prevents the frail fall into the unmarked grave. It is an advent that must be fixed, in the specific sclerosis before life can breathe its last and becomes other than itself. The story of Narcissus is about the transmutation of the event, from impredicable to categorial, along the lines of the performance staged in child-Narcissus's ritual murder. The *élan vital*, the life-force, must be reduced to a standstill and survivorship ended. This means that Narcissus's love must be consummated and a new entity conceived. Life minimalized to image must surrender a last breath and rest on nothing, the nothing. In the radical displacement of tradition, Narcissus loses everything including his capability to die and be done. He becomes other than himself and other to the image of himself. If, in the ill-success of the killing, Narcissus were to behold *himself* in the water, he would fall out of love, cease being an object of fascination, transgress the law no longer, and return to the world as scion of a rich and famous household. This too is impossible since at that very moment Narcissus leans closest to the limpidity, he is at the maximum of self-absorption, of obscurity to the interior that is his signature, and most lost to appearance. At that moment in his demi-divinity, he is most fully human.

Significantly, the sacrificial killing is syntactically signified in a present progressive, "A child is being killed." The act can be inscribed only insofar as it progresses without progress toward a completion that, unachieved, is no less incomplete than it would ever be. It never departs from being ongoing, going on without coming to a limit, border, or shoreline. This is an infinite present (an infinitive), distinct from the *nunc stans* of theology, rather the perpetual return of deferral, the backwater eddying of Dasein's entanglement (*Verfängnis*). The French language has a further subtlety: the progressive construction of *venir*, to come, is rich in allusions of nearing, welcoming, inviting, approaching. It engages, as Derrida examines at length, the *da-fort* interchange, the movement that extends from presence to absence and back again.[6] The semblance of a shared space breeds an unlawful crossing of borders that do not predate the forbidden encroachment; the action (of killing) can advance only by removal of its instruments, which is to say, desire. The child being killed must of necessity continually survive a murder that yields no corpse. Narcissus, like Orpheus, is a figure of the gods and their peculiar immortality. He lives in the debacle of his own demise because his immortality is irrevocable. The killing consumes the present in such a way that nothing can come of it; or alternatively, the present is so distended that no end can be done. There is nothing to come and because of this, the ritual that would summon the next intelligence (beyond the opposition of death and deathless) is inoperative. Could one say that Blanchot himself is the recipient of such a gift? That his work, the *oeuvre*, attempts to repay this (as he says in a late *recit*) "injustice"? That work is the repeated affirmation of the sacrifice or its actual enactment?

Once retold to include the protagonist's murder, the Narcissus myth has an unexpected consequence. Ritual conjunction of the living with an image of the living produces an entity distinct from life and image as well as from any resemblance to life (or image)—the neuter. The neuter is not a category added to language or an attribute of the world; it can be given voice only in a suitably inflected grammar unknown to a transcendental ego. It resounds as a distinct linguistic mode in that it does no work in the making of sense and disseminates its inoperability throughout linguisticality in general: *desoeuvrement*.[7] A neuter statement stands in need of infinite qualifiers to repair the unserviceability. That infinity "names" the neuter, which otherwise remains hidden in the very name. Undermining disclosure, the neuter is concealed from the world whose order assumes a relation with there above, sidereal space. When the astral link is broken (although unknown), there are consequences: the *far* cannot be made *near*, cannot *come* close, cannot await the *to-come*. The mark, for Blanchot, of *désastre*, a ruptured linkage between life here below and "life" on the plane of the starry heavens, is "errant disarray, and yet the imperceptible but intense suddenness of the outside, as an irresistible or unforeseen resolve which would come to us from beyond the confines of decision" (WD, 4). Its entry (non-entry of the dysrelation) into human affairs would attest to the dying (of life, of desire) that is the intrigue of the neuter voice, if it were equipped to bear the attestation. Between Narcissus and his image, moreover, there exists an incongruence. In a mirror (as Kant knew) if the left is to correspond to the right, the figure must be flipped through another dimension. The other space (other than space) is the neuter. Can one say that the myth's impossible death rehearses the impossible genesis of neutrality?

In the killing, ritual marriage, and entombment, child-Narcissus never recognizes the image as of himself (itself). In this regard, the account diverges from Ovid's telling (and Lacan's adaptation where the mirror-stage inaugurates the scene of narcissistic impulse). That the image (of erotic fascination) is an other (not the same) transforms the nature of the conjunction; otherwise, his lust remains self-love, *amour propre*, the same conjoined to itself forever destined to remain the same, that is, impossible to conjoin because already conjoint. The transmutation is strange in how a living being is attracted to an inanimate image, groundless and without origin. The estrangement stems from a fascination that welcomes an image as image, not as semblance of life. Living Narcissus falls in love with the watery figure not because it looks like him, with his bright eyes and curling hair, but because it only *looks* living but is really other than alive, neither life nor death, because it is like nothing else. The shimmering face attracts with an absent presence, a surface not bounded by the law of the world—resemblance—but in a different way unbounded by the lawlessness outside, beyond the impossible step over the border.[8] Here, Narcissus is less perceptive than Orpheus, who recognizes the obscure object as Eurydice; Orpheus knows the *Als Struktur*. For Narcissus, it is enough to love a stranger, to lack understanding, and to be lured by attraction. It is almost enough that the other return his gaze, that the image fix its sight with avidity on him. The look from the other beyond life is returned to his life with the addition of nothing, and having been seen, Narcissus (Blanchot writes) "dissolves in the immobile dissolution of the imaginary . . . losing a life he does not have" (WD, 126). The killing cannot proceed until Narcissus takes his eyes off his beloved. As long as Narcissus holds to an identity of his own, it cannot be replaced by the image and he is absolved of surrendering life to the non-living.[9]

The image, furthermore, may be non-dead but properly speaking neither living nor dead. Living dead? A human, Blanchot says, is not so much made in the image (of God) as unmade, returned to the elemental horizon which is the un-de-distanced nearness of things, and thus rendered far from an incarnate self. Narcissus's love underscores a distance from interiority that defines childhood; nothing can be near. The child reaches to touch the world only to discover it is out of reach; once touched, the world is no longer palpable. The haptic self that would feel this or that ceases to exist; the child has no credence in the soul. Attraction to the otherworldly stirs fear and dread of dissolution. The "ancient fear" is associated with the living dead, underworld crypts, and voices that speak in the neuter. Narcissus is a naive hero to the extent that he suffers that apprehension and does not waver in the interval while fascination attenuates, while the child is being killed. If it did fluctuate, the murder would have been committed and the advent of the neuter forestalled; Narcissus would have retained the power as a living being to give love a discursive voice.

Nevertheless if attraction persists while the child is being killed, the withdrawal that institutes a new economy or an-economy would not take place. Once no longer active, Narcissus is gifted with a passivity beyond the opposition of active-passive. A passivity radical enough to foster Narcissus's erotic surrender to the image, to wed it, and to become other than himself and other than the other. To accept a passivity of such a degree is impossible even to a demigod, and by reason of an impossible acceptance the new Narcissus, transmuted or transubstantiated, comes into being. The passivity unmakes the child as it marks the trembling between alternatives (near/far, present/absent, living/dead, day/night). Entropic and gray, it vacillates and is unresolved in restlessness. It dissembles life, a remarkable breathtaking beauty haloing the scene. The magnetism of a space that cannot support the projected world spawns dreams of life; Blanchot remarks how inspiration—breathing in the second night—weaves oneiric tableaux. Unearthly dreams as when the mortal coil has been sloughed: dreams beyond earth and conquest. Utter passivity, in Ovid's version, has the child-Narcissus fatefully turned into a flower.

Does killing kid-Narcissus transgress the law that forbids annihilation of desire, a particular desire, erotic-self-love, or of auto-eroticism? Desire can only mutate, never die and be gone. Transgression is internally linked to desire, to ensure that satisfaction does occur "by posing a new and always higher law, which made of this infinite passage from the law to its transgression and from this transgression to another law the only infraction that upheld the eternity of his desire" (SNB, 24). The absented desire inaugurates the disaster in which resounds an incessant reference to origin, desire's link to sidereal space. Its would-be eradication (the ideal of Stoic *ataraxia*) signals a breakdown in the relation to there above, and thence come the death camps, Holocaust, Hiroshima, genocide, ethnic cleansing.[10] Flaccid desire moves under the guide of indifferent values. The breakdown is tantamount to refusal of remembrance, preservation of the event of awakened life *as* event.[11] Refusal: that forgetting that falls away from a living memory (*mnesis*) and submissively gives over to dying. "The disaster is related to forgetfulness—forgetfulness without memory, the motionless retreat of what has not been treated—the immemorial, perhaps" (WD, 3). This is a rich statement and will call for a deeper analysis. For now, Narcissus has been relieved of ardor, passion, and his flesh, and rendered a thing of fascination for an image that mirrors his love. Can it be said that he is guilty of forgetting—himself, the *who*—in endless dying of reference, as if the thing dissolved as soon as the word appeared? That he is so undone by forgetting as to cease to be, and yet bypasses not being? The abdication of care (*Sorge*) yields unconcern or insouciance that conditions writing (of/in) the neuter voice.

Desire killed is desire renewed and the absence of desire is yet desire but in the form of despondence, depletion, or detumescence—on the way to non-desire. Like the child whose death perpetually nullifies coming (*viens!*), desire can be animated only through dying when it lingers in the throes of non-arrival: the repetition of desire's narrative.[12] To desire to kill desire: this too could be non-desire, a desire for the self-killing of desire (in turn repression of desire or desire's wanting to repress itself). *A desire is being killed* would be an alternate title to Leclaire's text. Narcissus's relation to his own desire must be viewed through the admonition against suicide and the overreaching of self-mastery into the realm of utter passivity.[13] He must necessarily defer eliminating desire and instead attend its attenuation with absolute patience. Doing nothing: non-desire.

Narcissus's desire, moreover, is expended without limit in fascination; the subject subsides unto forgetting, falling outside itself, first lured then mesmerized into a passivity. The polymorphous perversity of all desire has a potential for flaccidity and insouciance. Forgetting himself, Narcissus remains poor, destitute, and powerless—on the way to patience. No wonder he fails to recognize the image as his own; the event of self-recognition has removed itself beyond erasure, toward erasure of the mark of erasure.[14] The movement passes from the advent of awakened life to a profaned and unfinished dying. But the child is not there, he has abandoned *Jemeingkeit*. Narcissus has forsaken the lot of victims of ritual murder, since by tradition, the chosen needs to be a subject of sacrifice, a supplicant. As soon as passivity mounts and subjecthood wanes, the ceremonial knife must be dropped. Wakefulness is the warrant of a sacrificial death. When a command from on high corresponds to an act here below, the stars play out their stories in the human heart. But Narcissus sleeps like the apostles in Gethsemane, and, therefore, is no candidate for the killing, the writing, the struggle of the logos, and being(-in-the-world) itself.

Consider desire more narrowly, as autoeroticism. Again, passivity and forgetting take Narcissus's gaze outward toward an object of fascination. Not the image as himself because he fails (by divine decree) to recognize himself in it, nor the image as image, in its immateriality and groundlessness, Narcissus loves (by divine decree) only an other that is himself. He does not know himself whom he loves. He has withdrawn from the interiority of the corporeal mass in a movement toward the impassible place between organism and mirage. Within the flesh, he is moved by the object-cause of desire and it is for this earthly impulse that he strives; but that is neither the shimmering reflection nor the pulsing tissue. Well before the *conjuntio* that transmutes ignorance to unearthly wisdom, dying to autoeroticism, Narcissus already has engaged the *pas au-delà* and crossed to the outside.[15] Narcissus inherits the capability of the neuter voice and participates in the neuter, its lack of power and possibility, through the legacy of the gaze. Then the disaster has taken place without happening but "leaving everything intact." Since no event eventuates (an evental other does), it leaves no memory trace of it.

The infatuation of kid-Narcissus inscribes a break in the relation between above and below, "the starry heaven above and the moral law within." What cannot be held in memory and remembrance establishes the rupture with other dysrelations: near/far, presence/absence, in/out, life/death. The cosmic nature of interruption, its dissemination throughout language, the ruin of expression: reverberations echo without an originary sounding. One could say that "relation" has been shattered, hence any citation re-cites the blow and augments fragmentation. Language disrupted and displaced, "cored," fails to work for truth, but is insistently language, perhaps the very language that dissimulates the giving of voice to reality. Language that suffers diversion, cannot seem to find itself, is slack in intentionality, and remains preoccupied, is language that falls short of functionality and slips into uncanniness.[16] Like the disaster, the weakness is unexperienced. Like the disaster, it "is what escapes the very possibility of experience—it is the limit of writing" (WD, 7). Its weak force enters into this very writing, the disastrous remembrance that necessarily breaks under the light giddiness of forgetting. It is not an affair outside the text. It is not the case that killing the child rectifies or reduces the *fatum* that is Narcissus's destiny. The force that waits patiently or is patience itself far exceeds his or anyone's desire. It is constantly on the verge of installing a relation of the third kind, a relation that exempts itself from relating its terms (Levinas would say, "absolves").

After entombment, the conjunction produces a hybrid, neither image nor living being, but one who lives on and remembers. What is kept in memory Blanchot calls "something like a presentiment—remembrance of the disaster which would be the gentlest want of foresight" (WD, 6). The small gap ineluctably disrupts wakeful solitude. The gentleness is in excess and leaves a faint, almost illegible mark; there is nothing to remark but a slight disorientation toward projects. In this sense, Narcissus's transmutation is the disaster's perfection, a slight insinuation always already having infiltrated thought.[17] Beforehand, need is confusion, lack is disarray, and a sense of cosmic immensity has given way to "stress on minutiae" (WD, 3). If wakeful sovereignty is possible, so would be the arrest of the disaster; then powerlessness no longer a threat, the disaster would be neutralized. But arrest is an excess of activity that swallows the primal passivity of the outside to interiorize it. The arrest would be feckless, the arrest of an immobility, always already arrested. There is no defense against the disaster.

The salient want of foresight (*Vorsicht*) recalls the Heideggerian *Entschlossenheit*, resoluteness.[18] It is the "presentiment" that draws together the two texts—*Being and Time* and *The Writing of the Disaster*—as two thoughts on memory that turn from one another. Heidegger's reinvestment of sovereignty through a recognition of the lack (*Mangel*) looks toward remembrance. Blanchot's intuition follows the expenditure and depletion unto the point where the master is forsaken by all mastery. To guard against the incessant slippage of Dasein into the neutral impersonal form of *das Man*, decisiveness, for Heidegger, must be in play. The leveling of the event of being coincides with the dimming of disclosure. The aperture of truth, *aletheia* (whose essence—against forgetting—is the revocation of amnesia) shuts. With closure, the present no longer exists. Attestation, contaminated by refusal and eviscerated by dissimulation, is no longer reliable. The witness who, in singularity, stands apart from the temporal flow ("vulgar time") is reabsorbed into generality and predication—gentle thought. That unique activity, presencing, is simultaneously consigned to language and condemned to dying. One look at Narcissus, before the child in him gazes out, can recognize a "natural" self-containment. In the presence of presence, he follows a law that demarks a possible frontier, with greater or lesser definition, within which existence is given. There, an originary openness measures availability to forces that gather unto being. The burden of remembrance carries the moment (*is* it) and is, however, always already weighted with forgetting's void, imminence, non-relation, and unsurpassingness. Narcissus remembers the verge of oblivion as the gaze issues from him, clandestinely withdrawn, as he pulls back to regain sovereign interiority.

Entschlossenheit is the fundamental position of care, the essence of Dasein. The English translation misses the main point in Heidegger's choice of terms. The German comes from *schliessen*, to shut, as though passivity were a seepage that could be remedied through appropriate action. The word is related to *Schloss*, castle, reminiscent of Eckhart's idea of a safe haven, moated and unassailable, of divine presence. It is cognate to *Erschliessen*, disclosure, in the key elucidation of truth. *Entschlossenheit* is a decisive closing to the outside of the event of being (*Ereignis*), a damming within of the force of remembrance, amounting to an *epoche* or reduction. An emphatic double negation, one cannot not do. Resoluteness renders sovereignty irreducible since without it forgetting (*vergessen*) would ruin things, including the power to speak of ruin. So inscribed, the approach of forgetting, nearing without leaving off distance, is marked with a call to responsibility, always already the enunciation of Dasein's freedom. The preliminary call of conscience "watches without sleep" in a twilit sovereignty threatened by nighttime entanglement (*Verfängnis*). The "gentlest" want of foresight is unavoidable and names a particular stance of Dasein—not wanting a conscience: refusal.[19] Only the obligatory, that which correlates with one's ownmost potentiality, can trump avoidance; here Heidegger sides both with Kant on duty and Husserl on intentional correlation. *Entschlossenheit* safeguards what is closest ("ownmost") to interiority, the possibility of return, recurrence, repetition. Foresight translates into anticipation (*Vorlaufen*) in the struggle against *lethe*. The lack in it necessitates *Verfallen*.

Child-Narcissus's fascination turns responsibility on its head. Fascination, paralysis, inertia, passivity, dispossession by being possessed (possession in the passive): a chain marks evisceration of the will. "*Drifting without shoreline*" (SNB, 64). Blanchot's principal category should not be viewed as an advance on willing, abnegated and molded in the image of the divine, a nod toward *Gelassenheit, apatheia,* or absorption in God. An access to presence would not empty Narcissus of determination but heighten it. Releasement is activity, albeit receptive, not the void of purpose. For that, the *ergon* must be extirpated and the child left in lassitude, rudderless without desire, the "child being killed." As the image takes possession of interiority, voluntary impulses are crippled. Work (*ergon*) becomes inoperability, *desoeuvrement.* He has passed to the exterior (allowed to pass) and responsibility withdrawn. Surreptitiously the inoperative condition has been in force since before the first sighting of the beloved, at the very petard of resoluteness. Analogous to Orpheus's retrieval of Eurydice, the murder of narcissism is doomed before its onset. Eurydice cannot be grasped as dark image and Narcissus cannot relate responsibly to an other that lacks identity, distinctness, and existence—radical alterity. Responsible to no one, least of all the contradictions within, he is condemned to writing. Here is an indication of a relation between writing and narcissism: writing continually inscribes the summons as well as that for which one's dying to desire is summoned.

Responsibility's other, the other of responsibility, is dative, not genitive. In Narcissus's case, this means to respond to the image, love for which dispossesses him. The passive possessive opens a language of estrangement. As responsibility immobilizes action without altering the imperative, suspended indefinitely prior to discharge, the distress of inertia roils conscience—"bad conscience"—and leaves Narcissus troubled and ineffectual. Seduced by the image's gaze that automates auto-eroticism, he can never be gratified by pleasure or duty: the horns of a Kantian dilemma and without the wherewithal to resolve its conflict. Although thwarted by an impossible response (responsible to the impossible), he is nonetheless not irresponsible. The other of responsibility, the dispersed possibility of responsiveness, ceases to be confined to night that would forbid the power of responsibility. It could be said that revocation of that power is the other, or that it "others" all possibility. Revocation as the other to invocation. Narcissus is left selfless, a troubled subjectivity, cored and decentered, yet paradoxically undone by inscription that is obsessive. On the verge of being stripped of name, falling into an anonymity that never arrives, he provides a site for conversion. There, words demark the absence of experience. Responsibility is mimed by a linguistic capability as language veers toward nominalism. "Name the possible, respond to the impossible."

The Dream's End

The alchemical dream, kid-Narcissus's being killed, confabulates an equivocation. It purports to join the two lovers, living being with image, and from the conjunction engender a new immortality, a half-breed not subject to earthly law or "vulgar" time. Such an account would be what writing has to offer. Under one hypothesis, the ordeal places a seal on the destruction of narcissism per se, thereby eviscerating the return, that is, to remembrance, sovereignty, and the dialectic. Absolute passivity is the remainder. Its excessive nature infiltrates interiority, the citadel of *Entschlossenheit*, neutralizing any activity opposed to immobility.

Phenomenologically, the event that identifies intentionality with life concomitantly delineates the field of possibility and power. A chronically enfeebled purpose, a dying increasingly thwarted at each step, a non-arrival at completion: a state of unassayable turbulence (*Wirbel*). Dying, however, does not take the place of life since it offers no alternative (non-living, inorganic, dead) and cannot since it occupies no place in the present. Dying supplies no supplement; it will not supplementally replace living. It is an empty categorial ineffectual in predicating a being; its usage is that of (Blanchot says in another context) a canonical abbreviation.[20] It is the remarking of a totality whose absence is so global that it makes no difference to what survives (it withdraws difference with it).

Ovid remembers the second hypothesis, the alternative reading of the alchemical dream, when (in a late embellishment of the myth) he states the other part of the gods' condemnation of Narcissus (prophesied by Tieresias): to "turn him away from himself." To let narcissism perish is to root out narcissistic desire, specifically, the desire to not see oneself, to blind oneself to oneself as well as other privations of self-affection, self-consciousness, or self-knowledge. "Vulgar" narcissism is the counterimpulse to the Socratic care for the soul (*melete tou thanatou*) that calls for dropping pretense in favor of forthrightness and sincerity. Narcissism installs attachment to the world, concern with appropriation, accumulation of capital, and aggrandizement of power. From an analytic view, it would manifest as temptation (*Versucherischkeit*) of such impulses.[21] Incapable of self-seeing, narcissistic desire fares no better in seeing the other as self (self as other) and yet the implicit rejection of alterity would seek to annul the difference. Blind to self as self, without sight of the other as other, vision gives impetus of xenophobia, expeditions of conquest, pernicious rivalries, and competitive animus. Extirpation of narcissistic desire coincides with restoration of sight or sightedness (*Sicht, Sichtlichkeit*) as well as bearing witness. It would constitute the eminent return to a life that simultaneously reinstates past and future, for which "present" is much more than a canonical abbreviation. Presence, mastery, ownmost potentiality, I: these are capital gains of renunciation (if it is that)—as expenditure of infatuation. As the eye of fascination closes, the seepage of *Sicht* to the outside together with the projection of the desired image is arrested. The event of being is returned to the how of its becoming. In anticipation of the death of desire (*Vorlaufen zum Tode*), the reflection of the pool would cease to trump Narcissus's renewal through the alchemical marriage. Once again he would forgo death by dwelling in the disaster, that is, by dying.

That is not all. Narcissus who desires to not see himself as object, instead sees not as object but as a cloud, nimbus, or pixilated visage: the invisible when brought to sight. The invisible hides by being seen as indecipherable, blurred, broken, scratched, ripped, written over, encrypted, or partially erased. In shadow, bright or dim, behind corners, over hills: its blindness inscribes its mutilated appearance. Toward where do Narcissus's eyes turn to look away from himself, to suffer the lack of an image of his appearance, a nonappearance? This can be said, that he is given to see a certain nonappearance of himself, a manifest void of interiority.[22] Narcissus's gaze is on the invisible—faced away from subjectivity. His gaze is the recursive object of his gaze. It is his meeting with alterity.[23] He does not see his visible self (illuminated by sun or *lumen naturale*) but his invisible self that is incapable of being an object. Unable to stand over and against it, de-distance, and accomplish the reduction, he does not *not* see it but sees the transparency that encloses it. Narcissus takes invisibility in through the gaze of fascination as it unfolds empty space that "contains" all images, auto-affections of primal forces—while lost to the eyes that reflect his. This is a potent arrest of the law that had held him reversed, delineated, and cast aside. It frees him to an invisible neutrality. He is lost to the interior that he could have found (by some counterfactual) had he turned around, so that when he does, he sees no one. He identifies with the absence then and there, a "one or it—*il*," and finds the possibility of return "to himself" expired. He—"a borrowed, happenstance singularity"—is freed to that which has no escape (WD, 18).

Can it be said that Narcissus has "advanced" toward self-understanding by relinquishing the gift of sight? Blinded by narcissism's desire to not see itself, he sees what cannot be seen, nothing. But the nothing is not abyssal, is not the *Nichtheit* of panic attacks and bad conscience. When intransitive, vision sees the possibility of visual experience, the "a priori conditions" that regulate the transcendental object that conditions the being of light (*Lichtung*). The nonobjectified vision abandons the play of traditional perceptual forms and sustains the emerging form itself as explored in painterly experimentation from impressionism and pointillism on. At the same time, Narcissus's sacrifice that leaves him *sichtlos* also leaves the visual field without a center by which to order the deconstructed forms. Loss of the "I think" that must accompany a possible sighting means that he lacks the means to say, "I see this," but only, "That, there." The transcendental unity of apperception has been jettisoned, and although real blindness sees through to the absence of ground, Narcissus is not in possession of that experience.

Naïveté prevents a new vision of how the subject is left out of the picture. He who gains the invisible and its enigmatic interweaving with the sighted world gains no new grasp on things but serves its errancy.

Unlike Tieresias (or Oedipus), Narcissus's blindness grants no prophetic powers or second sight. Sacrifice of vision does not open to a future (future anterior) but to a time not privileged by presence: the immemorial or "most ancient." The invisible is not a giant display case of things once seen or awaiting seeing, static, immobile under God's eye. Deprived of the condition of visibility—which remains (however transiently) in some place—the facticity of the invisible never dwells anywhere (*Aufenthaltlosigkeit*). Narcissus blind-gazes endlessly across depths, abundantly traceless, unnamable, an amorphous presence of the voice that retains the patience of passivity but no order and no inscription. That it long since lost memory of fascination's thing does not slow a search in which nothing is sought. Its unquestioning character is inertia bereft of the essential lack from which questions arise. Correlative to the same naïveté that overlooks the noncongruence of self with self, the indifference seeps into the interior. Narcissus is incapable of suffering inquiry and becoming adult. The neuter voice has inoculated him with intransitive impotency, a vaccine against senescence. Henceforth, Narcissus shall remain *puer*, child-Narcissus. Never will he grow old. Long live the Kid.

Vision without object, immune to the law of identity, respect and propriety, of beings in the world, non-focal, diffuse, without borders, aperspectival. An ontic consciousness without the onus of *verfallen*. For Heidegger, falling prey, which means having "fallen *away from itself*," is identification with the world.[24] Narcissus's sight, however, is no longer of the world. Having passed, bypassed, or surpassed, by way of the *pas au-delà* (is there a "way"?), beyond proper limits of presence, vision is not disclosive but shot through with an unrehabilitative *lethe* so devoid of memory that it is forever ineligible to become *aletheia*.[25] Perhaps an untruth too closely linked with truth to become other than errancy. Blind seeing, moreover, is not so much auto-affective as hetero-affective. That it arises unmediated from an alterity makes it resemble the *intuitus creatrix* that Kant reserves for the deity; hence the many allusions to negative theology. They are beside the point. The entire visual apparatus that Blanchot utilizes to illumine the "second version" of an image differs from a model for the ocular function that requires minimal sensory input, some "outer sense." The ab-ocularity has to do with mundane forgetting.

When Narcissus sees without seeing himself, blind seeing, *Sicht* does not take place in a heedfully circumspect manner that links meaning to use (*Vorhandenheit*). The being of the question (Heidegger would say) is absent. Properly speaking, attribution of the first person singular pronoun is deferred in favor of the third person impersonal, one or it, the French *il*—Blanchot dubs it "narrative voice." The narrator: one (it) who (which) is putting in writing the thought of narcissistic desire, on the stage of transcription, who (which) is performing the venerable role of scribe, Anubis in the Egyptian. To write is to be blind to both the sun and inner light and to be attuned to neither, joining by disjuncture each sight to the neutral, the third that neither wants nor waits. It is to recall interiority to the mortality of writing that inscribes the passing of what passes away, the dying (impulse, force, power), senescence or aging (what is re-begun); and, moreover, to abide for no reason, "without a why," to participate in the event of repetition, the repeat eventuation of the event, without needing to make sense, abandoning the *Sinngebung*. It is to honor repetition of the headlong plunge of Narcissus into the oculus of the image.

Infatuated, Narcissus doesn't perceive an image at all, but a faceless swirl traced by an equally formless reflection. He is lured into the cataract by a gaze that cannot let go of his—or of itself. In this case, delirium follows, and the haunts of suicides: Ausable Falls, Golden Gate Bridge. Madness upon leaving the shelter of dialectical discourse and entering the precinct of the neuter voice.[26] Narcissus's fascination passes through the portal of a defaced face, a face of the invisible tracing an absent presence vigilant to his passage. The look is a gift given without expenditure, for he who has nothing is dispossessed of the damp spark of initiative. Not given, the gaze remains occluded, behind tensed forms and intentional consciousness, before an impasse guarded like Kafka's door of the law. Its forfeit of intentionality, however, does not merit assignation of a nonintentional consciousness (as in Levinas or Merleau-Ponty); the depth to which it plays is not the unconscious either, a reserve furrowed by gratuitous desire. Absorbed by the inhuman—and inhuman violence that will be abated only by the second violence, the language of being—the gaze is drawn forth, extending the languor without deposit as it roils, desire imaged as both its unsustainable cause and its unattainable gratification.

Where the two would cross (but do not), the sightless look of Narcissus and the ab-ocularity of the deep, there is recognition in neither the one of the other nor the other of the one. Mutual nonrecognition calls dissimulation into play. The scene, de-scribed by the still-life, *nature morte*, that the painter (Cézanne, for instance) captures to render the gaze pictorial. Narcissus is the figure in the mirror that doesn't self-remember. What is specular in the look that doesn't see himself is that there is no *amour propre*. The one he loves is alien. On the threshold of recognition, the mirror scene resembles the elation felt in his heart, and that he believes felt also in his beloved's heart—as if a complete mirror-transference had taken place and he now lived the life of a looking-glass creature through Alice's looking-glass. The risk in the (failed) chiasmus is that the mirror is untrue, the remembrance remembers only the forgetting.[27] It illuminates with nondisclosure while it traces the extinction of being, the cataclysm that leaves everything intact because it changes nothing at all. The defective mirror or mirror defect: a trope for the transcendental. Yes, the doubling, the *moi-même* of "is" instantiates a new interiority, renewed being and will, and ontological weight assembled by resolve. The potent mastery and ecstatic time is a totality in spite of transgression of its laws, anarchy that evokes the repeated explosion of form and continual deformation that follows laws of travesty and derision. The mirror that reflects twice, once with the image of being, once de-imaging the same; once child-Narcissus, once the specter. Is it safe to say that Narcissus sees neither, but a space of errancy? That, were he to speak, he would give voice to the neuter?

Seen otherwise, the (non)crossing of the two gazes, image and being, aligns each askew to the other, neither in relation nor in dysrelation. Strangely, each is unable to be nonintentional since intentionality flexes even in latency and is expended on the other's uncanny absence. Such a chiasmus invites nomadic singularities to the site (sight), and they cluster round. It must also be that the tonality is revealingly heightened so Narcissus's gaze verges on confession, prayerful in mood and stance. He is disclosed as weak, unmindful, and entangled in the dread of anonymity.[28] As one prone to transgression done in excess.

The analysis of the gaze relates thus to forgetting: forgetting the desire not to be self-seen is a double negative that would recoup remembrance. The confession that forgives concealment is a call from one's patrimony to serve. To unwork the desire is to render it inoperative, dysfunctional, inefficacious, ill-accomplished, and poor in spirit. Forgetting is the holy drug *moly*, Hermes's anodyne that clarifies the need to remember. Need is not desire and not moved to excess. The weakness of need is contested by robust desire, which is a sign of balance of good health.[29] This sounds like the "active oblivion" of Nietzsche, in which forgetting delimits dialectics where things enjoy the safety and wisdom provided by ecstatic time. Time allows for the abatement of suffering. Forgetting opens the passage to a surrender to the neuter voice where time bypasses the present. Here, time has no lapses, does not elapse, and neither accentuates nor ameliorates the ordeal of experience, *erleben* or *erfahren*. This means: time is incapable of bearing a mark, hence nothing to be remembered. The immemorial: the reserve that forgetting leeches. In this case, forgetting absconds with Narcissus's desire and clears the way to the reduction.

In the other case, killing child-Narcissus would weaken or eradicate desire *tout court* as well as gratification, the primary impetus of intentionality. It would result in a deformation of serviceability, that is to say, its ontic relevance. To deny caring for things that satisfy—self-sacrifice—opens to the need to be (*Selbstzusein*) and the experience of the lack (*Mangel*). The turn from the world, its collapse, would usher in deep anxieties that contextualize the advent of being and its specific responsibility. Here, the challenge of paralysis makes for strange bedfellows. Is there a homology between the Stoic *ataraxia* and the "ancient dread" whose mantra Blanchot repeats in the voice of the neuter? The incessancy and inefficacy of murder, moreover, make the dangerous repression apparent. A partially disabled, wounded, or debilitated narcissism yields a train of specters to supplement the beloved image. They recapitulate the history of a repeated homicide, its story in symptoms and representations that belong to the unarticulated (suppressed) portion of the myth. Ovid's allusion to the unconscious becomes evident in Narcissus's declamation, "Possession dispossessed me."

Dream Vision

Taken to the exterior through his eyes, Narcissus has always already turned from his subjectivity. Beyond it, through the desire to see, the scopic drive (*Schaulust*), he exemplifies the imminence of concupiscence. He would at each moment say, with Augustine, "Finally I must confess how I am tempted through the eye. . . . The eyes delight in beautiful shapes of different sorts and bright and attractive colors. I would not have these things take possession of my soul. Let God possess it."[30] To mortify such desire, to kill child-Narcissus, is to introduce blindness . . . or second sight. Augustine: "I resist the allurements of the eye for fear that as I walk upon your path, my feet may be caught in a trap. Instead, I raise my invisible eyes to you so that you may save my feet from the snare."[31] But the object of "invisible eyes" is ambiguous. Augustine would have it the holy and divine, but hasn't Narcissus inverted the greed of vision into the insouciance with which he beholds the nothing? Distinctly or indistinctly, the image, anchored ironically in the indeterminate, floats on the void. Its lure mingles with a freedom from concern, an abandon of ontic and ontological commitment alike, lingering on shores neither bordered nor unbordered, where there is a languid engagement with the *pas au-delà*. To drop consideration (relation with the sidereal), he looks past shape and color (figments of the world) toward where they have been annexed to grey indecisiveness. What is seen has no counterpart in reality, represents no thing, and is marked by a haunting self-resemblance, a nod to semblance (*Schein*) as such. The sight, moreover, does not illuminate another world, more or less beautiful than that of "beautiful shapes," where one might conquer a longing by the familiar route of appropriation. Vision entrained in the neuter voice is second sight.

It is not, however, the clairvoyance of either Augustine's God's-eye vision of omnitemporality or Tieresias's of the future. To end concupiscent desire is to culture a blindness, or better, a neutrality with regard to the object of sight. Otherwise it degrades to *Gerede*, curiosity as distraction. The excess of *Gerede* infects all senses since their knowledge is modeled on vision.[32] To not identify with the appropriative mission of desire—to be available for a relation with that which is absolved of relation, God, the One—is to effract the sidereal connection, source of astral force and the call to sovereignty. This blindness sees but in(to) the neuter. Its vision is subject to an other time not constituted (unmarked and unremembered) because its sheer transparency evades disclosure. In the neuter, the subject sees at the limit, the horizon necessary for disclosure and itself impossible to be disclosed; the encounter with impossibility. If this time exists, it evades history. It can appropriate no site, as if it were "slipped in" between instants of recordable time, an *entre-temps*, a meanwhile that belongs to an alternative temporal movement whose lawfulness differs from "vulgar" time. An aporetic time, never dwelling anywhere (*jemen sich aufhalten*), unsettling, disintegrative, oblivious of presence, "dreadful."

First sight, narcissistic in focus, sees things that snare it in order to snare them. More precisely, it sees by virtue of the signifier that designates the appropriation. Dialectical language (since Hegel), directed by identity or nonidentity, would operate the apparatus of sight in a "heedfully circumspect" manner to make out what is near at hand. By contrast, sight allied with the neuter voice (second sight) gives way to imprecision, indeterminacy, ambiguity, amphiboly, equivocity, and the multiple, all refractions of the ne-uter. The object of desire has absconded and taken on an obscure dimensionality that undoes self-identity. The essence of concupiscence is clandestinity, the secret tryst under cover of dark. This is the case with Narcissus's infatuation. His eyes' ravishment by a beautiful thing, an exemplary play of seduction, seems provoked by a well-lit image but in fact the focus has grown distracted, toward the unlit and hidden—a defocus. The other in turn is deprived of a "there," an indistinct survivor of the ambiguity: Is it any more than a figment? The night of essential solitude does not sustain a penetrating discernment; it preserves the secrecy of the beloved, an identity cloaked in desire. The *who* in neutral vision is dispersed and cannot be gathered unto a thing, named or nameable. To say Narcissus loves himself and himself alone overlooks the impossible depth that he would cross in order to achieve union. The secret in neuter vision of "primary narcissism," its force of concupiscence, survives the exhibition because it is faceless, labile, and infinitely malleable. If he could enunciate, it would be an "impeded speech," and the object of infatuation still undiscerned (SNB, 85).[33]

Concupiscence, excessively desirous, calls forth the other, the "clandestine companion" who is neither there nor not there (*celui qui ne m'accompagnait pas*).[34] Under that condition, giving voice takes place in a language other than the one presently inscribed and whose vociferation would require "that it stressed and cut off every word"—that is to say, whose enunciation, emphases, and articulation work against signification as known (SNB, 85). Since linguistic handiness no longer provides mastery of objectively present, serviceable items, to speak is to be "tested by the risky words that we had intentionally pronounced about them: *dangerous* words, words of the blind" (SNB, 79). The danger in abandoning nomination and naming then blocks disclosure of *what* is said in order to unveil a world. Voice is a dysfunction that enunciates de-nomination, unnaming—perhaps the "verbal" in Levinas—but especially a language of discretion, excessively hesitant when it comes to revelation. Conversing with his clandestine beloved, Narcissus's speech is "most open in its obliqueness, through interruption always persisting, always calling upon detour, and thus holding us as though in suspense between the visible and the invisible, or on the hither side of both" (IC, 31). Blind in the sense of a blind alley: no exit, terminus, or destination. Blind also in the sense of bearing no witness to events, divulgence of which would satisfy idle chatter, rumor, and curiosity (*Neugier*)—double blindness both discreet and protective. To be clear on what blind words protect: forgetting. Why speak of it? "'You torment yourself in speaking.' —'If not, I would torment myself in not speaking'" (SNB, 91).

The clandestine companion repeats a simple question, "Are you writing?" Obliged to answer in the negative, the reader is primed to wonder whether it is a call back to Narcissus from his fatuous languor, to retract his focus to the still-blank parchment. Or whether it is directed at Ovid who transgresses the deep law (like Homer, like Orpheus) by averting his gaze (blinding his vision) in order to uphold "the eternity of his desire" and write within the invagination that is myth. In both cases, the language of clandestinity by which Narcissus converses with the image and speaks forgetting of forgetting is that of writing—which is not to say, written. The language of "the language of writing" both is and is not the language presently inscribed. The other language resounds as neuter *through* the sounding of this language, the one at hand, the other, in the rhythm determined in spacing. It writes *différance*. It writes what is there by virtue of being elsewhere—not there—in the deployment of current usage, exemplary of linguistically available options. The language of the other is destined to write in the only language at hand, everydayness, since the other "language" "is inaccessible only insofar as every mode of acceding is foreign to it" (IC, 245). Its writing performs an erasure of the trace and is nothing other than that effacement. It puts into question the fact of citation; what is to be written has always already been written. If there is a totality (or quasi-totality) of language (arche-language), it would encompass what is possible to be written; it defines that possibility as such. As if there were a book of creation, a book in the future anterior, of memory to come.[35] Writing in everyday language, however, writes in reverse. It is exemplified in the day journal, the anodyne against forgetting.[36] It honors the record, to preserve, sanctify, or sanction with memory; at the same time, it is not the writing of transgressive, concupiscent desire. Narcissus keeps no diary. If he did, Blanchot says, his writing would "not be destined to leave traces, but to erase, by traces, all traces, to disappear in the fragmentary space of writing more definitely than one disappears in the tomb" (SNB, 50). Picture Narcissus in front of a page of text, artist gum in one hand, ready to "write."

In the relation without relation, relation of "the third kind," relation in the neuter voice, the companion of excessive desire recalls the writer to write the forgetting in the midst of forgetting. The impossibility of the summons incorporates a novel demand, presence without anything present.[37] The writer cannot be an I (Blanchot, Narcissus, Ovid) who is engaged resolutely with interiority, language, and work. Such subjectivity remembers traces, marks of difference that *à la* Freud get etched on a suitable psychic surface for recall (remark). Possibility (of mastery, decisiveness, sovereignty) lives on, awaiting the act of designation. With impossibility, the writer is retained by an impossible time, the temporality of the *pas d'impossibilité*. The companion orients the writing, measured by the *entre-temps* "between past and future, the absence of present ruled in the simplified form of forgetfulness" (SNB, 16). Within the high tonality of excessive desire (desire of the otherness of the other), the alchemical dream is finally realized—a new being that has interiorized both the law of sovereignty and the otherwise than law. That it is a being that never has yet nor will have appeared and that does not quit its nonappearance at birth, means that it has been delivered over to writing. "Born to write"; tasked by birth to a specific work. Blanchot: "[M]an sees himself assigned . . . the status of his new sovereignty: the sovereignty of being without being in the becoming without end of a death impossible to die" (IC, 209). Beyond the penumbra of ontology, one inscribes marks that strangely undo themselves and the world they affect. This is not a virus that injects havoc in programs but imbues the operative (or inoperative) with the power to effect a radical reversal of forgetting and reinstall . . . memory of disremembering itself. It is the conundrum of the border—unfixed, indecisive, labile, mobile—that disorders sovereignty.

Remembering Forgetting

To die, to awaken, to be reborn. These invisible crossings affect child-Narcissus's ritual murder ("the necessary destruction of the primary narcissistic representation").[38] To cross the line, to flood his vault with light, dispel the ambiguity of everydayness, its "refusal" of memory, and chase the ghosts and *Doppelgängers* from the scene: this would free the soul for God, or at least *Jemeingkeit*. But the trans*a*scendence that puts itself forward as sovereignty disdains the zero-point of power, the "uncertain obsession that always dispossesses" (SNB, 36). *Vergessenheit* accedes diffidently to the pathless insignificance in everyday obscurity, Narcissus's amnesia returns him to an impersonal anonymity that antedates both his name and the peculiar silence that will dissolve as soon as the ear turns to listen. Although oriented by an invisible magnetic north, *Alltäglichkeit* is Godless and without an I.[39] It is sovereignty in the neuter voice, that is, as Blanchot channels Bataille, "Sovereignty is NOTHING" (WD, 90). Pronouns and proper names belong to the day that conjoins subjecthood and presence, thereby delimiting interiority from exteriority. Forgetting, however, is not excluded from Narcissus's experience but rather nullifies the power to suffer it. Emphatically, "It is not beyond the trial of experience, but rather that trial from which we can no longer escape. An experience that one will represent to oneself as being strange and even as the experience of strangeness" (IC, 45). In its nonterminal trajectory (endless dying), it provides no alternative to sovereign survival but a nonmagisterial de-mastery of life. As if in letting memory fall apart, a countermemorial were set in motion, one whose dis(re)membering were in the relation of supplement to living memory.[40] It serves the survival of interiority, or more precisely, an alternate means to return to living memory. As if to *sur-vivre* were "to live on; not to live or, not living, to maintain oneself, without life, in a state of pure supplement, movement of substitution for life, but rather to arrest dying, arrest that does not arrest, making it, on the contrary, *last*" (SNB, 135).

A countermemory? However unmarked, effaced, or expunged the trace is, it necessarily differs from no trace, its nonoccurrence or –recurrence. Although no retrieval is possible (it could then be remembered), there is a quasi- or an ir-recognition of its supplementarity or non-passage in things. Countermemory responds to what replaces life, takes its place, takes over its place, and in the untruth of its dispersal recalls life to living.[41] It serves as a specialized perceptiveness, affective, kinesthetic, or proprioceptive, of the "movement of substitution" that triumphed over the deadness of forgetting. Call it the spark that iterates the forgetting; the scintilla or *punctum* able to repeat the same, the difference in the same: *différance*. The perception would be in excess to life, sovereign existence, master of the *Umwelt* and the Heideggerian workshop; it would be non-circumspective. Beyond possibility, it would have already crossed the border between doing and undoing (*desoeuvrement*) via the movement by which the difference is established.[42] It is almost nothing.[43] It is that which, though lacking the right, would arrest the non-event of dying, put it to work, induce it to recount the trans*de*-scendence, and make it set out toward the impossible act of regathering.

Survival (testament, iterability, remaining [*demeure*]) delays both death and life, remembering and forgetting, by obfuscating a clear-cut opposition or stable non-equivalence. In the life-after-life, it is (like) *différance* in how it differs and delays the beyond of identity and difference. One could say (speaking from psychoanalysis) that its play is within the "uninterrupted wake," behind dreams, outside consciousness-unconsciousness (WD, 59).

The pure supplement, "almost nothing," slips backward and forward across the bounds of its own making and allows survival of remembrance. Think of it as a memory that disremembers, unworks memory, but must itself remember to effect *that*—at the very least, in the form of an iterability. Levinas calls it "sovereign forgetting" though he fails to see the equivocation of it.[44] It is duplicitous. It acts lawfully, as supplement, at first augmenting the remembrance (prolonging, growing more repetitious) and reinforcing the *Entschlossenheit*. The retrieval of the question of being (the being of the question) from the murk of the perpetual wake (relation of the third kind) is a triumph of living over dying. It reanimates desire, if for the purpose of killing desire (the ongoing murder of kid-Narcissus) even as the entire dialectical structure is resurrected.[45] The supplementarity, an excess of remembering, however, is like the *pharmakon*, both cure and poison. It both supports remembrance and blocks it. It extends and serves remembering by arresting the forgetting (without arresting the arrest of forgetting). It is that *x* that lives in memory, comes alive in memory, brings memory alive, but is never remembered. But contrariwise, it reprograms forgetting by adding a new link to memory. It takes over forgetting and turns out simulations of remembering, the passage between, and the dream of full presence. In effect, it assumes the subject, assumes its voice (transposing it to the neuter), and replaces the first person singular with the third person impersonal. For forgetting it substitutes . . . writing.

The form of supplementarity is writing and writing is supplement— *the* supplement—to living memory, not in the sense of preservation (what would that be of?), but in attaching a program for unmaking forgetting: an unworking of unworking, negation of negation, that is the last affirmation, yes to yes, a double affirmation, an affirmation equipped with its own echo and nothing other than that, for example, self-consciousness. The event, supplement, writing, unforgetting, as an attachment, consists in nothing but coming about, going on, and being gone. Such is its "purity."

One could go farther. Intentional consciousness constitutes both active and passive voice to install the master discourse. Voice in the neuter is the supplement—almost nothing—that, added on, is priceless. Lacking intrinsic worth, it contains no "beautiful images" that lure it to a narcissism. Added to the master discourse whose heedfulness (*Besorgen*) is personified in the mother (tongue), it is potentized as an operational assemblage of talent.

"Sovereign forgetting" inaugurates an aporetic relation to possibility, that of impossibility. Where does voice in the neuter voice manifest but in writing? Writing, the supplemental possibility of impossibility, is responsible to an alterity omitted by active or passive voice. Responsibility to give voice to the neuter, to offer it vocal *force*, lies exclusively in writing, more precisely, in putting in writing that to which voice is given. Short of putting it in writing, that to which the neuter would give voice would be on mute, inaudible, lost to an unfathomable silence—a counterfactual. Yet no sooner is the neuter voice heard than it blends listlessly into background sound, a murmur clueless about things. The neuter voice is too reticent, too timid— too unjust—to be audible.

The disaster (void of recognition but already having taken place) that is forgetting the event (the event of forgetting) being put into writing, is the event of voicing the neuter, is not consciousness of being—an onto-theology based on war of opposites and death—but an aporia within the forgetting that severs remembrance, scarring it with the ghostly vestige of the real relation to the starry heavens.[46] That relation can never be known since it exceeds the sign system. An inoperable *cogito* is, however, a condition necessary to inscribing a meaning that necessarily forgets the presuppositions of rational discourse. "How could one know the law," Foucault asks, "and truly experience it, how could one force it to come into view, to exercise its powers clearly, to speak, without provoking it, without pursuing it into its recesses, without resolutely going ever farther into the outside into which it is always receding?"[47] Put otherwise, forgetting liberates writing from the *Sinngebung* whose coherency acts as a refutation of what the neuter voice would inscribe. Here the borderline of poetry awaits entry.

Narcissus (like Orpheus) looks into the whirl of primal energies and from that relation (the unthought) speaks to only himself (the prohibition against speaking with another). He is bound to give voice in the neuter and, moreover, find that he can no longer speak *as* himself—but as an '*il*,' an it-or-one. Deposed of mastery, given over in servitude to another to the maximum of voicing for it, his vocality unknowingly serves an alien. Narcissus discovers that knowledge too along with power has been stripped. It has become hearsay (*Gerede*), ambiguous or straightforwardly deceptive. There is more. The neuter voice is also the voice neutered and desexed. Desexing does not leave voice erotically unattractive or attracted, voice of a eunuch, a computer-generated or stenographic voice—eros a dead theme. In the neuter, eros is displaced as the voice tries on masks (*per-sona*). A favorite is thanatopic. In Blanchot, writing is dying and the trope, macabre, morbid, moribund, or medical: "the burn of life which cannot burn out" (WD, 105). As if death is erotic, as for Plato, it dies, is reborn, dies again, all within a single day.

It is the movement of forgetting that writing would intend (if it could) to inscribe (unmaking the book as a valid, completed, totalized text). The killing of child-Narcissus vociferates the neuter, as if being and desire were coextensive adjuncts of interiority and the annihilation of the latter at once closed access to being and cancelled the struggle of opposites. Active and passive voice, agents of the law (of being), are put on mute. The outside of law—exteriority—is not, however, lawless anarchy. There, a more rigorous lawfulness rules, the law of the neuter, the neuter itself if the neuter were capable of ipseity. The logic of *ne-uter* that comes from the upsurge of *différance*, not from Aristotle, Hegel, or Frege, provides a law "that can be posited only in its own transgression."[48] The strictness and rigor allow no grip for possession of power. One illicit move is assertion and one such power, to state "this is how things are." Truth and untruth become unfixed in relation to each other. There outside is a lethargic murmur, unpleasantly hypnotic, in which the material of thought is colloidally suspended. The law's errant influence is that to which voice must comply. The remains, an infinite conversation, cite an inscription from another text or a copy of a fragmentary document that will have been written. The charge demands a surrender of designation, as if the link between word and object had been corrupted and sent error messages. As if the nominative didn't work; the names it named name nothing. Naming nothing doesn't prevent naming, but causes naming malfunctions, sometimes going attributive, sometimes imperatival.

A Supplement of Forgetting

The play of forgetting is equivocal and duplicitous. To view Narcissus's forgetting as loss or privation of mastery—the unitary potency of the I—reads Blanchot's texts as books of memory. They would then constitute a primary response to the Heideggerian problematic of being: "But are we nowadays even perplexed at our inability to understand the expression 'being'?"[49] At the same time, they serve as exercises along Nietzschean lines in the dismantling of memory as keeper of interior sovereignty.[50] "Forgetfulness without memory" displays forgetting, not as counterconcept to remembrance, but as its own thing (WD, 3).[51] Nietzsche posits an "active oblivion" that clears the slate and empties the space where retention (repression) lodges a replication of the event. It clears the spool of memory from the entanglement of events. Remembering is subject to exploitation by guilt (*Schuld*) and the set of prohibitions and prescriptions that constitute the law of slave morality, the law, period. Although memory is a potency of intentional consciousness, the counterconcept of forgetting draws power from a traumatic encounter with nothing, *das Nichts*. The value of memory lies in attestation and the witness through the internal relation to mortality, "my death" and the possibility of the impossible. Remembrance testifies to self-presence by attesting to one's being mortal. Self-presence requires a rigorously dynamic law of identity, an identity that will have come to be, and in addition, the self-movement (auto-affection) of intentional consciousness.

An iterative memory of the simulacrum (image in the "second version") screens the subject from the outside. Forgetting in the supplementary sense surrenders remembrance, with its anterior guilt, "bad conscience," and other bourgeois masks that dissimulate unity. There can be no *one* in position to witness. The end to attestation frees interiority of accusation and indebtedness (*Verschuldung*). The delirium of an exchange based on such debt will have been exorcised.[52] The I can suspend its misplaced effort to gather a self in front of what is present and to honor synchrony. The absent, or better, the forgotten witness no longer impedes the border crossing proclaimed by "bad conscience." Transgression and contestation are permitted. Freedom from the haunt of guilt describes a life without suppression of the excess, an excessive excess. Since forgetting withdraws power from death, the possibility that is impossible is no longer possible. Death de-potentized marks the impossibility of possibility, that is, the impossibility of arrival.[53] Nothing comes of anything; embarkation is an aimless sojourn without destination, a nomad plunge into uncharted terrain. The freedom that has become unbounded in the absence of marks follows a light, meandering trajectory; this needs emphasis. It is exemplified best in reading. "Reading does not produce anything, does not add anything. It lets be what is. It is freedom: not the freedom that produces being or grasps it, but freedom that welcomes, consents, says yes, can say only yes" (SL, 194). Unconcerned to the point of distraction, reading engages *Gelassenheit*.

Forgetting as renunciation of mastery, as freeing up or disencumbering. The latter undercuts the sovereign subject by negating the operation ("bad conscience") that supports the solvency of memory and refuses to reinstate the latter's primacy. To block remembrance is to disengaged the apparatus of attestation and being-toward-death.[54] Amnesia comes into its own when Blanchot alludes to "inoperative forgetfulness, forever idled, which is nothing and does nothing" (WD, 85). It is conceived on a par with the inoperative community, lacking intentionality, under the law of an other time, and partaking of interiority through means different from remarking. To speak of a time that does not deposit memory traces (immemorial time) is misleading. As with the relation of the third kind, in which terms are absolved of relating, a non-employable forgetting leaves no traces—because the marks are too light or the "medium" too labile. Without bypassing *différance*, "idle" forgetting is indifferent to consciousness and independent of the conscious-unconscious opposition. It is an effect of the disaster "in leaving everything intact" (WD, 1). At the same time, engagement with *différance* promises a role to the neuter voice, that is, in writing and what can be considered as a result of being written.[55]

Excursus on Myth

One could say, with Bataille, with Nancy, myth interrupts the repetition of the world established by self-love and auto-eroticism, in order to reinscribe an account of the killing. Myth interrupts in its absence. Myth is defunct, "Great Pan is dead," the gods have departed in a retreat that doubles the betrayal of humanity by humanity. Myth is a missing portion of the *epos*, and in its absence, what is said says nothing of the mystery of transparence. It leaves intact its respect for the depths of experience that necessarily overflow the bounds of signification, that is, the sacred. The excess that would be myth is unemployable by the dialectic of interiority. Hence, where myth would "speak," it tells of the sacrificial murder, the alchemical protocol of transubstantiation, that yields a novel voice. The disruption occurs because myth invites linguistic force through a direct, less mediated fashion than discursive language. A speech of oracular discretion that respects countersaying.[56] Further, all myth is arche-mythology since it gives an account of the movements of the starry heavens. Loss of mythic figuration, due to amnesia about archaic time, leaves human experience susceptible to the breakage whose abbreviation is the disaster. But myth is not a panacea. Blanchot warns that it offers more than it can give.[57] Myth does not inoculate the dialectic against severe afflictions, e.g., "Outside. Neutral. Disaster. Return" (WD, 57–58).

Playing with seduction, the Narcissus myth shows (without telling) the double fold of an image backlit by otherworldly darkness—and a third between intentional and non-consciousness (consciousness in the neuter). The story lends itself to dialectic but contains a parasitic supplement that proves fatal to ontology. As with other myths, narrative discourse disguises an otherness that must disjoin itself from everything. Myth, the alien forever alienated, would dwell beyond and between active and passive grammars, a *gramme* that neutrally vociferates. Myth as a nomadic shelter, mobile, ephemeral, discreet, within which the force of nondisclosure can be somewhat attenuated. Myth is not the explosive *chose* but its cloak: the slurring sibilance of images, the event concealed beneath a high emotional tonality. Myth is not yet a book so it explodes nothing.[58] Child-Narcissus is captivated and makes himself in accordance with the image, smiling when it smiles, scowling when it scowls. But seduction unmakes the seducer, exposing him to the illusion of memory that is a paradoxical forgetting with which he remains fitfully absorbed. Oblivious to death, the tragic and catastrophic, drained of will, Narcissus faces only the misapprehension, repeated. His thought seduced by a perennial immaturity, he is given to an immobility in the face of dying. That he lives forgetfulness is precisely what makes him primed for transformation. The myth de-scribes the reduction of reality to a phantom, a miraculous life to a dying of immortality and desire to responsibility.

2

The Mirror

"The Sky, the Same Sky, Suddenly Open"

We can always ask ourselves about the neuter, without the neuter entering into the questioning.

—Maurice Blanchot, *The Step not Beyond*

Identity and *Différance*

What value to assign to the sky in the *recit*, "(A Primal Scene?)," [or: ("A
Primal Scene?" where placement of brackets and parentheses affects meaning)]? It occurs at the precise center, the fold, ridge, center, median, crest, or
midway point of *The Writing of the Disaster*; its placement is not fortuitous,
but the play or gamble of the book. It is an italicized document folded
into the two parts of an essentially autobiographical (autothanatographical)
work.[1] A conspicuously ambiguous document, even within the Blanchot
corpus, given its narrative appearance: Is it story, *recit*, true account, memory
laced with childlike hyperbole, part of a theory, record of a dream, conceit,
or ruse? Does it offer testimony or ruin testimony? Its border on both the
earlier and later halves of the book provides a threshold or passage that can
be crossed in either direction. The title (barring the question mark) makes
reference to Freud's "primal scene," an initiation by witness in which the
child first sees the sexual activity of the parents. A witness's perception
of a transgressive event, when, moreover, attestation cannot be mediated
by judgment or knowledge. Therefore, a mediation without the benefits of

mediation. An event whose taking place is in question, but which, whether attached to an actual occurrence or not, globally affects desire, especially erotic desire. Does the typographical mark (?) make a questionable allusion to Freud, suggest an attribution of primacy or originariness, or contest what constitutes a "scene"?[2]

At the fold, there is nothing, no text, only the topological effect of folding. In the doubling, which comes before and which after is left indecisive, permitting reading backward as possible or as preferred. In which case the incipit would become the final sentence of the book, "*Shining solitude, the void of the sky, a deferred death: disaster,*" a likely frontispiece (WD, 146). The first fold leads up to and ends with a meditation on child-Narcissus interpreted psychoanalytically by Serge Leclaire and Winnecott, and the second in a penultimate segment presents a reading of the myth itself. Midway through the second part, the longest italicized fragment of the book gives detailed commentary and analysis of "(A Primal Scene?)." As if to emphasize the aporetic space, the middle of the narrative speaks of a sky "*absolutely black, absolutely empty*" (WD, 72). At the fold, at the center of the fold, there is nothing to cross, absolutely no way a reader can advance, come, or pass over. It is a *mi-lieu*, a midpoint that is a no-place, where a nomadic wandering over unmarked (unremarkable) paths never guarantees arrival at the other side and where hazards abound for reaching a destination. The words of the companion echo:

> To say that I understand these words would *not* be to explain to myself the dangerous peculiarity of my relations with them. Do I understand them? I do *not* understand them, properly speaking, and they too who partake of the depth of concealment remain without understanding. But they don't need that understanding in order to be uttered, they do *not* speak, they are *not* interior, they are, on the contrary, without intimacy, being altogether outside, and what they designate engages me in this "outside" of all speech, apparently more secret and more interior than the speech of the innermost heart. (TOW, 321–22)

A fold whose doubling adds nothing except by performance of its supplement. Whose massive ineffectuality recalls the incipit or opening of the book: "The disaster ruins everything, all the while leaving everything intact" (WD, 1). There, the disaster functions as a border zone whose crossing is at every point of the text and whose greatest risk is at the "point of no return," the midpoint. Prohibiting movement across, it is a limit that arises simultaneously with its infraction. To make matters worse, it is not a known limit or law, or an unknown one whose limitation though indeterminate is nonetheless there, or even one that limits by indecisiveness. In the zone where ruination is universal because it has always been, to transgress is to discover that the movement had been accomplished unendurably long before setting out, and, therefore, cannot presently be undertaken.

The fold in the center is inserted in the volume at the place of opening. A book naturally opens to the centerfold. In the center is the void, "absolutely empty," without words, able to unsay, there to undo (*desoeuvre*) language—to express the death wish of language in language, both language's desire to die and the death wish's desire to be a linguistical designate. At the same time, the center (of earth, of the cosmos) is by tradition the spawning grounds of creatures, as if poured from that site in the ebullition of the creator. As if, when the book opens to the "absolutely empty," it is to the holy of holies, the site in the Temple, forbidden to Gentiles, that Pompey imperiously entered, only to leave its vacancy puzzled and unverified. The possible coincidence of the most holy and most destructive (disastrous), the height of the aporetic, would then define the central threshold or border as troublingly enigmatic, abusive with regard to belief, and paralytic to thought. The immobilization of that point, the point at which the operative *Sinngebung* of language gets stuck, is precisely where the step—the *pas*—of passivity is taken.[3]

That can be otherwise stated: the book opens to the unworking of itself—that inessentially is the disaster. Simultaneously, the disaster comprises the theme of investigation; in the destitution to which it opens and is opened, there are actually two disasters. A double disaster: disaster of the double. The first is by constatement, according to current terminology; the second by performance. The discourse constates the particulars and specifics while in its performativity, the text is always destroyed utterly as soon as the reader begins. It is possible to read the book from beginning to end, in the right order, including the centerfold, and fail to see what it exposes. This is a "proof" that the disaster changes nothing, ironically and literally. Which is to say that the forgetting or disremembering of the I qua sovereign is a non-event, incapable of eventuating since it belongs to a time that evades self-presenting.

The scene with the sky open, moreover, is not set panoramically, from a shore or mountaintop, in relation to the earth, but rather is framed through a window, "through the pane." Viewed through a portal from inside, the event of enucleation yields a situation that defines the mortal human Dasein: one who dwells being-in within being. Between viewer and view, the window normally mediates, lets light in, and keeps night out, excludes other elements, wind, water, particles of matter, ultraviolet rays. A space of interchange (picture a Vermeer interior), it can equally attenuate the harsh elemental outside or celebrate a ritual of life within. By the same token, the frame de-distances (*Ent-fernung*), making the far near and placing it circumspectly within the world of serviceability. Distance is not thereby annihilated, but lingers as an anxiety. The exterior world becomes a picture hung on the wall, a *nature morte* or part of a cinematic sequence, the real as domesticated, en-framed (*Gestell*), under control.

The window frame augments an infinite gaze, fascination with the dark gaze that looks back. The look goes out, insouciance to guide it, an unconcern that is discreet with regard to abiding indeterminacies. In an effortlessness that erodes the being, the attraction disperses to the far horizon and beyond. The window thus invites a further penetration beyond its contents or quasi-contents since part of what is contained isn't there—nor is not there. To follow the movement out defines the vector of exteriority whose aggravated passivity of *Gelassenheit* empties an intentional consciousness that resists impoverishment. Attraction opens obscurity—hidden, encrypted, camouflaged, disguised, masked, sacred. Accompanying the frame are fissures, gaps, rifts, cracks, and other stress-related tropes. Through the window, the appearance of nonappearance can take place; the blind that catch sight of the invisible. The painterly eye has a view of this window-effect and can create the subtle resemblance to the scene that is on the canvas.[4]

Of greater import is that the window pane (*vitre*, compare *vivre*, to live), the glass, has a double effect. It is both a barrier that prohibits full sensory contact with the world outside and a reflective surface that mirrors an image of the interior. The duality restates the enigmatic nature of glass, a physical substance that is a liquid maintaining itself as a solid. There is always a (perhaps subliminal) reflection in need of an account. Unless the interior is totally dark, the viewer who looks directly out receives a faint image of self, a phantomization that observes, not the sky, but the observer. Wherever there is ambient light, the image, the double, is there, gazing back. With the force of the image looking in, the inward turn is indicated: the turn away from the looked-at object and the detour in the direction of an imaged source, a source of image—point of origination. This image, superimposed on the scene, can be taken as exemplar for the curse of Narcissus: that he is obliged never to see directly but always around corners, eyes averted, looking away.[5]

The other image, of self as other: intrusive, indiscreet, voyeuristic. It is there because it is not there, it has no *there* as far as seeing goes. It doesn't show up. It spies. And then, by a sudden lighting effect, a new slant, and it is there by being not there, having disappeared into the vision of the viewer. Viewing has turned focal while the double survives only by virtue of non-macular sight. By not being there, it magnetically influences what is regarded, the particular focus of concern. In vision—but never with apodictic certainty—the other's image is obscure, a self-portrait partially effaced, to Derrida's eye, the blind leading the blind. But the obscurity is shared in that the chiaroscuro of the living I mimes the flutter of primal dark, deep unconsciousness, intentionality drawn back in support of vital function, *sur*-vival. That fluting of bare being, the *il y a*, resonates unto the conscious life of the subject and provides it with a lowest border.

The image "under glass" evokes a basal note: the haunting presence of the face. It is inappropriable. It cannot be grasped and presents itself as elusive, evasive, fugitive, marginal, insignificant. It is there to dispute. No one responds to its contestation and insistence to the point of vanishing. The image doesn't fade away altogether, it stays there (grin of the Cheshire cat) and goes dark. One need only look at the dark face of the glass to sense that it is there still, the *there* is there still, the *there is* is still there still. An intelligence whose motives are beyond the ken and whose radical ambiguity figures a face of terror, "sedentary dread" (SNB, 66).[6]

The double who peers in is a secret self. It is not invisible but the viewer alone is in a position to see it. Not that it is recognized or perceived as such. The one in the glass, moreover, is quickly repositioned in the imaginary. The attraction is a magnetic phenomenon that Lacan celebrates and places at the center of his thought on child development. The interiority that is secret, the secret within, is as though it were an image assigned to a reflective surface, for instance, the face of another. To speak with it requires a secret language, not the mother tongue whose general usage is supported by law, but one that respects the singular silence of the gaze.[7] It won't do to try, as Horatio with the phantom of Hamlet's dead father, while speaking in the usual way. Because of the singular secrecy, language itself must be superseded or supplemented with an other's voice. To turn toward the secret self by turning away, to converse, requires the neuter. There, words will have ceded their attachments in order to exhibit a free suspension within the flex of meaning; moreover, whosoever uses them is no longer an I since the first person singular conjugate no longer functions. This makes the secret "neither another self for me, nor another existence, neither a modality or a moment of universal existence, nor a superexistence, a god or a non-god, but rather the unknown in its infinite distance" (IC, 77).

The window-glass replicates Narcissus's pool or stream. As soon as the look meets glass, an event of primal narcissism is called forth. Below the threshold, invisible, the image is returned to act in its turn upon image maker, to ply its recursive structure in front of the one who attends, then without name or pronoun. An unworked image undoing the forward intention of mastery, its deployment is a stick in the spokes of time's wheels. Primal narcissism desires an indeterminate something of the secret one. The lack of definition is paralytic, as if the Medusa head had the world turned to stone. A hobbled desire, an impeded mobility that produces thwarted, inconsequential undertakings, as well as the regret of an asymmetrical look.

The sadness of Narcissus, it must be said, is not wholly due to unattainable desire, frustration, or obsession. The infinite gulf that separates his beloved, which he is forbidden to cross, congeals that. But also, his sadness is because he forgets, fails to keep a mastery, and finds it necessary to lose hold. He lets go in distraction (*Gelassenheit* improper), relaxing on autopilot whose programmed control is the default. He suffers an absence linked with an indebtedness, lack of competence, proficiency, and possibility. As if devotion to the other cost him a birthright, what is "ownmost" his: remembrance. Like a gift never given, it is the trace thereof, moreover, that gnaws at his well-being as it posits the alchemical dream of transformations and its economy. Never again will his reserve of desire be superabundant.

The book opens to the center, the nothing that is a sky as viewed through window glass (vitrine) that reconstitutes itself as "almost nothing." Substance in commonplace transparency is not transparent enough to forbid image making. Obtruding at the vanishing point that reverses the line of sight, a ghostly replica situates itself—a self-portrait—that watches the observer observe, an observer's observer whose observations exist only by transference, another looking-glass operation. A face "hidden in the sky" like a child's game (Find the Hidden Objects in the Picture), whose image the viewer can approach only under specified conditions, for instance, low lighting. The glass front is invisible, difficult to de-distance, and confronts sight with a mediation that must be seen through or behind in order for the intentional object to appear. This occultation is also a superimposition, one appearance on top of (*sur-*, *sur-vitre*) a second.[8] The effect is a scattering or dissemination of facial features across the sky; they "scatter like sand" (DS, 143). It persists as long as the look does, through the fullness or absence of the sky, highlighted when superimposed over the latter.

At some point, the gaze is violently ruptured. This occurs at the advent when absence makes its unintended appearance. It shows up in the largest possible container, the sky. Suddenly the sky is not there, the *same* sky that just was. Blanchot underlines the law of sameness—*auto-*, *selbst*, *même*—meaning that it is not a different sky, an earlier one, for instance, that had changed with the weather. There is an absence of change, a no-change, an insistent sameness or insistence of the same, that is striking: that the empty sky doesn't produce a different one but one and the same. The same remains one and the same. It is not replaced or supplemented by the empty sky; is it a change in the *autos*? It is a survivor because of its immunity to change and is unresponsive to threats of indiscretion. As if its substance could now simultaneously bear contradictory attributes, as if the laws of thought were suspended (*epoche*), as if the retreat or reduction to a more originary sighting annulled without annulling the appearance. The same-not-same is the last possible mark of a border (a lowest), the mark before illegibility and forgetting. The next step (*pas au-delà*) would be lost to immemorial time, time not remembered: forgetting "of the third kind." That time paradoxically holds the key to remembrance. But it doesn't remember this. Time that does not allow for intentionality doesn't allow for folds; everything unrolls flat. It is a time of (infinite) discretion since by discretion one chooses not to remember things such as remembering discretion. Secreted in its vault, the memory of how to remember evokes no remembrance or self-presence that constitutes an ownmost potentiality of being: singularity. The secret is empty of itself, contains nothing, has nothing to tell, as if there were no secret. Therein lives the secret—but this conclusion is too hurried.

At this border, on the way to the irreducible, the subject is susceptible to the onslaught of forgetting. The encounter evokes a terror that shatters the world and leaves the interior with the high tonality of the fall—into nothing. Blanchot calls it the "fragile fall," fragile because the intensity might exceed the limit, inducing a limit-experience—threshold crossed already and no turning back. The fragility is measured against the dream of reality, the dream the dreamer dreams who passes through the obscurity of the everyday (*Alltäglichkeit*) with devious remembrance. It is the dream that the fall is easily broken, landing soft, dying deferrable, and return guaranteed. Furthermore, the calamity has been held in reserve by the glass pane.[9] Apparently durable, its material property is to fragment on sudden impact. Something shatters in the same. It remains the same, it cannot change or be otherwise. But now it is empty, absolute emptiness, the perfect void—words that are not void signify without resemblance. The words dissemble. They give an index, point, but do not express. To realize the fact of language with apodictic certainty is a step beyond the step beyond shattering. It engages the "errant disarray, and yet with the imperceptible but intense suddenness of the outside, as an irresistible or unforeseen resolve which would come to us from beyond the confines of decision" (WD, 40). The sovereign forgetting (with)holds a decisiveness, double and duplicitous. To unmake the fall or to fall in errancy toward the neuter outside, both interweave and conjoin the outside's dis(re)membering force.

The sacrificial remembrance that instantiates the alchemical dream of transmutation is the indirect approach to proximity whose infinite detour leads through writing. The sacrifice is not voluntary inasmuch as volition defines the I and its dialectical finesse. Neither willed nor unwilled, the gratuitous non-event of the disaster slips by unnoticed; the suddenness of the fragile fall, completed before it begins. The fall is repetitive, the fragility irrevocable. Yet each time, ruin must precede the event, supplementing it with a pretext, a foreword or parergon that cancels the meaning of the body text, the event, like a spoiler. Things get told before they are supposed to be said: exhibitionism. Only through sacrifice, with its aporia, is the highest affirmation possible, Nietzsche's *yes* to *yes*, as Derrida channels him.[10] Negativity does not come to an end with absolute knowledge and the identity of identity with nonidentity, as Hegel. It must be borne beyond, unto the final contestation that castrates the father. But, and here's the catch, the father survives, the cut is to-come, an advent. The double *yes*, the affirmative of Nietzsche's last man, is a messianic performative, which is to say, an *après coup*. It will have opened to the event before it will have come. Or, as Blanchot, "I don't know, but I have the feeling that I'm going to have known" (SNB, 112, repeated at 124; italics omitted).

Remembrance meets with sacrificial death when desire strives to unite with the desired, narcissistic gratification, when the gaze becomes enraptured with the outside, when voice enunciates in the neuter. The threatened desire subverts self-enclosure by slipping past passive receptivity and active grasping alike; both are distracted by the appeal of the thing. Each is torn by impatience, wanting to name and to render the image dialectically sound. Concealing an impossibility too discreet to enter the fray of everydayness, unconcern, heedless of desire, alone can respond to the neuter. This is the menace of narcissism classically understood: it subtracts from, rather than adding to, interiority. It opens to the outside. There, remembrance is lost in a vain search for traces. The desert bears none.

Remembrance and Writing

Voice in the neuter exists only in writing and vocalizes only when writing the inscription at the very moment that the voice-writing speaks and (simultaneously) the one writing transcribes what is inaudibly vociferated. It comes from far off, like Heidegger's *Ferne*, designating conscience. Although it preserves distance, the neuter voice resists *Jemeingkeit* by unworking the reticence in which that voice speaks. "To speak in the neutral is to speak at a distance preserving this distance without *mediation* and without *community*, and even in sustaining the infinite distancing of distance" (IC, 386). The words vociferated are one and the same (like the sky), but now in a voice more ancient than discursively oriented vocalization. Older, antecedent, sacred. Writing supposes the voice always there already, but what does this mean? That it surpasses the exigence of being? —Yes, "the exigency of the neutral tends to suspend the attributive structure of language: the relation to being, implicit or explicit, that is immediately posed in language as soon as something is said" (ibid.). To voice the neuter in writing is to inscribe emphasis in all tenses. The neuter insists.[11] It will never not insist, refusing (the first step of contestation) to make peace in the war with the onto-theological project.

Sacrificial remembrance is necessitated by its attachment to living memory—re-marking the moment in the moment—an attachment that mirrors Narcissus's posture. *Mnenosyne* leans over to look at herself looking, fascinated by the sight, giving over infinitely in an abyssal movement.[12] This serves as exemplar for both intentional consciousness and the death experience (in Hegel's moment), the self-aware I whose dying forgets death and opens to the passivity of the neuter. The neuter voice does not surpass the appropriative voice; the two are incommensurable. Furthermore, it is the *same* I (voiced neutrally) as voiced dialectically, now absolutely vacant and unknowing—the aporetic frame of the window. Interiority is there, guarded resolutely, and at the same time, not there but replaced by an other, uninscribed, non-linguistical, antisymbolic, that would give voice non-acoustically on its behalf. The subjunctive "would" conveys a force of responsibility. To serve the other, the writing mirrors the selfsame absence of place, dwelling, and power that alterity suffers. The sacrifice responds to an "unlimited call for help," Blanchot says, and "causes me to disappear in the infinite movement of service where I am only temporarily singular and a simulacrum of unity" (WD, 21). To meet an unnamable responsibility, interiority exhausts its infatuation with closure and welcomes the unforeseeable: the outside.

The obligation to the other may ineluctably lead to the ethical mode, as in Levinas. There, the subject is a nonconsenting hostage who substitutes for the other (*Autrui*) on the basis of a choice that predates the possibility of promise making. In a withdrawal that defines the same, an irreplaceable I takes the other's place without ceding its identity. Just as the alterity of absolute emptiness remakes the sky the *same* sky, so too otherness fixes the sameness of the first person pronoun, pronominal presence, interiority, and selfhood. Called to service by the other (dispossessed, without means or relations), the I is I no longer but one conjugated in terms of anonymity, stripped of biography, powerless and susceptible to persecution. That one, the other to the other, is an unmade identity and forced to answer for irresponsibilities committed by the stranger, even unto murder. Bereft of initiation, including saying, the I-no-longer is nonetheless assigned to responsible action: this high paradox defines Levinas's sense of the ethical. It asks a difficult question: whether a relation so suffocated, a relation of double reversal or betrayal, is to the other as other or whether the relation is to a who or a what that is an impersonation of the (former) other. Is alterity the sacrificial lamb on the altar of the ethical whose remembrance is sacrificed for a bowl of pottage? For the new master is obsessed with destroying the self that the subject used to be. Blanchot asks: How does this thought differ from a despotism of the absolute ego?[13]

"The subjectivity of the subject is persecution and martyrdom."[14] Here, sacrifice—the killing of the I—would be an affirmation of the other (*Autrui*).

Prior to any act, the other's poverty obligates the subject to end its usurpation of the other's "place in the sun." The nexus of activity is dissolved by the moral imperative that distributes the subject's possessions (its genitive) among the needy. "A borrowed, happenstance singularity," she is left to wander in the other's generality, alien and unwelcome, and to endure a temporality that does not lapse (WD, 18). On the road to sagacity and magisterial wisdom, one renounces the paradise of kings and enters the purgatory of slaves. Such would be the lot of child-Narcissus if killing his fascination were in the script, for the murder weapon that Levinas provides is in fact the substitution of Narcissus for the other, the other that is not the image but other to the image.

Sacrificial killing, according to Bataille, yields an ambiguous result. It aims at a spectacle of death to produce an understanding of the forbidden, which, for Hegel, is negation. The negative dies, removed by prohibition from direct experience, and is raised to dialectical power. There it is instrumental in the investiture of subjecthood. But there is an "unemployable" portion that evades the achievement.[15] Annihilation of narcissistic impulse is adjunct to remembrance since the subject bears the thought of death in mind, the *Sein zu Tod*. The individuality, however, cannot have lived through death, which "belongs" to forgetting, and the death of individuality, rather than borne in mind, is given to be forgotten. Between these two deaths, the space of the neuter voice opens in which two phantoms roam, the ghost of the subject and the ghost of the subject's forgetting.[16] Inasmuch as writing inscribes itself in that space, it is haunted both by the living dead and the immemorial dead. The reader recalls the familiar faces that crowd around Odysseus in Hades—his mother, the dead boatswain—as well as the faceless others too numerous to be counted.

While pane glass keeps the secret image of Narcissus, the window takes the place of the sacrificial altar. In one sense, the sky is sacrificed. Although given in sacrifice and inalterably removed, the gift is not in the least changed. There has been no exchange: that is the aporia. The sky is one and the same, the self-same sky. At the same time it has been offered and taken: sky is not "there." It can no longer be de-distanced and no longer dwells in the everyday. Nothing is changed, therefore, everything is. In another sense, the sacrifice is performed on Narcissus himself. What does killing the child accomplish? What is given to sacrifice is the living body that is the resemblance of Narcissus. As with a cadaver that replaces the body after death, it is *in the image*. The image then is "in" the body until it is liberated at death. Think of it as one of the nine souls of ancient Egyptian thought, perhaps the *ka*. Similarly, Narcissus gives up his body to be joined to the image: superimposed, we would say. He wants to sacrifice his own position in order to survive as a superimposition. That way, Narcissus would gain access to what no mere mortal can, a direct death experience. He could experience, contra Bataille, his own death, stage by stage, as he ceased being a creature of earth and became a palimpsest. Could one say that he would gain wisdom of an imagistic or imaginary kind from super-imposition as he keeps watch over the comings and goings (*fort* and *da*) of "image after image"?

The abnormal economy of sacrifice conceives the ritual murder as a great benefit to the victim. Release from discourse originates at the hidden point that attracts the attention, draws it beyond itself in fascination, opens the border already open, and waits for the future to catch up with the past. The wonder lies in a new-found enjoyment in the work of putting into writing what already was put into writing but then without recognition. Avidity is relinquished as voice is neutered, it is true, but in an aporetic vociferation that must eschew audibility and is scarred with the mute rumble: background or limit-condition to sonority. The inauguration of desire-free writing, or desire paralyzed but whose inner core lacks access to the springs of action, ends the play between image and imaged that underwrites inscription. Narcissus as a superimposition on the self-image occupies the position newly assigned to inscription. Neither living nor non-living, he has renounced life in order to survive as a conjunct of the imaginary. With it but apart from it, he interiorly transcribes the image outside: "What happens through writing is not of the order of things that happen" (WD, 62).

Crucially, the imposture in the superimposition puts the non-order of the imaginary into writing. So many puttings and placings . . . Fraudulence, fakery, trickery, phoneyism, counterfeiting: writing is the appearance of the nonappearance of an event (the appearance of the non-event).[17] It inscribes what doesn't take place—a naive definition of fiction—not constatively but in performance of the empty non-place. Its description is dis-scription. It transcribes a superimposed diapositive in relation to a beloved image, a deposition that attests to the narcissistic devotion to love. What writing posits, however, is less the imaginary and more what is owed the superim-posing of the real (a bad definition of the surreal). The real is the image primed to explode into non-acoustical voice that momentarily nullifies the work of sense-making, high privilege of the symbolic order. *"There is no explosion except a book."*

Narcissus's going "under glass" is an imposition as well as a superim-position. It presents an imposition relative to a full view of the scene. It occludes or occults with a stubborn, in-the-way attitude. It asks to be seen and insists to the degree that it will not be seen; such is its intransigence. Annoyance, distraction, diversion. It is an imposition to the convenience of everydayness whose ontic reality is conveyed by a two-value logic. The image remains a thorn in the side of dialectical truth that derives from disclosure of what is. The amphiboly of glass, its two images (representation and nonrepresentation), defines the field where the contestation of the imaginary and the real is played.

There is correlatively an amphiboly of translation: the neuter as expressed is the neuter imported into the active-passive matrix. The neuter in itself, or rather, without "*ipse*," inscribed anywhere, the neuter without itself or lacking its ipseity, speaks "language qua language," the other language that differs from this language by the least minimal difference and which gets entirely lost in translation. What does this mean? The neuter resists discourse; it remains a companion apart, in excess, repetition of contestation, and challenge to a philosophy of being. As Blanchot writes in his review of Bataille's *Inner Experience*: "If the questioning arms itself with this reassuring perspective, challenges the vague and superior authority (God) that has given it its form, suppresses any hope in life and outside of life, it is the very fact of existence that is now called into question" (FP, 38). That contestation entails fragmentary writing needs emphasis. Enunciations from different points, sometimes radically inconsistent, fragments are the "pulling to pieces (the tearing) of that which never has preexisted (really or ideally) as a whole nor can it ever be reassembled in any future presence whatever" (WD, 60). In combat with ontology (onto-theology), fragmentation expresses *différance*, that which is the precondition of the "there" and of the world.[18]

Narcissus's ability to live through the death experience and be conjoined with (superimposed on) the beloved image is of a piece with an interiority that lives "under glass," the looking-glass one superimposed on the viewpoint of the observer. Like an unwanted window on a computer screen that won't go away, he is on the threshold of the imaginary, as if peering in at the *Sinngebung* version of the image or reacting to the absence of one. Upon crossing the uncrossable border, the desire for the gaze or for a vital, organic mingling with the lifeless entity doesn't weaken. But passing over, he knows what no mortal knows, and this makes him—even more than Orpheus—the Blanchotian hero. He knows the noncoincidence of death and dying.

As pure radiance, the superimposed being is not fully image. It is dependent on the laws of the physical universe that are part of the symbolic order. By contrast, his beloved exists apart from materiality (light by tradition is identified with nonmateriality). The infinite gap remains, repeated in the transcendental realm. The irreducibility is the deep cause of Narcissus's sadness. The duality cannot be expunged, not even by death.

If Narcissus's sacrificial murder is to provide a spectacle and by extension an indirect experience of death, there must be a spectator. The one who watches over the spectacle of his own death is Narcissus. That is his teaching: resurrection takes place upon receiving the gift of death. Resurrection, the desired end, is without beginning and end. The one who watches is the already departed, given over to the greater exigency of the void. That there is nothing to attract him doesn't diminish the fact that he is nonetheless infinitely attracted. The amphiboly arises from the coincidence of spectator and spectacle and ordains the performativity. It has to do with an excess that escapes the one but not the other. Coincidence and dissymmetry. The spectator sees more than is seen in the spectacle.

Immortal Writing

The empty sky marks the destruction of verticality. One can no longer be oriented by an above-below axis. There is nothing above, no above, no position relative to an above, nothing higher than the level of earth. Life is reduced to Flatland. Sky-earth, mortals, gods: the four no longer prance in a Heideggerian round song of existence. There can be no trans*ascendence*, no mounting the rungs or the rocky incline with Plato's hero, to a vision of the Good. Only trans*descendence*, exiting below to the outside of the world-line, the totality of what is: evacuation of being. To descend, moreover, without the celestial compass point, the north-south of the celestial sphere. Flatland creatures are mystified by the uncanny intrusions of the dimension of height. No compass by which to plot a course, but the nervous, fretful meander through an unknown place, if "through" has any meaning left. There is no pole star—the single stable point required for classical order, *ordo*. Descent has to be understood by way of deconstruction of that constellation as well as all *Verstellung*.

Absent sky together with the rejection of height, a there above.[19] Infinity will be planar, the receding horizon, if it exists at all. A "bad infinity"—though not the indistinct, indefinite *apeiron*—in an ever-deferred limit of a law poised to set a limit to be executed. A *terminus absconditus*. The law that will have been put into law without execution. This is the loss that will become gain, once the law takes effect, the limitless become contained and sheltering. The return, of sky, law, limit, God, has become messianic. In this sense, the neuter voice records the future anterior; it will have happened. The empty sky is the beginning of duplicity in writing, the contestation of a voice that preaches mastery.

On closer examination, the sky and the absence of sky are the self-same, in that their nonidentity is given by the principle of the non-identity of indiscernibles. Perhaps its ecstatic discovery is exclaimed when Blanchot writes of the deep joy that overtakes him, impressing the rest of his life with its mark. It is essentially an Eckhartian moment. Blanchot has previously extolled Eckhart's thought by virtual recitation and cites him in

the particular absence of the divine—the divine absence—whose vociferation is the work of the neuter.[20] Nothing—worthy of one's complete absorption yet completely undeifiable—survives its work of rejection. Not a thing.
The sky speaks of an emptiness that is incessantly emptying, not growing
more empty but emptying the *more* of its comparative power, neutralizing its
potency, leaving it weak and ineffectual, a wimp, a loser. Hyperbole (and the
via eminentia) doesn't survive either. An excess of the trivial to the point of
trivializing a trivialization of itself, so marginal a reproduction of text that
it is worth no comment—a marginal text, at the margin of value, putting it
in writing for the reader who would normally extract value, barely coherent
and of such low relevance that the act of writing it down exemplifies an
absolutely minimal inscription that hovers over vociferation while trying to
survive the effort of survival, the evacuation of language to the exception
only of the exhibition of the absence, which nonetheless must be inscribed
in putting it in writing, the presence of which is the necessary condition for
a freedom sufficient to the task—of entering upon the freedom of putting
in writing the voice that is being put in writing—here lies the question of
the authorial identity and its means of inscribing what is freely espoused,
freedom from a censorship or management of voice-writing via the speaking
nib of the pen, the repeated proof of survival and productivity within the
stringent rules for a text, rules of grammar, style, rhetoric, shadings, affirmation and denial, and so forth.

　　　The freedom is frail because it is, like a ghost—the holy one—super-
venient to the scene of writing, wherein the words are dictated by a voice
not recognizable until the words present themselves, as if the one writing
has first to have them read in order to know what is written since she
herself inscribes anonymously, invisible and speaking behind the veil, making the words happen as written in the very action that centers on the
nib—from where author materializes, becomes matter, matters, matters more
than anything, yet is nothing; with the trial to become something, there is
the forgetting. Forgetting, moreover, is the impassable gap between writing
and reading. The one who writes does so from a site beyond the world,
life, knowledge; the one who reads, with the fiat "*Lazare, veni foras,*" resur-
rects the work that lies before her eyes in the state of alchemical death.[21]
Forgetting, moreover, forgets the freedom that initiates putting it in writing, which in turn reports the condition of freedom, inscribing the freedom
of inscription, where the inscribing alone matters—the narrative voice is
thoroughly opportunistic, seizing on anything to turn, detour, upturn, over-
turn, and return, relying on gratuity, where chance is master, and yet other
than randomness, and at the same time purposelessly possessing a trace of
justice.[22] It comes to voice by an impulse that matures into and produces
the inscription of putting in writing what the voice-writing is dictating.

The act materializes an articulation of spirit as it faces the appearing of appearances, as if the putting in writing and its refined discernment were a later bloom on the blanching of manifestation, duplicitous, luring astray in deception, deceiving with the truth, but in all cases, exercising the rigor of writing, writing the ordeal of writing as it is being undergone while assisting with the writing, not leaving its side, not abandoning it to forgetting, but by contestation, affirming the freedom of the anonymous, non-desire as its condition, and one, moreover, that reduces conscience, comprehension of the divine by the mortal, to gratuity.

The blue sky is the everyday ("Why is the sky blue?") sky. It could represent the ceiling (*ciel*) of the dwelling that shelters humanity, the "house of Being." It is the site of uncanny manifestations—deities, angelic messengers—and while establishing limits beyond earthbound borders, grants visibility to the unlimited, the starry heavens. To shine through and reveal the infinite enigma, tinted with a frail memory of abandonment . . . by God, by the alien intelligence of sidereal space. That is the manner in which Blanchot thinks. More precisely, not God but the One, Pythagorean unity that has no second. "God" has been derelict since the disaster, no, before; "I knew that to think of him, to claim to protect him, was only a sly way of revealing him, and I also knew this: unmasked, he could no longer be anything else—but me" (TOW, 318). There is, furthermore, a relation that everyday life enjoys with the sky. Heidegger makes reference to it in *Gelassenheit*. If one gazes into the horizon, it recedes into the distance so as to defer presentation of a limit. It cannot be de-distanced. It thus opens to what cannot be negated, the outside, beyond the law of limit, the law of the law. To imagine the movement is to undergo the same feckless embarkation as that of the image that suffers inconsequential nonlinearity. The sky, apprehended patiently, opens precisely (is this right?) at the point that isn't there because it has absconded and deconstructed, its former elements now heterogeneous, decentered, and dismembered. This event parallels the mega-event of an empty sky, that is, it opens the question of "sky" and the slippage that has been taking place linguistically. The words *star, sidereal*, change meaning. In the limit-experience, a virtual absence is disseminated over the body of experience (*Erleben*). The absented sky is attestation to the fact.

The statement, "'The blue of the sky' is what best expresses the sky's emptiness," recalls the concealment of the secret identity: everydayness is obscuring and most obscure (WD, 133). At bottom, it would seem to involve a Hegelian logic, the identity of identity and nonidentity. The conjunction of the everyday with the limit-experience yields, however, not Hegel's universal but a singular secret confided to the boy who gazes out and who accepts confidently to write in its confidence. The gesture—call it belief or counterbelief—cannot be overemphasized. It expresses the faith that Blanchot puts in writing, which performs what is right, to defer divulging the secret.[23] To write keeps it by giving the secret away, by marking its secrecy in commemoration; this is "truth" for one who writes. The writing of everyday life capitalizes on the disastrous forgetting that would annul the *Umwelt*. Perhaps in that sense must amnesia be viewed as contestation, that is, of "nature's sacredness," and therefore of moral consequence. Within the web of discretion and memory, faith is inherently connected with linguistic confidentiality, that which not only must not be said but cannot be. It is fidelity to the singular in the face of temptation to the universal.[24] The word does not begin and end with *silence*. Confidence, the *fide* of language, is grounded in attestation of its vocalic disengagement from the bare murmur of existence—a specific *Hören*. The specificity has to do with utter passivity, hearing devoid of grasping at meaning, the ear freed from constructivist habits.[25] The sacred lies on the borderline between the two, voicing and hearing, the neuter and the active-passive, a relation on the verge of slipping out of itself into nonrelation. Faith preserves the sacred by hewing to the neuter voice; there inscription resides at an indefinite distance from truth-value and content.

The phrase, "The blue of the sky" is caught in the use-mention web where it appears to be a state of affairs describing the sky's color. A definite description whose logic of supplementarity requires that it stand for and replace the thing. The grammatological account leaves out the violent nature of dis-scription: killing is involved. The link between dictation and inscription is broken as soon as there is an attempt to read the meaning: *Noli Me Legere* (SL, 22).[26] Because the latter mark is illegible, desacralization is deferred. In the rupture lies the confidence of language. Language writes off the loss but doesn't show it. What is written appears no different from disclosure of the apophantic function. The secret concerns the tragic loss that makes no difference: dysrelation of voice-writing with the mark, now a nonrelation in which the *same* writing persists. Fascination with the nonrelation (Blanchot calls it friendship) is the forgetting at (un)work, as it erases a repressed violence. Albeit frail, the violence—second violence, the violence of language against the primal violence of sheer being—undoes mastery, turns to disaster, and evokes the neuter voice. Use of the name "sky" yields nominative power, but (another Hegelian insistence) only when the thing named is dispensed with, eliminated, iced—when the "right to death" is exercised.

In its fashion, language keeps a confidence. To the ear, it repeats a murmuring that draws fascination to the outside. The one who puts it in writing follows the turn or detour that marks the inner ear's perception of the words dictated. Dictation signals a split in the operator. *Without media-*

tion, hearing is correlated with putting it in writing—the event—ceaselessly spoken in a language not apposite (because of its vulgar singularity) to representation. Language yields to dictation entrusted to put it in writing yet the one who writes may be ignorant of its meaning—the scribe, stenographer, or court secretary. During the attentive wait prior to bifurcation, the writer has a taste of duplicity; what appears phonically is not subject to erasure and what is so inscribed bears the trace.[27] Each linguistic particle together with the whole of writing persists in the shadow of oblivion. Each well-formed sentence bears oblivion within it, repetitiously. Each work is unfinished and incomplete, due to the infinity of oblivions it contains.

Language keeps a confidence. This means: an event takes place unmarked by language. Language tells without showing; it indicates without expressing. Strange, an apophatic language, a language that is through and through disclosive in narrative, never shows what is really going on.[28] One can veer from telling stories. As if to describe (the showing of the shown) were to dis-scribe, to undo the link, enter into the relation of nonrelation between voice-writing and inscribing it, a relation that undoes antecedence and consequence and renders synchrony impossible. As if vociferation and the scribing function belong to separate, nonintersecting spaces and meet without comprehension in the mark. Or, as if a single event split into two and disseminated into an infinity of virtual iterations. The absent common ground constitutes the *punctum* in and through which the secret is insistently resurrected: the secret resurrection and the resurrection secret. The secret of death: of this, language "knows" and keeps its confidence. Insistently, it can tell and still conceal. Revelation is discreetly withheld. Language is not forthright enough to show death or exhibit its imperceptive forgetting—hence, showing is its ever-fascinating dream.[29]

Marking the absolute difference between showing and telling, faith maintains the paradoxical claim that nothing is revealed. If the secret is preserved, discretion then acquires a sacred function. One definition of the sacred: "That which escapes without anything being hidden" (AO, 42). The appearance of nothing (the event of nonappearance) elicits the image in the noncanonical, "second" version. Faith is structurally related to the sacral nature of images: they are an appearance that conceals a nonappearance, and not the replication of an appearance. It can be put thus: an image of concealment that mimes the sacred, like lying by telling the truth. Faith is concerned with the mystery of confidence whereby language proclaims the openness of being without mention of the dark night. The presumed disclosure renders dialectical speech profane in its assumption of power; its egological function (Levinas). The speech of voice-writing, by contrast, is concerned, not with what is (the ontic) but its forgetting. This can be pursued farther. Voice-writing forgets attestation and the witness (that constitute the subject) and frees the one writing from the guilt inherent in the subject (forgetting in the supplemental sense).

"The one who writes is not I." What does this mean? Within the yes-no, active-passive linguistic matrix, "I" is an abbreviation of the binary self-world.[30] This could be said thus: the one writing is a subject that is not I but enucleation of the I (to provide for the null space of alterity), and engages, like the *same* sky, the antinomy. Voice noncoincident (by contestation) with passive and active mimes in writing the other voice that is neither the one nor the other. In the unmarked poise between habit and forgetting, within the latency of remembering, the scribe waits. There, a voice remains distinct from the one waiting to inscribe—recall Derrida's postcard image of a Socrates who dictates to Plato, writing. The neuter voice enfeebles presence absolutely, the interior slipping away so as to leave a barren, depopulated zone in which no interest takes root, in which one vainly awaits an interest in immobility. There, non-desire, intransitive desire, objectless desire, primal process, non-life itself under the guise of life, invests a narrative that neutralizes the play of desire. In the neuter voice, even the gaze becomes immobilized as it aimlessly wanders in search of the obscure object-cause.

Freedom to Write

What meaning is to be assigned to the sky in light of Blanchot's observation that the *moi*, the "selfsame" "was as if fissured, since the day when the sky opened upon its void" (SNB, 2)? Blanchot confesses that with the dearth of desire, writing begins.[31] Writing whose law establishes the transgressive limit between day and night, mastery and impotency, nomination and anonymity, living and dying, whose limit will have been overstepped once the writer clears the penumbra of remembrance. There is to be sure the day to day writing, the journal keeping, what the healthy hand chronicles while the sick one flaccidly records the trajectory of fascination. That is directed interiorly by the I in authorial command of the discourse of existence. The frail fall, the movement into forgetting, is double. It is at once a dis(re) membering of the I and an awakening of a memory that concerns a nameless someone.[32] Forgetting under the guise of impotence does not surrender power altogether, that is to say, it erases not itself but the everyday. There results a fourfold relation: "The one who, forgetting, is effaced from us in this forgetting also effaces in us the personal ability to remember; then the impersonal remembrance is awakened, the personless remembrance that takes the place of forgetting for us" (AO, 38). Writing bears the second remembrance firsthand, and the first remembrance—of life—only by memory. It is always essentially co-memorative; it celebrates living through mediation while it celebrates dying immediately.[33] The neuter voice, Blanchot likes to say, speaks incessantly of dying.

Someone without identity who bears the second remembrance, an *il*, may find it less odd to call it remembrance, a power of sovereignty. More a memory of impotence, it is as susceptible as the inner ear is to voice-writing, in wait, as though these were conditions necessary to an unknown inscriptive event. The event is forgetting, that memory follows when it takes the *pas au-delà*, the transgressive step. There it will meet the "submissive luminosity" of forgetting, relinquishing a hold on light and giving over to the impenetrable night of auditory perception, inscribable through absence.[34] The gentle resonance of words, culled through inner audition, vocally embodies attendance. The special hearing has been on pause since the event of the *same* sky, ruined by the fissure that undid the logic of identity. But then *but then* something is made ready for inscription, the act of which concerns no one in particular. Remembrance of the transgressive variety surrenders the reins and finds an itinerary (if that), perhaps a remembrance of the unknown. It is a voluntary amnesia that just happens to remind.

"Forgetting, the acquiescence to forgetting in the remembrance that forgets nothing" (AO, 33).[35] A "remembrance that forgets nothing" operates duplicitously. On the one hand, it is a perfect memory that diabolically loses track of the most important thing. A forgetting by necessity since even if perfect, memory cannot remember what hasn't happened, the forgetting needed to recapture the turn or detour of writing. Always imminent, this is a forgetting of what is to come, messianic in character: the forgetting to come. On the other hand, it constitutes an amnesia of the void, there by virtue of not being in the world (not being, not in the world); the second remembrance casts out the bedeviling emptiness. It would deny the sky's radical evacuation, a quasi-transcendental condition for writing. In both cases, the memory that accedes to forgetting agrees because it remembers its supplementary nature, an impersonal remembrance beyond its limits.[36] There is a circularity that is not vicious and not hermeneutical. One remembrance recalls the infinity of the I that endows it with plurality without inflation, the other, the *il*, subjectivity without the personal subject. One recalls dialectical negation, the other, "unemployable negation." The encounters with alterity are distinct in that for each, the sovereign or the scribe is an attempt to penetrate beyond memory. As are the outcomes: in mastery, deification; in writing, withdrawal unto fascination.

The event of fissure at once doubles sky and self, and persists in *dedoublement*. In the impersonal remembrance of writing are two entities, two presences without presence, Blanchot recalls, united in separateness. One is a site of voice, the second, of hearing that would write or writing that would hear.[37] The conversion of aurality to inscription, an aid to memory as Thuth told Aman, that would enhance forgetting, as Aman told Thuth. The gift of remembrance is thus doubled. Parceled out once, it is given to voice to say that which is impossible to remember in the daylight world (to name the possible); and, to audition, to let be heard that which has been in wait to be remembered (to respond to the impossible).[38] But neither takes place on behalf of interiority charged with the return to pure presence. Inner vociferation and audition have a different agenda: to engage writing in a time that waits in temporal indifference. Since it has erased the marks of difference in time and has nullified choice of one moment over another, it is patient. It need be because its sole accomplishment is failure. The work of writing fails for two reasons: first, because language itself, duplicitous and indiscreet, not only shows but always already tells of the world; second, because language may not be a faithful reproduction of hearing inaudible subvocables. As Orpheus discovers, as Narcissus learns, the motive for union with the beloved other is not pure. It cannot be, since non-desire always contests desire, and since the trajectory of desire is avoidance of the thing. To empty desire, the *same* desire and substitute emptiness for it: that is the agony of the writer. Only then does waiting attain the intransitivity of the fragile fall into the space of writing.

The scene of writing is, against expectations, not the "essential solitude" of the hermit at the writing desk, but conversation, a turning toward one another that belongs to the fissured self, the *moi*. Strictly speaking, however, the I isn't split since in its majesty, no deviation from self-identity is permitted. Through attestation, it has the possibility of knowing itself up to the limit. As it returns to a breached interiority, voice and ear, linguistic articulation and its aural comprehension, appear as dissimulations of alterity. Speaking and hearing—the constellation of voice-writing—manifest in the empty place toward which fascination is attracted. The strange attractor of non-desire, desire emptied of desire, desire without an object, whose non-Euclidean (Reimannian) curvature guarantees that the fascinated attention will never get to the conversation, likewise lacks coordinates and place on the otographic map. Any "finding" is immediately placed *sous rature* and discarded like the gesture that empties waiting of being awaited. The waiting doesn't diminish the attraction of forgetting or of a scene of conversation. Thence, words attempt to converse with the other despite the fact that everything will be forgotten; in the wait, they are gleaned from the muted murmur that will subdue those reckoned suitable for inscription.

A conversation, *entretiens*, a holding between (the French says), is cognate with *entretenir*, to maintain, staying in relation to a central point that may not exist. Conversing is somewhere between keeping together what is separate and separating what is kept together, which is to say, giving credence to the interval. It is faithful to the ambiguity of voice-writing, its subvocal speech and hearing of inaudibles. "*Qui parle?*" one interlocutor of *Awaiting Oblivion* repeats. From whom (what) do the words come? There are three sources of linguistic capability: dictator, author, and the I. The first two involve a binary relation. They aren't found apart from one another even though they pursue different orbits around an absent center. Where one speaks, the other listens and inscribes, there can be only vicissitude. "Vicissitude is essential; it is a matter of holding firm and maintaining the equivocity" (IC, 30). One speaks, sometimes saying words for the other, of the other; the other mutely ventriloquizes the first. Boundaries are exploited and exploded and exported. As identity loses an icy grip on meaning, the confines of the one intermingle with those of the other, and a line drawn is in violation of the border. Yet there are two, unknown to one another, that face the exigency of the confrontation with alterity. Only at the limit does conversation find a voice. Then it is conversation as *entretiens*, the response respectful, however flagrantly, to the nonexistence at the middle—to the loss that mandates an economy of excess. Which in turn necessitates an encounter where the alternatives are stark violence.[39]

The present text belongs to a conversation inscribed at this very moment in a voice that mimes the neuter. Written mimetics take place in the neuter voice and excursions into that voice are mimes. The present voice is not in the neuter itself since there is no neuter *as such*. The *Als* structure is not a grammatical feature of neutrality. It can be stated that the neuter doesn't exist. The fact has been recited recursively in the self-same conversation that this text records. The nonexistence of the voice, moreover, does not affect the work of miming. It makes it more contested whether the voice is good, bad, or indifferent. Undecidability is a permanent antagonism of the neuter, which is to say, the neuter is underdetermined. It cannot be pure or complete since it must traverse and to a degree lose itself in opaque everydayness. The present text might be a recoding or remix of the present conversation with segments of other *entretiens*, real or imagined. There can be no truth or timbre of the neuter voice that separates it from other voices. It has perfect cloaking.[40] At same time, the conversation, mimed successfully or not, exposes the voice that waits. It is from waiting, suspended passivity, that voice is given—*from* and not *to*. From waiting come destitute words, worn down, drained, used up, no longer able to do their work. The waiting voice, voice on mute, exhausted before the first word, nonetheless speaks to whoever listens, pen ready. It speaks first and foremost of its proximity, its obscure immediacy, and discovers that words give only weak indication of the crepescent reality. As important as their signification is their rhythm. The drone of parataxis is an onomatopoetic presentation of the resonant emission of the thing on which conversation centers. Soon after, to be named the siren's song.

To recapitulate: the relation of the binary to the monad, the subject I, is repeated in forgetting. Interiority must acquiesce and surrender access to the archives of identity; remitting remembrance to amnesia when granted comes bundled with the condition of return. The I must subscribe to self-erasure and embrace without memory the nocturnal luminescence that makes effective action impossible; can this be voluntary? The I cannot be a contemporary of forgetting although there is the gentlest exigency of prescience or pre-sensing. The presentiment of an unknown event that lacks the power to divide time into before and after is not enough to sustain the subject.[41] More frequently, anticipatory resoluteness meets a quick, silent, and indecisive end in the "stress of minutiae." Never included or clearly delineated, the border is where writing again begins. In the nonidentity of the subject, in its fissure, the meeting with the other would inaugurate inscription (or murder.) The language called forth must accede to the law of the limit that denies passage except by transgression. If the binary of writing (the *moi* and the not-*moi*) respects that limit, it morphs into the question: of writing. Is writing taking place or is it the linguistic jugglery of journal keeping, the scriptural exploitation of the written word, legitimated by the said? To write lawfully of the limit is to forget the law, to accept the demand on attention to follow the fascination wakefully. The work of language under the acute passivity, "the self gangrened and eaten away," speaks in the voice of the other; the neuter sonorously demolishes the logic of active-passive dialecticism. In forgetting the law, that voice finds inspiration.[42]

It unworks by penetration into the deep, where two points cease to define a straight line (Riemannian space). The trajectory bypasses active and passive and seeks the point "between" that is nowhere, its trace everywhere. Orpheus seeks Eurydice as active (the one to follow him back to earth) and as passive (the faceless beauty of the night), but "finds" her only in the failure of his mission—to disobey the law of desire. Nevertheless the trope of depth misleads. The neuter voice is the shadow-second of each and every point, a resonance, double and mechanical, that cannot be appropriated. It is conceivable, as in Agamben, as a halo that englobes each being. There it is other than being or presence, but strongly attracted to the world. The attraction does not derive from a transcendental purity that a paradoxical vocality, protected from empirical accidents, might possess. Voice in the neuter has no possibility of living apart except by patiently awaiting, or dying, Blanchot would say. For what? There is the example of Eurydice as she follows her lover's gaze that penetrates the night and is ruined when he returns hers—the detour of impossibility. She waits insouciantly to return to Hades, where she is more shade than image, more image than dead. In an exemplary fashion, a halo of impossibility (as well as irresponsibility) surrounds each and every image. It could be considered a sign of the holy.

Writing forecloses the event. There is no event, or an image of one borrowed from forgetting. The event-horizon opens to allow the writing to pass. It will afterward close, when writing is ended (before it begins again). It ends at the first hearing, which may not be of the voice, while the ear vigilantly scans the horizon for vibratory reality. It might be a diabolic simulation of voice: computerese. But the voice's resonation, the *elle*, signifies a specific space that the archaic world reserves for the scribe. On alert, this community, belonging to the "deep past, never long enough ago," is again operative upon the sounding of a specific audition, on mute. An invisible image that doesn't summon the eye but the ear, it is an auditory image—and bears further study.

3

Death as Instance

·•·———·•·

The Firing Squad

To write is no longer to situate death in the future—the death which is always already past; to write is to accept that one has to die without making death present and without making oneself present to it. To write is to know that death has taken place even though it has not been experienced, and to recognize it in the forgetfulness that it leaves—in the traces which, effacing themselves, call upon one to *exclude oneself from the cosmic order* and to abide where the disaster makes the real impossible and desire undesirable.

—Maurice Blanchot, *The Writing of the Disaster*

Death and Language

If writing requires a polestar to which constant repetition orients it, it is *this* death that belongs hyperbolically to time more past than past, that has not finished (will never finish) its accomplishment, and that exerts an influence from within the interstices of being. The I that has died is not marked, except in rare cases, by personal memory. Immemorial, the most ancient temporality that is nonattributive and not attributable to a syntax of personal pronouns where it is sited without situation, archived in what could be designated collective or unconscious. Although it has more to do with what the I disremembers (the dismemberment of interiority) than that to which it recalls itself, *this* death is intimately interwoven with memory of self, specifically as memory to be avoided: aversion memory. A memory that turns from interiority with the *same* gesture of child-Narcissus as he turns from identifying the watery reflection as his own; death of desire, objective and subjective genitive. The turn, furthermore, is from the window full of sky to the *same* empty window. Thus, an anomalous memory—Freud thematizes it as the "death drive"—whose engagement is its disappearance in the uncanny abolition of its trace.[1] Yet whose disappearance fails to remove it from proximity, from where it insistently calls attention to itself: the death I cannot die because it isn't mine, though I am its. An anomaly because the I seems to recall a quasi-event that never took place in personal history. As if I had access to human history and could remember things like the taste of an apple in my great-grandmother's mouth.

The anomalous nature is made more complex by the fact that *this* death is marked by the loss of remembrance, and conversely. It enters experience as a blockage: not being able to remember death, that is to say, self-erasure. The text always appears self-erased, an empty folder, without a semantics file. It is there in that which is inscribed, illegible and untranslatable, but nonetheless abiding: remembered but inaccessibly "on the tip of my tongue." *This* death finds a way of archiving itself "within" each and every text, augmenting it in such a way that the attention is detoured around it, distracted from the impulse to grasp the special archival content, track it, and pursue it to comprehension. The unconscious aversion affects thought indelibly with the mark of proximity, appearing in what Levinas calls the reservations of thought.[2] Its uncanny, hidden force, unworking and deconstructing meaning, loosening its joints, destabilizing sense, wielding great indiscretion, and disrupting the calm of reader's abiding in the textual dwelling. Indiscretion: to speak indulgently about what one doesn't know (*Hörensagen*). When one speaks of *this* "death," language turns from its sense-giving function toward mimicry of good sense, then simulation of reference, then dissimulation of definition. That is to say, language returns to an image of itself, not precisely "an imaginary language, a language no one speaks," but one where all bets on truth and sincerity are off.[3] The revolt of the simulacrum, recommencement of the spectacle.

This death comes (*viens!*) in the event of forgetting death (or: of forgetting, death), as if the forgetting mimes a memory of something without existence. In its wake, when "death" is enunciated, the cipher has been purged or corrupted. The utterance draws a blank, the reader cannot attach meaning to the word because she feels excluded. Estranged from linguisticality, forgetting formally appears as a local language aphasia that precipitates a general meltdown of meaning-production, for instance, breakup of rules and conventions. Language ceases to be a reliable vehicle for communicating the (vocal or subvocal) intentionality; it ceases to partake of the father's name. After the disastrous loss—remembrance betrayed—"death" becomes an ambiguous site in the semantic field. Formerly archived, the null site, *non lieu*, designation without place, phantom designation, acquires a mobility not barred by friction. "Death," the fatherless son, can go anywhere. Its movement is the trace whose erasure is the trace of a trace. About it, there are many stories . . .

The (non)event of forgetting, death, constitutes the dis(re)membering of the event of self.[4] In a complexification of Heidegger's *Jemeingkeit*, the self-possession of the I as unique and singular is irrevocably modified by alterity. Hitherto, its own being and death, the destruction of the *conatus essendi*, assumed primary importance. It brought the hope of a stance against the proximate menace of non-being.[5] Now, the other to whom the I is bound by an antinomous relation speaks phonemes obsessively attractive in dispersion and powerlessness. The other possesses nothing, not a personal pronoun but an *il*: the *persona* or mask perforated. With a force that renders Narcissus immobile and Orpheus weak-willed, the other-in-the-self redraws intentionality so as to dilute and attenuate its focus on indivisibility. Eviscerated intentionality—like nonintentional consciousness in Levinas— is dysfunctional to the degree that it does not mean what it says about egological reality. Its power castrated, such intentionality is not up to the onerous task of self-presence. The *same desire*, which had become pure or proper in the act of self-attestation, drifts away from the "natural" order, is made inoperative, and succumbs to "the pressure of the undesirable even in the most desired" (WD, 47). In the transfixing gaze, rule-regulated language employed to voice interiority gives way to gratuity as law.

As event, the self dis(re)membered, un-mastered of memory, portends an account in which the subject cannot be justified by an exigency demanded by a proper death. This is the thesis of Blanchot's final recit, *The Instant of My Death*. The narrator (in front of a firing squad) both describes and performs a psychosis, in Levinas's sense. In the loss that aggravates and suspends the law, the self is bifurcated, not unitive, the-other-in-the-one. While the recit recounts the saturated event of splitting, the writing is a scene of double-voicing and offers (two for the price of one!) a performance of it. Since the other is otherwise than voice—cacophony, acoustical phenomena scoured of signification, counter-vocality, the murmur—writing is effected by hosting a parasitic guest. The proxy author specializes in the violence of cutting and pasting. Poetically, writing gives voice to the sirens' song, the abundant inarticulatable reserve of sonority, the matriarchal *khora*. Since voice is in the neuter, vociferation is always and everywhere accompanied vocal alterity, a nearly inaudible drone: the mother-voice that does not recognize her son (daughter) as speaker. In Blanchot's psychotic, the other is not the *autrui*, the poor, dispossessed stranger (widow) to whom I owe the shirt off my back and the bread in my mouth, as with Levinas. Nameless, related by terms that absolve themselves of relation—like *autrui*—the other is that which (who) dictates the writing that traffics snatches of identity across the page. From the ethereal larynx of the other, *il* comes to a voice whose acoustical properties display in writing. Inscription is the maternity ward that alone supplies the "organs of speech" for the neuter.

The otherwise than voice is not silence, in whatever degree or pitch.[6] The resonance of the *il y a*, for Levinas, Illeity or God, the primary process, id, or the matrix of vibration, provides a reservoir of semiotics, a kinetic hodgepodge of semes that is the play of forces, known or unknown: the prehistory of the word. Semiotics: the semes are images that, unlike signs, do not possess the linguisticality presently in use. The image-swirl lapses into the telling of story, the epos; the former is a verbal as opposed to the latter, a nominative, language. If language is thought as signification, the semes or images interrupt meaning-fields, where discourse makes sense of the world. It is helpful to think of the *khora* within the economy of vociferation. *Khora* names the non-place from which semes enter to disseminate breakdowns across discourse. Image is disruptive because it would give birth to death to challenge reason's deft defenses. Judgment is compelled to distinguish between real and fantastic, intelligence and fascination. The fertility of the seme pool, the mobile forces that precipitate disturbance into thought, marks *khora*. It retains the word before it was given voice, speaking that antedates itself, *après coup* speech. It follows the protocol of writing, where everything is written in reverse. Such articulative force subsists primordially, effable but not yet said. The not yet defers the voicing forevermore.

Within the firing squad scene, a second alteration of voice is produced.[7] In Blanchot's love of the double, not only does the phenomenon of double-voicing appear, but also the voice-writing remarks the source in the imaginary. Lacan speaks of the imaginary as a vocalic dynamism of image that is initially triggered during infancy; the fold of intentional consciousness in proximity to the origin. Blanchot's thought flows from the same reserve. The imaginary operates with a force of dissimulation independently of the symbolic order, the "system of signifiers," as if there were an agon over voice. In contestation, the one is at variance with the other, displacing, congealing, compressing, and eliding the elements of recognition until language loses precision and warrant, and is cast into the role of a refugee. The agony is located not in the fact that the imaginary has its "own language," but on that playing field on which two adversaries put voice in movement (forward or backward).[8]

If *that* death meets death by the firing squad, there must be the remains. The death of *that* death is clairvoyantly marked: in the image of sleeping humanity, humankind destitute of its orientation toward being, humanity undone by its image. Without the vertical axis, average everydayness, "the fury and mire of human veins" is a purgatory for writers in search of the neuter voice. That death, the passing away that is mine, *je meines,* the being possessing a me, happens often. It is the frail fall into forgetting, disremembering the resoluteness when present to itself and to the other in itself, the psychosis. That death is not mourned until the work (of mourning) is encountered in writing, after grief.[9] The gift of that work, the disaster, is given when someone is sent forth, naked of the world, into exile, pen in hand. Since its acceptation is perpetually deferred, it is a work doomed to lack finality. The writer grieves what is to come with unfulfilled grief that awaits the event of mourning to arrive.

The death of death is an inflection that conceals a radical ambiguity. It refers to release from finitude or life in the present; "if death no more, then immortality." It also speaks of the inoperability of reference. As Hegel (or Blanchot) thinks, with the sign's marking the event of death of the signified, the signifier comes to replace the thing. If, because of a successful vaccination program, the signified were immune to death, language would become a babble, total *glissage* with nothing to hold the pins in place. Voice would lose contact with its rhythm and be a wayward copy, mime, or nth generation product. The death of death means that language lacks a founding condition. If foundationalism constitutes a principle metaphor of any semiotics, and if it is baseless, doesn't language belong to the imaginary (not an imaginary language), for in the image there is no death? There, moreover, "death" doesn't exist because it lacks the image, because it, unlike things of the world, is not subject to expiration. Can one say, the image lives in inspiration and that inspiration is drawn from the ruins? Is it possible to love other than the possibility of ruin?

Because of the death of death, writing is necessarily fragmentary.[10] Because the place between mastery—there where is death—and the death of death—impoverishment and dispossession—yields no totalized totality, in body or form, writing is repeatedly in the throes of breaking off. This should not be mistaken for incompleteness since the concept of totality is inapplicable. There are moments of lucidity, interwoven with intervals when the body text has been lost, maimed, injured, broken, or is legible under unusual conditions established before the inscription commenced.[11] Each fragment comprises an epitaph. Each fragment writes an obituary on death, commenting on its incapability of dying; or said otherwise, a declaration of the flaw of death (the double flaw squared of death). *The Writing of the Disaster* is an exposé of the weakness of death ("Death be not proud") that contests its reserve vis-à-vis acts of remembrance—even as it contestationally writes. It asks whether writing, in its most potent form, can bear witness to death since it is the chicanery of death to absent itself from the transparency of inscription. It asks whether writing can contain a work of mourning, if beforehand it unravels infinite mourning. "I write, therefore I don't exist."

Witness Writing

If a fragment offers proof that death is withdrawn and cannot present itself (imminent but not yet), then the question of testimony becomes pointed. Blanchot writes "I"—"I remember a young man"—and apparently gives attestation (*Bezeugung*) to a privileged view on the part of the person "prevented from dying by death itself." There are two separate problems. The first concerns whether to witness is to be in attendance to a singular event whose secrecy and singularity prohibit disclosure. The act of inscribing the event necessarily violates the law of the witness (*testis*)—a law of irreplaceability—and produces a text whose claims to truth apparently lie with reproducibility. As with a duplication of the singular, the secret holds itself immune to attestation. The prohibition, moreover, is as absolute as the secret; any advance on it or move to transgress it highlights the uncertain border between truth and fiction. To resort to putting it in words is to disavow the secrecy. By example, Abraham's silence throughout the journey to Mount Moriah performs the avowal to preserve it: to not speak of the secret commandment to which he alone is witness and that summons him and Isaac to that place. There is contradiction or paradox between the witness's recitation of what took place, publicly or privately, and the irreplaceable event that eludes identity. Drawing from this crosscurrent, Derrida locates the possibility of literature in a most unlikely place, the institution of law.[12]

Writing, moreover, proceeds through a withdrawal of presence. The I forgets and is forgotten, etching effaced, and falling fraily to an oblivion bereft of possibility; it forgets itself. With it goes the "ownmost potentiality for being oneself" and the magnificence of a death of one's own. The I written is the code for what has the absolute sharpness of the imperceptible; through the agencies of language, it can allude to attestation, "Yesterday, I saw . . ." In allusion, the I writing never is personally "in the flesh" in attendance to what takes place. Separation in time makes recourse to memory (recall, replication, remove) necessary. On closer examination, the inscribed "attestation" is not that of the witness but a simulation of witness, a witness "on paper." As Blanchot puts it, writing is *testifying for the absence of attestation*" (SNB, 76; his italics). A version of testimony that absolves it of personal responsibility and binds it discreetly to the secret. It is the witness that speaks hyperbolically in the neuter voice: attestation without attestation. Yet what guides its ears or eyes is a respectful observance of a command, a gratitude of receiving before knowing: the importance of the witness.

What looks like attestation in the neuter voice in fact is an acknowledgment of its nonoccurrence, attestation to an absence, or to absence itself. Attestation to the facticity of no attestation. In the work of writing, the subject is in an impossible position from which to attest to the event of writing these very words because the I has ceased to remark itself (if it ever had) and has been rendered powerless. "It is attested" replaces "I attest," or more precisely, what is put in writing is an experience without experience.[13] In contradistinction to Derrida's admonition, attestation occurs without a first-person subject.[14] What passes for attestation bypasses conditions of truth and justice. The quasi-attestation reports that I forgot that the subject is forgotten, together with its thrownness forward, its project, ultimately its presence before death in the guise of the awakened one. It is not the attestation of a self-remembered Dasein, called from forgetfulness and guilt to be present so that it can bear testimony to the existence of the one called to—or gazed by—remembering; but instead is of the one who gives voice in writing *as it is being put in writing*. The synchrony that gathers the voice writing unto a perception is a rare occurrence. In most instances (instants), the statement of testimony is made in the name of the *il*, the nameless one/ it able to attest without attesting.

The *ergon* or work in writing foregoes the power of attestation except in the exceptional case, the single exception noted: the power to attest in writing to the absence of such power. Writing is—in contrast to juridical proceedings—surprisingly inept in the task of bearing witness. Because the subject, critical to testimony, has been replaced (by the *il*), the I inscribed is in double error: in both attributing to interiority the work carried out at this very moment by one nameless, and being beholden to a (mistaken) belief that it performs the work of witness. The one writing must stand apart from nomination if it is to summon the inscription . . . without falling frailly back into the thought that interiority is capable of the inscription. The one that writes the testimony is not available for legal depositions, taking oaths, et cetera, and, moreover, is a teller of tales.

That the prelapsarian position requires a remarkably high degree of rigor seems part of Orpheus's error. As he gazes at Eurydice, an obscure point in the other night, indistinct and perfectly released from her attributes (vivacity, litheness, warmth), the work of writing is poised for inauguration. All that is needed is stylus and tablet. No entity that is her can be appropriated and brought back to the daylight world. Up to that point, in the gaze's carefree (non)desire to embrace the desired, Orpheus has forgotten subjectivity. He too has been swallowed by the other night, in astonished exile from the world of serviceable things (*pragmata*). Disseminated across galactic space, he has become inspiration ("a desire that forgets the law") for that which will have been written about her. He is unable to maintain this "cosmic" position; its openness demands more than he can renounce. He forgets: this is the disaster. He begins to perceive the first lines of composition, the semes align themselves in the mother solution. He grasps . . . already turned toward an interiority impregnated with the abyssal outside and away from the forgetting of fascination, dying the death of *Jemeingkeit*, which is to say, the death of death. Thus, Orpheus presages the position of the narrator (Blanchot, "Blanchot") before the firing squad: to abide in the experience of nonexperience without withdrawing to experience.

The second problem with testimonial writing follows the first. If the work is unable to yield full attestation (to mark its impossibility), then to attest to the "dying of death" is a feat of double impossibility. If "death" draws a blank, designates with no distinction, and thereby fails to name the detached, absolved thing, then the testimony is true only in the limited sense that it preserves the secret by misinforming the reader. One who reads the inscription is led to believe in the counterfact of what took place. "Death" the word cannot tell the secret because unlike "woman" that designates (à la Hegel, à la Blanchot) by killing the woman, death is already dead. You cannot kill a dead thing. In the work of writing, "death" is there to tell a story totally disengaged from intentional consciousness and outside the discourse of truth-value; and although the account does not qualify as a candidate for truth of testimony, it is not untrue either. The neuter voice attests without attestation but attests nonetheless.

The encounter with voice in the neuter demands iteration of the resonance that is neither active nor passive, present nor absent, sensible nor intelligible, but stays behind a curtain that conceals an acoustical space attendance to which is deferred. It vociferates in a voice so frail and timid as to be too reticent to manifest. Isolated by prohibition, it manages to appear intermittently in spite of eschewing appearance, and remains reclusive, elusive, and nondisclosive. The resonation is Levinas's nonintentional consciousness but without the moral status that he grants *vis à vis* bad conscience (that motivates remembrance). A consciousness whose discretion prohibits it from intruding upon the scene, it possesses a "discretion of presence."[15] Inasmuch as intentionality is the appropriative response of the I, a nondirective consciousness is not proper to it. The impropriety is precisely what calls to the neuter voice to put something in writing. The thing falls apart, internally alters itself, becomes other than itself: is not fit to be written. Thus, the face to face meeting with death—the venture of *Bezeugung*—must come by way of inscription whereby the date is perpetually postponed. Without death conferring its impossible possibility, without intentionality, there can be no attestation, no one to witness the forsaking of testimony, the witness of the witness (God the Father). This is the law of the law, the law that even those outside the law must obey. (The outside is not bereft of law.)

If attestation informs becoming to be and if renunciation of intentionality makes the context impossible, then writing is ill-equipped to perform attestation. —What is such an act? Presence of a sentient being to what takes place is a necessary condition. What writing is for (if not to empower the one writing) is the inverse, to disempower the subject, as if the work of the pen or keyboard cost dearly, utterly depleting her of impulse (desire, intent), so that the writer becomes anonymous and without distinction. Writing can attest to the fact that there is nothing to attest to, and that to attest to attest to (double attestation) that nothing—its emotional intensity—is to journey to the depths in pursuit of the obscure object. An attestation thus undertaken is rapture (*Entrückung*), an ecstatic event in which one self is annihilated and another reborn; the later birth gives birth to its progenitor. Rapture is transgressive—crossing the prohibited border in search of high tonality. Attestation as a limit-experience.[16] Ecstatic, it does not belong to the order of the subject that has been denuded, but to the one who (that) replaces her.

That attestation is a secret and the secret is an incorruptible attestation that gives proof that the disaster fails absolutely to eliminate testimony in its annihilation of witness. This has an important consequence. The witness cannot be destroyed and therefore needs no further witness—Celan's rejection of the third man argument.[17] That *that* attestation escapes experience contests an empiricism and brings to mind the experience of nonexperience, traces, gaps—"appearance in disappearance"—and the limit-experience of phenomenology. The absence of a presence in what presents itself "registers" in the recoil of being from groundlessness, as Heidegger describes.[18] One could add that it is the transcription of death.

What is striking is that attestation lives beyond its own death, when remembrance is absorbed and death forgotten, the forgetting of which is impossible. Death cannot not be forgotten since it yields the very impulse that is forgetting. Consciousness suffers irreparable loss of recognition in the absence of intentionality. Although death cannot be remarked after the release of releasement, through its free movement (once the grasp has let go) one can respond to the immemorial, a time resistant to the memory trace of intentionality. Could it be said that one then faces a different "death," non-pending, never to happen, without imminence—a death whose funerary arrangements would be in yesteryear's obits if there were witness there. It is a "death" borne on the wings of no testimonial element yet whose certainty is uncontestable. "Before I was I, I was dead." The attestation without witness concerns the fact that an obituary writer doesn't have to attend the funeral to get the news right. Inscription in the book of life was there at origin; the facts are there for the reading.

The *work* of writing does not consist of attesting to this or that. Instead, attestation concerns itself with a void at the site occupied virtually by the witness. Virtuality would take it to mean, not that there is no witness but that absence becomes the witness . . . to the fact that nothing takes place. The absent witness witnesses a time that suspends the everyday temporal flow, placing each moment in the closest proximity with every other, and rediscovers that "watching is not the power to keep watch—in the first person; it is not a power, but the touch of the powerless infinite, exposure to the other of the night, where thought renounces the vigor of vigilance, gives up worldly clearsightedness, perspicacious mastery, in order to deliver itself to the limitless deferral of insomnia, the wake that does not waken, nocturnal intensity" (WD, 49).

The absent witness means that there is no *there*, no *Da* of Dasein. No place is allotted for being's happening. All available sites are taken, reserved for this or that. That there is no *there* means that space has lost its Cartesian dimensionality and has grown uncanny. It is a no-place world, allowing no known spatial coordinates—inherent or superimposed—to be applied. Inasmuch as it resists order and maintains an improper unworkability, it takes on thing-like characteristics. It works neither by itself nor with the help of an other, although the other retraces the work and imbues the subject with resistance to it. No witness, no being, yet a space in which unseen forces determine visible outcomes and allot destinies. Heidegger speaks of the abyss, *Abgrund*, like that. As ground of the soul, for Eckhart, the groundless ground is the highest and closest to the source of continual creation of an intelligible universe. Although Blanchot's negativity when doubled does not yield negation of the negation or a higher synthesis, the special ground merges with the witness's absence.

The attestation of the work in writing cannot be accomplished by other means. In the world, the subject always already attests to the authentic presence of self. It repeats the mark of the ontological difference. In writing, this is suspended—an *epoché*—while other quasi-testamentary powers come into play, that is, powers *as if* possessed. Powers without power. When in play, they give attestation to the absent possibility of attestation, a power that resides in a subject that doesn't exist and lacks a place in existence—a unique witness. A witness that occupies no site and at the same time isn't nonexistent. How the testimonial posture is executed is as aporetic as the testimony, and reiterates the antinomous nature of virtuality in general. The quasi-transcendental act etched in the work of writing arises from and returns to the gaze of fascination. Its aperture is set to infinity. Then the law of desire is forgotten, inspiration is linguistically exclaimed, and in relation to the null place, the work produces itself. It mimes authorship.

The denouement lies in the meeting of death with death, as Blanchot writes, "As if the death outside of him could only henceforth collide with the death in him" (I, 9). Grammatically, this is an instance of crossing out, one death annulling the second to yield death without death. What is the syntax of "without," a favorite preposition of Blanchot, and how does it relate to virtuality?[19] Its appearance seems to signify self-annihilation. There, death, the destroyer, eradicates a colony or repetition of itself, its *ipse*. Regarding the theory of naming, the encounter is otherwise. Since the name names by killing, nomination correlates with nominal homicide. In the post mortem, the name acts as a supplement that, added to the thing, usurps its place. The puppet becomes the puppeteer. To kill or "kill" a woman by naming her—murder by designation—allows language to operate. What does killing the signified of death (the named), when the place is empty, produce?

The syntagm death without death is an answer to the question. Inasmuch as death cannot die, its quasi-immortality as a name indicates the deathlessness of death. "Dead—immortal," Blanchot writes to exemplify the fact (I, 5). The singular absence of the signified marks how death cannot be rid of. It ("death") floats free of gravity above linguistical activity, a priori disseminated and naturally polyvocal. As with similar moves to negotiate the issue—Heidegger's crossing-out [X] or Derrida's *sous rature*—the free play of death remains so radical that it escapes the law both of existence and of nonexistence. Death, the third (*tertis*), can impersonate one or the other yet is neither real nor unreal. Derrida assigns it to the spectral zone inasmuch as it "exceeds" the fundamental oppositions of present/absent, actual/virtual, and fact/fiction. With Blanchot, this is the place occupied by *mourir*, dying/to die. *Mourir* evades death and life; it is "the sickness unto death" that defers any outcome to another time and leaves the subject in despair.[20] It partakes of without belonging to an other time ("most ancient") whose nonarrival does not succeed in rendering it any less temporal. *Mourir* is death's witness unto life, the lens through which death sees life and through which life sees death. The lens, however, is asymmetrical. Life looks at death and sees power; death looks at life and sees impossibility. The interminability of dying *versus* the non-event of death. Death's witness is called to attest to its—death's—insignificance; life's witness sees its paramount importance. One never stops recommencing its happening, the other never begins to happen.

Immortality and Death

> To die according to the lightness of dying and not by the anticipated heaviness of death—the dead weight of the dead thing—, would be to die in relation to some immortality.
>
> —Maurice Blanchot, *The Step Not Beyond*

To proclaim the immortality of death—à la Blanchot (or John Donne)—supposes a thorough grammatological examination, rehearsed above. A dead death (a death that indefinitely remarks its impossibility) would no longer be subject to itself but would be displaced from the null space it had usurped and occupied. A disseminated nullity would show up as random degradations of spacing and episodes of an uncanny mis-spacing in everyday life. This should not be reduced to a drive, much less a thanatopic one, but conceived along lines of an alien and unassimilable force. Its alterity belongs to the absent father and manifests in the imminence of fascination—more imminent (*bevorstehend*) than the imminence of death. Since fascination, too, has degrees and finds objects ("dead deaths") of increasing depth and intensity, all gain in everlastingness from death. Eurydice is exemplary in this manner. The source of myriad immortalities, death is the khoraic force that ruins archives, loosens the hold of memory, and slowly hastens forgetting. Appropriately, death in its nonappearance rather than dying in its iterated appearance playfully exposes (without exposing) the outside. Access is fortuitously provided by the object of fascination, "the glad accident."

To turn back to child-Narcissus: to vociferate in the neuter voice, as he does in adoration, worship, and dread, gives his voice a spectral intelligence, which is to say, returns it to the passivity of the imaginary. It is essential that Narcissus speak in this mode with his ghost-reflection to which he is erotically bound. The erotic is not accidentally but intrinsically related to the neuter. The alchemical plot describes how the ritual killing of child-Narcissus, together with his beloved image, produces the immortal double, his *anima*. The wedding and consummation of the two (sulfur and mercury in an alchemical register), living being and lifeless image, wield, through the sacrifice, a deathless body with properties of neither. Body of life, body of death: this is the body proper to voice in the neuter. The immortal double speaks of the between, the *Zwischen*, and its concatenation of specters. Neither deathless nor lifeless, it voices the object of voice, toward which the one writing cocks an ear: source of inspiration and spectrality. Like the object of sight, such an object is unobtainable; it cannot be de-distanced. Like the mother-space, it is self-withdrawing. It gives a trace in the act of withdrawing the gift. Hearing, like vision, turns from what is given as it nears. What one "hears" is the dissimulation; the transcription is never on the mark (writing as sin).

The guilt absolved with the erasure of Dasein's attestation to its own lack is reinvested in inscription. The one writing is at the mercy of winds that cause unavoidable deviations from the voice dictating. How does one look at the breach of responsibility? The firing squad incident examines the question of the soul shamed by the survivor complex. Forever indebted, Blanchot cast as Aloysha feels more guilty than anyone else, namely, with "the error of injustice" (I, 3). To put the event in writing demands engaging atonement. Atonement draws near to subjection and abjection, as if hyphenated by these attunements. It gives up power, wanders dispossessed as an exile in an unwelcoming land. To write, to atone, to neutralize the guilt by a counterirritant—dread—so that the neuter voice is also—and this must not be forgotten—the voice gelded, desexed, spayed. Surrendering a portion of its humanity—the erotic and sexual—the neuter voice proceeds toward absolution from sin and liberation from time's passing. The further chain of supplements defers it from endlessly repeating the frail fall into guilt and rote living, the tormented unawareness of everyday life, where the obscurity itself is obscure and desire the moving force, and frees the one writing to respond to the impossible address of alterity . . . again to fail.

Spectrality is the register of sounding the voice in the neuter. To hear the ghost speak is to comprehend the neuter. Hamlet's father's "Do not forget thy almost blunted purpose" articulates a voice that antecedes active and passive, or, in Derrida's fluid metaphor, "overflows the opposition" and speaks in the midst of the step (not) beyond life.[21] The king's apparition on the ramparts at midnight is exemplary in how it recalls that, from a phenomenological point of view, appearance in general has a strong nonempirical component and equally strong affiliation with virtuality. With its "suspension" of external reality, the *epoché* subjects the immediacy of the real to question and "overflows the opposition" between real and imaginary. Husserlian thought thinks that fantasy operates with the same intentional analysis as the real. In a science of appearance in general, the spectral is not in opposition to what is the case. Beyond or before a division into fact and fiction, truth and literature, it speaks the neutral voice and by doing so constitutes the grammatical (grammatological) fabric of both real experience and its imposture. It speaks from the rift (*Riss*) that for Heidegger separates (thus joins) truth from untruth, and vociferates the primordial errancy or phantomaticity that rules all.[22] It antecedes and supersedes the dialectic and calls attention with repeated self-withdrawing incursions into the everyday to its peculiar nonexistence.

Because of the priority (without priority) of spectrality, its implication for written testimony is clear. If no well-defined border exists between real experience and an unreal (irreal) counterpart, then false witness (intended or undeliberate) and true confession can speak in the same voice. They arise bearing the indeterminacy effected by the unworking force of the neuter. Relation without relation means that the terms, though unconnected, are connected as if there were what there is not, relation.[23] Death without death says that although death fails to arrive, it is as if it did. The *as if* construction (*Als-Struktur*) grants truth of testimony a playroom with respect to justice, that is to say, broaches the question of injustice. It no doubt constitutes a severe challenge to the demand for truth and exigence of sincerity. It calls attention to the realm of vicarious experience, to which testimonial reading (and reading in general) pays homage. Reading is accomplished through an act of estrangement; the reader's "tendency is first to unburden it of any author . . . the book has become a book without an author" (SL, 193). The suffering of the one writing is effaced, as if it were a portion of the gift withdrawn. Inscription has returned to anonymity and disemburdened of the gravity that bore it to existence. The reader gains access to the event but without having to endure it, and comes to the "universality of the singular."

Reading of a failed execution by the firing squad, the reader can undergo the trauma but forgo the threat of real bullets. Commenting on the strangeness, Blanchot notes, "Reading is situated beyond comprehension or short of comprehension" (SL, 196). Reading is thus linked with desire; each deflects its satisfaction by falling short of or overrunning it, while comprehension remains tied to the "reality" of experience, experience *with* experience, experience *tout court*. The blessing of reading, "freedom without work, a pure Yes blossoming in the immediate," derives from spectrality's neutering of external reality by giving voice to the transcendental imagination (SL, 196). The benefice is related to reading's weak side: limitation of a reader's admissible testimony. She finds herself able to testify only to the absent attestation of the text.

Reading is a matter of ease because it defers a comprehension that requires "possession of the facts." Bypassing the empirical for the vicarious, reading takes the writing in by insouciance, freeing it from everyday being-in-the-world. Reading in itself is without agency though it may lead to high (or low) ideals. Lacking the understanding of projects (*Entwurfen*), its hallmark is narration that conjures a transcendental replica—the image— to substitute for the "real" thing, previously "killed" by the linguistic act of naming.[24] In its freedom reading calls the meaning (stripped of gravity) assigned to it by the work, and this invocation is miraculous. "*Lazare, veni foras.*" From the tomb where he lies dead—where voice in the neuter echoes the silence of the dead in the death of silence—Lazarus is summoned forth to another life; from the book's crypt, lifeless words are called forth to speak again what they once heard and inscribed. From the spectral apparition that "speaks" without flesh and blood to phantomical reflections that are potentially world-changing: Is this not a nonnatural movement?[25]

The nonnegotiable borders between experience, "experience," nonexperience, and experience without experience raise the question of translation, communication forth and back. Between the language that voices the neuter and, dialectical language (everyday discourse), reference is confused and equivocal. The problem is not that there will be more than one "analytic hypothesis" for the meaning. Instead, it concerns the subject or, more precisely, the subject place. When Thomas says, "And yet I was really a dead person, I was even the only possible dead person, I was the only man who did not give the impression that he died by chance," he refers to the I that has been taken from life, stripped of personhood, and assimilated to death's necessity (TO, 111). No one remains, no I, to de-distance and take charge of things at its disposal. No interiority folded into itself, able to distance itself from itself, present itself to itself in a *Vorstellung*, thematize, engaged in self-generated discourse, and remember. Instead, the infinite distance of proximity has drawn consciousness to the obscurity and calls forth the thought of Thomas's I that in its absence haunts the reading. Is it Thomas's? Drained of breath, the I reduces to image, seeming to exist, but is in fact worldless (*weltlos*), without everyday designation, comprehended without comprehension by a placeholder term, *il*, it. It belongs to no one. The story of Thomas is told without telling because of the absence of its protagonist; it mimes a story that keeps unraveling the tale of nothing it tells. The experience foreshadowed never arrives to fulfill the event of its taking place.

The absolute vicariousness of reading unworks the worldly doubling of consciousness. Consciousness conscious of itself—the for-itself—invests power, possession, and mastery. Self-awareness ("seeing myself seeing myself") warrants intentionality, the ability to appropriate the given for oneself, *Jemeingkeit*. It ensures de-distancing, bringing near the far without changing position. Penetrating the invagination of night, reading encounters an ungraspable distance, one not from itself but from what is never itself and cannot be comprehended. Expelled from itself, the proximate interiority is too close to be brought to view. Unfolded to a single ply, the I proceeds by participation, an unknowing knowing that no longer exists outside of the field of knowledge, and thus is enucleated. Sublimated through repetitive substitution, its sense blends with the obscure object—over there, over there—without site. It is ready for the labor of replacing the irreplaceable: writing.

The Weight (Wait) of Writing

The frail fall from remembrance into a dream state, delusionary, fragmented, impersonal, and anonymous. World mastery has been forgotten or is itself forgetting—with a lightness stunning in surprise. Dying, the unending non-ending of an indeterminate event—Is it still happening, when and where?—that is almost weightless. Combusted in grief and dread, the evental substance is a shell of its former constitution. Think of forgetting as a wafting motion, silk in the breeze, "a floating ribbon of cloth" such as Loie Fuller's Chinese dancers used. It is nonviolent and opposed to violence, which includes the traumatic intervention of the absolute other's call for a responsible response.[26] Unimpeded movement, free from obstacle or constraint, and aspiring to aimless motion—forgetting is the great seduction. The trajectory of desire toward a projected object is like that, a tauntingly anticipated conjunction, disappointing with failed union and meeting freedom as obstacle. What is more difficult to refuse than a free ride to the heart's wish, when death's little brother, sleep, plays second fiddle? The fall into immemorability, "nothing to remember," to partake once the center is displaced, has a hidden eroticism. This underscores the source of its gaiety: the spectacle one attends in the realm refractory to the light of phenomenology.

Gaiety persists in the vacuum of concern (*Sorge*) over equipmentality which bedevils the world. Absence of the Heideggerian workshop leaves the unworking with purchase: sapping and draining of intention, which must ultimately infringe on representation in language. At the heart of Orphic work lies an insouciance, unconcern: the forgetting of the day, world, and hope of retrieving Eurydice, life of Orpheus's life. How far does this go? Does it extend to amnesia of how to sing, to speak, to think, to thematize? —No, Orpheus relinquishes self-mastery and will to power, and his vocality becomes lightened. The loss or second loss of his beloved is reason for a passing grief but the lightness of his song—his work—allows it to rise to heaven and the gods. What remains to be said about him is said by a character in *The Last Man*: "If I ask myself: did he think more than you think? I see only his spirit of lightness, which made him innocent of the worst. A being so irresponsible, so terribly not guilty" (LM, 5).

Things without gravity are in the neuter voice since dispossession has stripped them of their attributes. Returned to *prima materia*—which lacks weight and mass—things are composed of ghost matter, matter phantomized, a material phantasm—or made quasi-transcendental—and dialectical comprehension annulled. Spectrality is expressed in the resemblances of the imaginary. More precisely, the force enters the world in the guise of a spectral alterity. Things in themselves may not be haunts but are compounded in the crucible of hauntology. Surrounding the substance of each is a halo that Agamben notices, a virtual replication displaces a least minimal difference from the entity. The incongruity is irreducible and necessary. Things are constituted in the neuter by giving withdrawal. There they are matter offset by prime matter in an essential bond: a palimpsest.[27]

The state of the world is light, used up, worn down, exhausted, consumed. Resistance disappears since resistant material substance is absent. With nothing to work against—work is the struggle against the inertia of time—there is no work. Blanchot's famous *desoeuvrement* restates the tautology that work in the post-resistance world is the absence of anything to work against. It declares the destruction of the possibility of work, not of work itself, and even if work appears as a signified *in absentia,* to read the inscription with understanding is impossible. Its essential lightness is closely related to the impossibility of grasping what is read.[28] A reading *necessarily* misses the mark, always ahead of or behind it, like Lacan's account of Achilles and the hare. At the same time, the absence of work gives the uncanny impression that the reader is missing the point that, though elusive, is there in the work. Hence, the disputes and disagreements about the designation of "worldlessness."

Things are deconstituted as intentional objects. Consciousness has become dilated, defused, and directionless in free association. Uprooted from everyday configuration, distraction has been transplanted into the neuter and put to use for the sake of disuse. To read the neuter voice is to subvocalize the distraction, a voicing heard only absent-mindedly, when attention is unable to maintain or preserve its integrity and entertains a lack of purpose—its own lackluster. The Blanchotian monotone places no demand on the reader's affect. Dampened down, throttled, muted, the tonality leaves no foothold for interpretation and analysis. The fact "frees" the reader and clarifies how reading is "situated beyond or before comprehension" (SL, 196). The mind uncritical of the transcendental illusion absolves reading of penetration into textual meaning which absolution alone makes possible the "innocent Yes of reading." Such reading performs the bare affirmation that the work *is*, that it *exists*. This is the maximum of reading's achievement.[29]

The reader forgets her worldly position in order to read. She reads in order to affirm the forgetting. In both, the fall into lightness is frail, on the verge of collapse. An awareness of falling is lacking because one falls out of consciousness into insomnia—because falling is the disaster.[30] The frailty of the fall lies in its *almost*: that it almost doesn't happen, and if it does, it happens almost without showing, out of sight, impalpable. And if it didn't fall? —Such is the question of the fall. Is it necessary and if so, why frail, why necessarily frail or frail necessity, a one that borders on weakness? A necessity that limps along, barely potent, causing confusion over its apodictic status.

The fall of the reader's eyes to the page is a free fall. The fall (into forgetting) is freedom, and freedom, the fall. From self-present mastery into the neuter, the fall enables without effectivity that which is read to be self-marking. There, reading relieves thought of its discursive focus, frees intention from harboring objects, and cultures pure distractedness. The reader reading in distraction lets go of probing the text for the work's meaning. Literal, metaphorical, or anagogical signification is not sought. Paradoxically not grasping the work, the reader allows it to be, to sink back into primal being, in the time before mode and attribute, undifferentiated, and to seek no more from it.[31]

Reading and forgetting are bound by an internal relation. Forgetting (passage to the neuter) and reading (participation in the neuter). Does reading's "effortless liberty" have an analog in forgetting? —It does (SL,

196). Self-oblivion resets memory for the time that antedates the human: the empty, nondifferentiated presence, the "profoundly forgotten point from which every memory radiates" (LM, 85–86). Excessive inattention insulates the reader from the writer's encounter in essential solitude with the anguish of the interminable and the vague beauty of the thing liberated from all ends—from which the work springs. The protection grants reading an irresponsibility leavened with innocence; childhood outplays maturity (Narcissus again). Its spell magically shields the reader from the work's open violence and yields a simplicity and ease of affirmation. There is neither will to power nor initiative to delve deeply into bedrock. This is happiness, "always saying Yes, of endlessly affirming" (LM, 70). Similarly forgetting, letting intentionality (the master's wand) go, solicits a passive gentleness toward what lies unreachably farther (the step not beyond). Anguish over death has been suspended, and so too are initiatives toward being the one to whom death is given. Instead, the "free fall" of forgetting assents to a Levinasian *il y a*, presence of absence that obviates consciousness and unconsciousness alike. As Orpheus exemplifies, a freedom from desire, an insouciance or an insouciant desire overcomes the laws of intentionality and seeks out inspiration, the in-breath of creativity, of the work. Here, inadvertence or loss of remembrance marks a movement of sacrifice. Eurydice, the obscure object of night, is sacrificed without ceremony, without benefit of the ritual concentration that celebrates the sacred. She is returned to the outside by the slightest of gestures, a blind that shifts the gaze. Strangely, it is the commonplace of inattention, in its inessential weightlessness, that officiates over the sacred event—the work's arising—and of indecision that breaks the law of return. Inattention, not counter to attention, "neither negative nor positive, but excessive, which is to say without intentionality, without reproval, without the displacement that time effects (the ec-stacy)" (WD, 55).[32]

The anguish of essential solitude—milieu of writing—creation's womb, is the battlefield where mastery devises schemata for success, and fails. Gravity joins with an incessant pull toward certitude and attainment. Strife's contention with resistance marks the condition. The forced march of resoluteness motivated by nostalgia for being defines the irresolution. Distraction that pronounces the forbidden achievement requires taut reins, an essential concentration, and a single direction, in order to be outdone. The impossibility of the work makes transgression an unavoidable disaster. In forgetting, one has already crossed the border, and, no longer the "ownmost potentiality for being" in pursuit of individuality, has ceded its authority (that of a "canonical abbreviation") unto the service of an anonymous vociferation. To surrender is not grave but carefree. Made not for war but in play, it is errantly accomplished by "rules" constituted as one goes. They are disclosed only upon being broken. Knowledge has weightiness since it must determine limits and prohibit ruses. By contrast, freedom returns the work to its inessential—response to the impossible. It is "the glad accident" that brings the work to being, the reading of which is an aimless joy (SL, 176).[33]

In the dark, death escapes the neuter—deferred as in the story of Ivan Ilyich—not because of its weightiness but its inconsequence. It is more airborne than the lightness enunciated by the neuter voice and floats free of the grip of expression. It is designated by "a feeling of extraordinary lightness" in the very midst of the death sentence, the suspension of action that infinitely defers its arrival (I, 5). It doesn't belong to the transgressive movement that oversteps limits ad nauseam. The rhythm of syncopation prevents dying from full actualization—which confers a peculiar immortality to living since life can never be completely extinguished. The logic is given voice in Blanchot's syntagm after facing the firing squadron: "Dead—immortal" (ibid.). The hyphenation denotes how exchanges of life for death and death for life are likewise without end, producing a gyre or a round dance. That lightness arises in the roundelay, where *that* points to a play of forces, dramatic and dynamic, that is at the same time effortless, altogether without exertion. The negative freedom from strife (*eris*) is augmented positively by the aimless dehiscence of the neuter voice in its inessential gaiety, charged with a crepuscular *eros*.

That death is not a serious concern promotes an estranged immortality, the immortality sought as freedom from life's finitude. The immortal isn't attributable to survival without limit, an afterlife in a second world, or the (Pauline) resurrection of the body. That death lacks gravity enough to make an appearance or withdraws in order for appearance to appear in the neuter voice suggests that distraction, weak intention, and diffuse awareness—"passivity"—constitute the immortal. Immortality is founded on death's ineffectiveness, not on life's potency. In the neuter, the Grim Reaper is off his game. Hölderlin's thought echoes here. He envisions humans' betrayal of the divine as alloyed with the gods' infidelity toward humankind, and the double reversal signifies a radical devaluation of immortality. Beforehand, men and women experienced their deathlessness through unimpeded access to immediacy (the eternal now) and the "measured favor of divine forms," which in acts of worship allowed them to join the gods (SL, 275). After the reversal, the human is thrown into the anguish of an empty time, a time that never ceases because it is forever on the verge of beginning, and that disorients and disables experience by contriving self-identity. Guardians there of the absent presence of divinity and humanity alike, persons survive by remaining between the double disappearance. They must neither follow the gods into infinite exile nor subsist in their former rootedness (*Verwurzelung*) of life on the earth, when death had its limitless power and sting.

For Blanchot, "the happiness of not being immortal or eternal" in an epoch empty of divine possibility invites survival of a different kind (I, 5). It is adequate to a life whose afterlife is indefinitely postponed, having taken place without coming to pass in a present unworthy of presence and nomination. Alternatively, one takes the step not beyond to find that the transgressive movement—beyond life, in defeat of death—has already occurred. It is the happiness (*bonheur*) of time's not being over before it happens and of being indeterminately measured, when subject to death's law that ineluctably distinguishes death from life. In the estrangement of logic, death's inefficacy is related to its visibility or palpability from which its power ordinarily shields us: its "obscenity." Its efficient function depends on death's utter separation and secrecy. In absenting both the divine and the human, death ceases to labor unseen and enters the day as *das Ding, la chose effrayante*, which the narrator of *Death Sentence* describes as "something absolutely terrifying for anyone to learn who was naturally afraid of the night" (DS, 24). Happiness is tempered and coincides with its being irrecountable. It is a happy thing when what is forbidden to be told is not told. It is a happy thing *perhaps* when the forbidden comes to pass without achieving a narrative, a telling. Happiness is the *almost there*, death's having become a specter of a word. Unpaired to death but to a death-ghost, life holds an indifferent happiness, aimless, unconcerned, gratuitous. Its pathos is imperturbability, the Stoic's prize.

This passion comes to designate that of writing, a happiness of living beyond the terms of an eviscerated immortality. In a time when the divine has vacated its august place, a cautionary note is needed against the attraction of a void in excess of all limits. Failure to heed is dramatized by Orpheus who sees into the depths and by Narcissus who turns away. The one writing must inscribe the separation, eschewing both an active pursuit of holy transcendence and a passive surrender to terrestrial *jouissance*. The neutral voice is written in the spacing that enigmatically relates two utterly disparate realities, empty human, empty God. Without remorse, the one writing plays the sacred guide who searches with humankind for the other (the other of the psychism). Replacing the shaman's, sage's, or saint's words of reverence or devotion, the writer performs a most high function—Orpheus for one "frees the sacred contained in the work, *gives* the sacred to itself" (SL, 175). The work holds an image, the holy tonality evoked by the encounter. That image, Hölderlin interrogatively suggests: " 'Is God unknown? Is he open like the sky? I rather believe so" (SL, 176).[34] Recall the role of sky in the young boy's trauma at the window.

The wake of passion lends a detached lightness foreign to everydayness. Excessive meaning (think of reading the First *Critique*, where words must be pulled back to their places in the semantic field) escapes gravitational pull by floating improbably away. It cannot be approached directly by the critical mind that needs weight, resistance, and impenetrability to gain a dialectical foothold. It lingers out of reach, a fascination to the reader, whom it invites to join in lingeringly. When the reader does, the writing, born autochthonously in the maternal firmament, is fulfilled as a work. Prior to that, it is conceived and executed (to whatever degree) but does not yet exist. Actualization takes place when the reader joins in and the (mother) space of writing is made legible under the light of her mind. The material inscription is a sketch of itself, a rift partially effaced for the reader, as if incised by a stylus's light pressure. Even here, the tendency is to be lured by the optical metaphor. It must be resisted. Think of metallic gauze as the writing's ethereal matrix on which the words resonate before they give voice. They are written vocality read by the listening eye.

The writing's work is light because the neuter voice lacks mass. Things don't fall to the center because no center exists. Or, an abyss is the central point (macula), a center both voided and approached in avoidance. The decentered core is not subject to centripetal force, but then, words don't fly off either. They chaotically derange themselves. The scattered assembly, the unthought, unreasoned order is the risk taken by the writing. Writing is a vociferated response inscribed under threat of madness. It involves a nonintentional play of language that has become radically disequilibrated and in danger of foundering. Was it ever in balance? Was there a prelapsarian time? The writing approaches the unconditional with an empty beggar's bowl. It is forever light, a knower of poverty.

No gravity, no center, no certainty. With the gravitational pull of literary space set at zero, there is no attraction to the origin, assuming one exists. In other words, there is attraction to a nonexistent source: the outside. Movement is lured toward the vanishing point except where impeded by intentionality, that is, the obsessional dream of mastery. The impedance is fortified by resoluteness, sincerity willing to face the death of one's own. It is a good time to reconsider the event of the firing squad, in which the narrator (Blanchot, "Blanchot") is "prevented from dying by death itself" (I, 3). If the thing of death as an end point is endlessly deferred (as *différance*), if it can never come into full presence, then *contra* Heidegger, it does not have a facticity that is imminent.[35] Instead, its imminence is counterfactual; it is *as if* death were about to take place. Or, its imminence is imaginary; death that cannot take place is imagined as about to. In both, the "always already" or sempiternal qualifies the imminence of death, not death itself (as if it has ipseity). The second is the "empty deep" that stultifies thought and presents the Gorgon head to the gaze. Within the space of Orpheus's failure wracked by random crossings of forces without resolution, the literary work can arise, "where the echo of the empty deep becomes speech" (SL, 176).

By the movement to the outside, death—not life—is granted immortality. In *The Step Not Beyond*, Blanchot echoes the thought of *Instant*—"Death delivers from death"—and immediately corrects himself, "Perhaps only from dying" (SNB, 132). While the survival of death (death in death) spells anguish for life, dying is a kind of solace. It "is this lightness within any liberty from which nothing can liberate" (ibid.). Dying to the attachment to an identity that interiority takes for the self lifts one outside the limits of the *moi*, to the neutral voice, the void of gravitas. Death as terminus or power would reinstate the law of identity and block the consolation. Thus, the immortality of death is not welcome since "death does not have within it that with which to allay death; it is thus as if it survived itself, in the powerlessness of being that it disperses, without this powerlessness assuming the task of incompletion—unaccomplishment—proper or improper to dying" (ibid.).[36]

On Happiness

The child of the primal scene (kid-Narcissus) has a vision that brings "the feeling of happiness [*bonheur*]" that is borne witness by "an endless flood of tears." In Derrida's account, the latter transform seeing to a higher, spiritualized form, exemplified by the *pleurantes*, women whose weeping mourns the death-passage. The eye's desire, concupiscence (Augustine), to see beyond the object to the conditions that make sight possible—to see invisibility itself—is transcended. An impossible desire (any desire) is transubstantiated unto the ethical. Scopic desire aims at the ocular blind spot, the point that fascinates and draws sight toward the outside with promise of unmediated contact. For Derrida, the impossible desire of the subject is exchanged for an ethical concern for the other that absolves it of ineffectuality. The *pleurantes* weep not for their own loss but to beg pardon for the other's. They see blindly but with second sight. For Blanchot, the transaction is more nuanced. While vision may still seek the step beyond, transcendence is secreted away; the child "will live henceforth in the secret" (WD, 72). The excessive happiness will remain interior, subject to forgetting, perhaps forgotten in the gift, but exterior to both itself and the interiority of the boy. The child's conduct will be marked by the trauma of the blind spot but with no turn toward the ethical. The thing of ocular desire always already will have been avoided, not without leaving the portal open to the outside and the invaginating pocket inside.

The secret recurs in the second *recit*, the escape from the firing squad. The narrator there relates "a feeling of extraordinary lightness, a sort of beatitude (nothing happy [*heureux*], however)—sovereign elation" (I, 5). Immune to analysis or naming, it keeps its life secret in the absence of the signifier, incessantly unfolding, turning interiority outside, then again dissolving. There is, however, a transformative opaqueness which reveals moral sentiment, both "the feeling of compassion for suffering humanity" and "the torment of injustice" (I, 5, 7). The crucial difference with Derrida lies not with the transmuting of feeling to the ethical but in the operation of vision—the scopic drive. What becomes secret for life is how the object, "absolutely black absolutely empty," screens the excessive enjoyment of the young boy. He wants to experience what is impossible to see (secret) but instead is given to see what protects against encountering the blind spot and its illicit and "ravaging joy." Henceforth, an anxiety will serve as border guard to the forbidden precinct. To gaze there, the narrator of *The Madness of the Day* reports, "I felt the scars fly off my eyes, my sight was a wound, my head a hole, a bull disemboweled" (MD, 198). To look at that place brings guilty enjoyment of a trauma, a secret *jouissance*. One must avert one's eyes. "Must" here functions both as "should" and "cannot," moral and natural necessity, or as neither.

The secreting of happiness (happiness's secret: the heart) reduces the question of attestation to a presence that lives a life of its own. The witness who marks what is to be seen because of being present to the event is thrown, and therefore may or may not arrive at its destination. If what meets the eye is never the fully desired object of vision, since that has been destabilized, then the witness is inevitably off the mark, marking what covers over the real and beholding only the wasted residue. The thing remains "the secret." Like Eurydice, it is an image superimposed on errant nothing, an alluring display that may or may not be captured by the ocular "throw." Sight drawn to it, lured to see itself, finds instead an ever-receding possibility of seeing—an impassibility—to which one is attracted as to a phantom: the rapture of utter passivity, "sovereign elation" (I, 5). Its capture is bound to fail since the "law" of sight forestalls contact with both what is absented and the absence that remains present. The witness's task, to describe the event, surpasses one's ability since sight is protected from the unrepresentable and lacks signifiers of the traumatization. "The witness never sees what she claims to see." If witnessing did, it would elide with voyeurism, the guilty enjoyment of an other's trauma.

The fact is that the scopic drive ("wanting to see") works in errancy (*Irre*). It will always evade what is sought. It will take the supplemental screen for what it seeks, letting it appear that the object isn't there. The omission is not only self-protective but also expresses respect for the thing's self-remarking iteration. According to the law of supplementarity, the object is concealed, hidden, not known, absent from thought and perception. That of which the witness owes an account fails to appear in description; in place of the omission, she gives a story. As a counter to the naive view that "a man who speaks and who reasons with distinction is always capable of recounting facts that he remembers," Blanchot's narrator exclaims, "A story? No. No stories, never again" (MD, 199). This is an ironic counterfactual. Since "the truth, the whole truth" is unavailable, the best testimony is to forgo testimony, that is, "attestation to the absence of attestation."[37]

What is seen, screen or supplement, is the image of the "second version." The function of the "first version" is replication. It is a stand-in for the visible object, a second or proxy. The function of the "second version" is to make the invisible visible, to satisfy the unsatisfiable desire to see the unseen. Its premise is "contact at a distance," touch in the absence of mediation, a direct impression: a reduction of sorts. By offering a tolerable enjoyment, the image defers ultimate confrontation with the thing desired and its mute suffering of the excess. The exchange is aporetic and produces what Blanchot calls the inversion of the gaze: the shift in vision from the possibility of seeing to the impossibility of not seeing. Here again, an important role is given to the sacrifice of satisfaction, seeing without ever coming to having seen, "a gaze that has become the ghost of an eternal vision" (SL, 32).[38] To gaze is to forgo appropriation in favor of the passion of intimacy, possession for liberation from care: "[O]utside of us, in the backward motion of the world that the image provokes, the depth of our passion trails along, astray and brilliant" (SL, 262). There is the destabilizing effect of the ambiguous passion. Deferring attainment, the gaze preserves the force of the scopic drive (its passion) as it embodies the submission and passivity (its passion) required to engage it. The gaze, outside before it is outside, subtracts the weight of vision, both material and ontological, lives in danger of floating away into the abyss, but is returned always to its happiness of dying. It has thrown its lot into the object's disjuncture and falling away it reaffirms its nomadic proclivities.

Life's Brevity and the Work of Mourning

The neuter voice is polyvocal and vociferated by the multiple. It resounds in pluralities, equivocities, and homonyms. Hence, the three readings of "dying" (*mourir*) that interweave and mutually entangle. It is important to separate and rethink each. First, dying appears in its Aristotelian sense of generation and corruption. Life dwindles from the moment of birth as it is prone to aging and senescence; "One is never too young to die." Second, in dying the subject cedes its place to an unknown other, on the way to dispossession and exile, nomadism and pilgrimage. The cessation is never completed and one inevitably fails in the transference to occupy the impossible roles that internally rupture, mime, and remark themselves. Of neither religious nor ethical import, dying absolves an ontological misunderstanding (indebtedness for one's existence) as it opens to an immeasurable outside. Third, dying reduces the ego from sovereignty to indistinctness (the object's obstinacy of not showing) while eschewing attachment, especially to self-identity. There, the subject, minus self-sufficiency, is no other than what Foucault calls "extreme attentiveness."[39]

Ultimately, the strongest impression of dying is of ineffectuality. Dying neither does nor undoes anything; it accomplishes nothing and lives in indecision.[40] Because of its inconsequence, the subject constantly forgets the fact of dying, how it tries to make changes without placing any demands. *Dying is fatally impeded eventfulness.* In the mirror, dying is the mortal face of the disaster. Like the disaster that cuts humanity off from the astral source of the event, dying is of no consequence. It ruins everything yet leaves no impression as it steals away like a thief in the night. Its radical and absolute exteriority interiorizes everything, including itself, causing it to utterly disappear. *That* night threatens in its imminence and yet persists imminently in its imminent menace. Its cryptic impossibility affects all things possible but not at the limit; rather, in the very intention it appears in the challenge of gratuity to deliberateness. In the heart of intentionality, chance lies coiled like a worm. Freedom confronts the I like a yoke and thus, is easily dismissed with reproach. The gaze stolen by night is replaced by the everyday look, as was Maupassant's diamond necklace by a piece of costume jewelry. At the same time, the poverty of dying—supplement to nothing at all—exerts a force of attraction. To succumb to the lure is to pay the admission fee for the neuter voice.

Aimless unconcern, gratuitous play, carefree utterance: interminability does not weigh heavily on a disposition to the neuter voice. Active oblivion, erasure of marks of presence (erasure of illusory marks) has a childlike quality, repeated naïveté, curiosity with interest. Is there a place for the work of mourning or is it, like anticipatory resoluteness, abandoned to the daylight world? Think of the work as Derrida does: "Memory and interiorization: since Freud, this is how the 'normal' 'work of mourning' is often described."[41] This means: to remember the subject that suffers the loss of the one to be remembered. Both aspects run into difficulty with the antinomous neuter voice.[42] Vociferating the outside, its perilous erosion of memory traces (Joshua's trumpet at the battle of Jericho), neutrality entangles in retrieval processes. Marks and remarks are continually demarcated, leaving a deconstructed surface uncharted like the ocean swirled by prevailing currents, a vague, free emptiness. The other's death is another "site" that is depersonalized and merged with thanatopic events of humanity at large that coincides with the subject-place scrubbed of individual biography. Interiority is furnished with a mike through which exteriority speaks in a tongue that produces ghosts of words, an apparitional language, or a language of image (image of language).

In this spirit Blanchot seems to confirm the exclusion when he writes, "The work of mourning: the inverse of dying" (SNB, 96). What kind of inversion? Remembering for forgetting, sobriety for gaiety, purpose for happenstance, appropriation for abandonment? To resist amnesia regarding the dead, a resolve is needed of the same order as *Entschlossenheit*. Whereas, as seen, the play of forgetting entails a weakened intentionality at the very least, or a demolition of the underlying structures of mastery (guilt, indebtedness) at the other extreme. Yet Blanchot's thought is more subtle. He writes, "The death of the Other: a double death, for the Other is death already, and weighs upon me like an obsession with death" (WD, 19). Counter to the lightness and unconcern of dying, the weight is capable of turning into a totalitarian persecution, wherein a powerful edict from the other ("Bear me in mind!") is heaped on a defenseless mourner who has surrendered her possibilities (including the possibility of impossibility) in substitution. But in fact mourning concerns neither a reinstatement of the subject nor its subjugation through compulsive neurosis. It is primarily a farewell (*adieu, a-Dieu*), never completely enunciated, that constitutes the relation of the living to the no longer alive. The relation challenges the opposition of being and nothingness, and in Levinas's thought, the valediction is directed to the other beyond being, in "what is signified, beyond being, by the word 'glory.' "[43]

Commemorating a leavetaking, the work needs be a valediction forbidding mourning, rather than an encomium on obsessive desire. Otherwise, the other's death (including the other in me, my "clandestine companion") exacerbates the tendency that dying alleviates, dread. Dread is not a call to presence and mastery, as in Heidegger and Kierkegaard, but a monster of the afterworld, an introjection of night. Whereas dying gives passage, dread stultifies. The Gorgon stare. Dying moves with life but dread, from beyond life, with "its immobile disaster that lets everything remain" (SNB, 120).[44] The forgetfulness of dying (the synonymy of the two) opens a space in which language is free to fill with reverberations of its being that, when filled, hold the emptiness of a tomb, perhaps Narcissus's. The being of language—cleared of Heideggerian misconceptions, the clearing of which is the effect of the disaster—comes antinomously forth. To a streaming vibration, noncompliant with any syntax, the ear of the one writing responds and, like a priest who attends the pythoness at Delphi (in her drugged, blathering frenzy), inscribes a meaning: the impossible play of translation. Although the signification cannot be true (due to the absence of the signifier), the enunciation can nonetheless "make sense." The relative freedom of the *Sinngebung* supports what is called literature. A premise of literary work is a non-obsessive relation with death and the various cults of the dead, including the work of mourning. The recurrent thought of death and its call to presence found an ontology of linguisticality that elides the voice of dying with the neuter voice of the outside. The "house of being" rings too insistently in the ear of the one that would write. To write becomes a disclosure of the world rather than a botched inscription of what neither is nor is not of it.

The inversion that a work of mourning performs on dying puts on the dress of attestation. The former would reinstall the subject as witness to the other's death, whereas language in the neutral voice is that which can attest to the absence of death, the witness, and the need for a work of mourning. Such a language has no fold: it does not return to itself. It is a nomadic language. Since it has no destiny or destination, its turning (to, from, away, around, inside out . . .) is gratuitous, like random Brownian motion. Its proceeding bears away that which preceded it since it is not given to collaboration, coordination, or conjunction. Neither is it complicated, implicated, replicated, or duplicated—all formation derived from *pli* or fold. Deprived of a doubling, it escapes consciousness and unconsciousness alike and speaks to an attentiveness bestowed independently of that axis. It is without any power whatsoever: language of the imaginary.[45] The witness is privileged "to see that I am seeing." It belongs to a fold different from the one it holds in view while sharing a relation of identity to it. Rather than aimlessly participating in the scene, it calls up the subject-object form (*Gegenstand*) to instantiate the separation, invoking the law. In that sense, mourning perverts dying, limiting the latter's erasure of attachment. It does not respect the weak power of dying nor the (Nietzschean) fact that weakness triumphs over strength. In a strange way, it suppresses the imaginary by charging remembrance of the departed to guard against distraction and a defocused consciousness. It forgets that the instant is madness.

4

Echo

•◆———◆•

The receiver gave out a buzz of a kind that I had never before heard on a telephone. It was like the hum of countless children's voices—but yet not a hum, the echo rather of voices singing at an infinite distance—blended by sheer impossibility into one high but resonant sound that vibrated on the ear as if it were trying to penetrate beyond mere hearing.

—Kafka, The Castle

The Auditory Image

The enigma of rhythm—dialectical-nondialectical, no more the one than the other is other—is the extreme danger.

—Maurice Blanchot, The Writing of the Disaster

Blanchot writes, "Speaking is not seeing" (IC, 25). Is speaking (writing, engagement with language) an act of renunciation, sacrifice, rational decision, whimsy? The statement has to do with the extent to which imagery is identified with vision and how image is shorthand for visual image. What is being given up? —Image as coextensive with vision, *imago* and *eidos*. At the margins, one begins to listen, to turn to the auditory on mute, as a genitive of image. With speaking or giving voice, images should be heard, not seen. This does not endorse, moreover, listening for descriptions of visual images, but for the image's sonic appearance, or better, its vocality. Auditory imagery is generated outside the breathing of language, in hidden depths of the (breathless) imagination that brought Kant to awe. It is also sublime, in his sense of the word.

The turn toward the auditory (phonic, vocalic, *vox* and *phone*) goes hand in hand with Blanchot's infrequent but highly charged mention of rhythm.[1] His fondness for a Hölderlin citation: "Everything is rhythm; the entire destiny of man is a single, celestial rhythm, just as the work of art is a unique rhythm" (IC, 30).[2] As if the image were sonically communicated through the materiality of words, phonemes and enunciations, their presence and absence, on mute. The senseless iteration and vibratory display of the outside—the vacuous power of the image—interrupts the dialectic of the symbolic order. The image, in particular, the acoustical image, exerts a force, an uncanny influence, on life in the world. Since that image "is not sensible" (and not supersensuous either), this is accomplished antinomously, by opening to what Blanchot calls "the mystery" (WD, 113). The acoustical image and the rhythm manifest in or by it operate in an ancient time capable of dephasing the temporal flow of everydayness. It is able to defeat the mastery of language wherever linguisticality is time-bound: always and everywhere. Rhythm and the acoustic image figure what is anterior to language—the arrhythmic rustling Levinas calls the *il y a*—that haunts it as an inefficacious double. Writing is the after-the-fact (*nachträglich*) account of the event of *arche*-language, a sensible record of the insensible, a likely abusive statement of the paradoxicality to which language bears witness. Writing then defines itself within the literary work.

The abandon of the visual image is not the abandon of the image *tout court*. Nor is it surrender of the gaze, that for which Merleau-Ponty constitutes the subject of visual perception, the given-to-be-seen. In the panopticon of the world, the thing has the subject who sees in its gaze anterior to its look toward it. My seeing myself see myself is constituted by the latter priority, that I am seen. The seeing thing need not be sentient or animate; it need not be visible since it gives itself by giving withdrawal. It need not be there, if the *Da* opens the serviceable world. The possibility of sight is an upsurge from the invisible and unremarkable. If "to see myself see myself" defines intentional consciousness peculiar to the human, then self-awareness depends on something other's gaze on me. For Blanchot, *pari passu* with hearing and the image peculiar to audition. Perception in general operates in duality, with primacy on the passive side, given-to-be-perceived. This thought can be extended. If one conceives the auditory gaze as a listening (gaze:look::listening:hearing), then the subject hears because it is listened to . . . by the things of the world. Things, moreover, in their silent, mute, inaudible being: mute because their voicing trails its resonation by immeasurable time. If Lacan is to be followed, then as the subject is constituted by the split between the mirror image and the sensate or proprioceptive *vecu*, its constitution is reaffirmed by the split between her voice externally and interiorly heard, the acoustic and the mute. Moreover, the voice "in the head" is originally (mis)perceived as an echo of the doubleness of the worldly voice. Here, one can exclaim, "Speaking is hearing." This matter returns in the sections on Echo.

It is the gaze that encounters the (visual) image; in the case of the auditory image, listening occupies the place of the gaze. In both, a passivity (that exceeds being and is not the opposite of an activity) is attracted and further undermined by excessive desire from the thither side of the thing. Beyond the auditory image, listening responds to a voicing whose alluring sonic resonance disorders the spatiality of inside and outside. As if ventriloquized from a source without location, it remains inaudible, a sound on the verge of or no longer reaching sonic proportions but whose attainment is delayed, diffused, or deferred—to the point of anxiety or trauma. Listening is being vibratorily possessed to the extent that the sense making (*Sinngebung*) is challenged.[3] It is the release of the intention to comprehend sound-events as *paroles*, elements in a semantic display. Inasmuch as intentionality defines a horizon of concern, it is a surrender to a horizonless soundscape where the incessant, feverish, uneven vibrancy of error has no purpose or origin. When a description is correlated with the listening, the auditory image discerned therein escapes, to leave a residue of a mysterious effulgence (fulguration), the hearing of which poses a danger.[4] As the ear opens to contact, the image recedes and breaks apart since de-distancing has been forfeited: contact at a distance, contiguity in separation. Although earthly coordinates cannot locate it, what becomes apparent in the apparition is a background of absence. What is listened to is not there, lacks presence, and yet is capable of producing a traumatizing sound-event. Its voice is the illicit excess, the "cut," of the signifier. Everything comes with more than it vociferates. Enjoyment (*jouissance*) of its illicitness names the drive that seeks the experience.

The listening object, the auditory image, lies at the point where distance fractures and exception of the listener from the scene breaks down. It is where listening itself is inscribed in what takes place—where the object-image "listens" to the one who listens. It is the point where dissimulation occurs of an objective line that divides one from the other. The unmasking of the illusion of perceived distance raises the problem of constituting the border that might divide interiority from the external world. Without the line (barrier, limit, *barrio*, boundary), the externality of the listener's ear to the thing heard is problematic, even as the thing becomes other to itself, remarking and disseminating itself. When the image appears to reverberate, it lays bare the denuded null place from where an impersonal listening unfathomably operates. The one listening is then subject to the effect of the anonymous exterior that has a duplicitous nature. It is obscene, desecrating in its vocal exhibition of the secret, hidden, intimate, de-cored outside—the sacred teaching of death.[5] And, it is uncanny, provoking the anxiety Heidegger discerns, where "the most elemental disclosedness of thrown Dasein . . . confronts being-in-the-world with the nothingness of the world."[6] But instead of inscribing a Heideggerian call to conscience, the dread of being draws away the power of the I, handicapping the forethrow and leaving the subject to endure the full impact of purposelessness.

The auditory image is carrier of excess, both excessive authority of the other's voice and of exposure of the ear. It threatens infection, parasitism. The voice image steps over the line, bypassing the resistance protective of interiority. Transgressive in its neutralization of the law, it appears inside without ever crossing the frontier that defines identity and its limits, and without authorization to enter. The excessive power resides in surplus meaning, the remainder created by the signifying cut. Endowed with power over and above that which can be accommodated by the symbolic order, the signifier transfers the "unemployable negation" to the image. Apparently innocuous, like kryptonite, the image is charged to immobilize, stultify, and stun linguistic performance. The subject is then no longer subject *of* but subject *to* the listening. Plea, command, appeal, persuasion, summons (*Ruf*): the voice of the other is implicated and folded into the interior. What is listened *to*, the auditory image, is from the outside insofar as it presents itself to consciousness.

The subject listens and is addressed by the auditory image, and the image listens and is spoken to by the subject. But there is an asymmetry between the other's vocalic imagery and the subject's listening—the operations of emission and exposure. As an excess, the image-object must be dealt with, either by incorporation or expulsion. In fact, no choice exists if the subject's voice is linguistically constituted. Here, the problematic of language acquisition rears its head. Mimicry of the signifiers is not sufficient to gain a capacity to enunciate with a language. The voice of excess, superabundant vocality exiled from the everyday world, stands in need of embodiment. The other's voice, the surplus of the signifier, the signification that doesn't "fit" into the world created by the cut, phenomenalizes the linguistic matrix with its differential calculus. Its power is that of the inverse, being no longer delimited by law. Incorporation of the non-signifying vocalic image means that the site of null signification is then and always interior to language, and language acquisition proceeds through this interiorization of nullity.[7] At the same time, it isn't that the image belongs to exteriority. More precisely, it belongs to a family of borderline operators that constitute the division into inner and outer, which has the power to explode the dissimulated integrity. The seat of rogue ventures is the imaginary.

Rhythm is the semiotics of the auditory image.

One can recall the terse Saussurean definition of the signifier: language may be content simply to contrast something with nothing. In reduced form, language is the minimal alternation of presence and absence. Having no intrinsic meaning, the signifier operates according to a differential and oppositional calculus. The meaning of a single phonemic element engages the totality minus one, namely, the element not there. The difference that signifies is the differential between the element's appearance and nonappearance, its positive and negative nature, its resonance and de-sonance: *différance*. To comprehend meaning, voiced or read (spoken "silently" to oneself), requires listening for the absent sound as much as the sounded sound. The silent spacing is as essential to meaning making as the phonemic content that it spaces. The fact that the operation of language depends on the emptiness of phonemic production provides the basis for the rhythmic alternation of units of meaning. This a priori condition is in force with each and every enunciation, read or acoustically presented to oneself or another person, with each and every natural (phonetic) language, at each and every point in time (including this one).

As the display of the non-acoustical image, rhythm plays with death, that silent null space built into the taking place of language, its *vox* and *parole*. The vibratory life of the phoneme is interwoven with the absence of that life; their woven texture, their warp and woof, together constitute the voice. To put it otherwise, phonemic life—the organic component of voice—is joined with a nonresonant—dead, denatured—sound in the production of meaning. Is this akin to the alchemical dream of Narcissus, the wedding of living and non-living in a festival of love? The sound of absence (abstention of organic vociferation) then behaves like a parasite that feeds on the phonemic "body," menacing its vitality. The invasive parasitism corresponds to the intrusion of the signifier into the corporeal and is unavoidable as long as *différance* is in play. What the intruder retains is not the nullity of resonance; death is not the absolute zero of vibration, motionless in a cold and frozen universe. It has its deep—i.e., rhythmic—pulse that has roots in the outside.[8] What death brings to the vocalic operation of language is the disaster, the vibratory potency of night whose power is the subsidence of intentionality (like sound in an anechoic chamber) and its replacement with random jabber. Internal to it, the jamming of meaning-making vociferation blends significance with the inessentially insignificant. Enunciation is increasingly gibberish. Ruination of the voice, drowning in vocalic residue, is the result.[9]

At the same time, the muted nonresonance attracts listening as to an "obscure object." Through the sonics of the nonacoustical voice, the terror outside produces a paradoxical enjoyment; *jouissance* is enjoyment in excess of the excess, liking exceeding the capacity to like. In the ceaselessly broken movement between opposites—here, there; light, dark; full, empty; true, false—the neutral passage enjoyed as reality at its barest, there is also shame. Shame survives, Blanchot says, as "a mockery of life as life's beyond" (WD, 53).[10] Think of it as the analogue of voyeuristic shame—écouteurism. One listens as it were at the keyhole to what is not intended to be heard. At the same time, hearing the voice of the other that listens (the voice of the ear of the other, the deaf voice) transfers its estrangement by inclusion to one's own voice. Excessive enjoyment calls the latter voice into question, dispossessing and expropriating the subject of vocalic power. One can imagine Socrates's shame at overhearing the voice of the daemon that ardently listened to his interiorized monologue.

Subject to this condition, the very taking place of voice must be understood. The ruined voice is the voice of one's own insofar as "owned," when returned to the speaker as though from an echo chamber: the void of the other. One gives voice and instead of hearing one's given voice, it is a nonempirical voice that resonates in the resonant void of alterity, in the presence of absence. It is as if the speaker's voice (with signature enunciation) had been extracted from the enunciation, blended with, and then substituted by the mix for the other's. Phenomenally, one hears one's words emerge from and sound in the other's "utterance," yet coming from one's own mouth. The non-acoustic voice of the other's ear, its listening voice, operates as a sonic mirror. It is a surface that reflects vocalic events back to the source of their emission. That voice, the voice of the outside, is the vociferation of the *il y a*, terrifying, enticing, traumatic, desired. It speaks in audible imagery and is antinomously sourced in the imaginary.

The taking place of voice, then, is not a simple product of the signifying, teamed with the system of signifiers, but involves a significant "detour" or inversion. The enunciation must be echoed back to the speaker by an alterity in order to become voiced by the one who gives voice. Just as the face of the void acts as a mirror that sends the visual image back to the source of the image, so too does the "ear of the other" for audible imagery. In both cases, the source is null and void. Images arise wherever, auto-affective as they are. Ex nihilo, made of nothing, ethereal: they are multiple swirls of forces crisscrossing in neutral space. Voice emerges in the exchange or conversation between meaning and its other, between the giving voice and receiving the echo of it bounced off the ear of the other, not without effect. Voice takes place reflexively in the minimal sense that the echo deconstructs the subject of the voice and leaves a different one to reflexively relate to itself. The reflexive intervention of the other's listening constitutes the making of voice in freeing itself from productive subjectivity, animating, "breathing" on its own, transforming the meaning of "voice."

Intervention takes place in a strong sense. The absence periodically repeated intervenes to co-originate the event of vociferation, and that absence makes the rhythm of voice. Repetition is the order of the day as soon as the differential system of signifiers is in place. Recall that a pulsing of every grammatical particle, each seme, is generated by the hidden oscillation, on and off, of meaning-making units.[11] The pulsation is almost (but never) audible, on mute, a mumbled disjoint of vocalic matter with blurted snatches of emotion and cries of excess. Correlated with the pulsing, a non-acoustic ghosting of *Sinngebung* that is the other or double of the phonemic saying, there is a tempo. In the correlation is the generation and corruption of rhythm. Produced in the intervening absence, the phonemes' pulsion that flutters through the voice box of language is originary.

Finally, the pleasure of rhythm (is all pleasure rhythmic?) coincides with the attraction to excess, to a desire that lies beyond the plenum of enjoyment, the exceptional desire. That void is constitutive of the pulsation or pulsion that is the rhythm of voice. The attraction to the miniscule absence of phonemic content—the off of meaning-making—is active throughout the event of voice. Yet fulfillment is impossible without collapsing the entire scheme of meaning. Production of phonemes without spacing may yield a cry, scream, shriek, groan, or chuckle, but not a word. As with all desire, the desire for unlimited presence of absence meets impossibility; the drive is inherently misdirected. The work of the other's ear enables a posteriori the vocal work that takes place a priori, emphasizing the antinomy of freedom.

Is there a rhythm or family of rhythms that gives the signature of the neuter voice? Could one say that the "faithful" inscription of what the scribe hears dictated is bound to incorporate the rhythm of the other's voice, and that fidelity consists of phonemic decisions that do not obscure it? "To write is . . . to welcome the passive pressure which is not yet what we call thought, for it is already the disastrous ruin of thought" (WD, 41). Pressure, compression, pulsion. That basal rhythm, perhaps metaphorized as a carrier wave of a radio signal, extends throughout a word-choice put into writing. Its influence, like that of a weak force, is perceptible through the manifest linguistic content. It is inexpungible because of its self-erasing mark. At the scene of inscription, the neuter inscribes a double voice, that of the one who puts it in writing and that of the other, the other who hears it. The writer who masters the neuter voice is no master at all, but rather is indentured to a double dictation and a double listening. She must have an ear good enough that it can turn in two directions, "naming the possible, responding to the impossible." This is the case with Blanchot, the writer.

Double Voice

Let me return to the first recit, "(A Primal Scene?)," as inscribed with a question mark. In it, the voice makes an almost inconspicuous appearance.

Addressed to an invoked someone, "you who live later" (the reader, the narrator who recollects a childhood event, "Blanchot"), the voice demands listening intently since that life is "close to a heart that beats no more" (WD, 72). The required acuity is more likely to register the sound of a silent heartbeat, of a heart whose repeated pressure and release—the systole and diastole audible to the subject or the stethoscope of the physician— has come to an end. Imagine some EMT person, ear to the chest of an accident victim, trying to detect signs of life. A dead heart, the heart of a dead man or woman, but not necessarily. It could also signify the heart of one heartless and without compassion, an unpardonable heart, stricken or frozen, in its expression of humanity. Or, a heart that has skipped a beat in an interminable arrhythmic episode because of trauma, inner or outer, that stretches into an immeasurable future. Or, the heart of the child of the recit, who together with his child-heart metaphorically dies in the passage to adulthood. These variations on death are less important than the mute resonance, the absence of aortic pulse, the timed interval that ought to be filled sonically with the coronary rhythm. For a heartbeat is the voice of life.

The sound of a heart that beats no more, an inexplicable auditory phenomenon, a de-vociferated and deferred voice, is the seed around which the narration is formed. At the recit's origin is the traumatization produced by a voice that is both no longer and not yet, a voice universally recognized as that of life's pulse. The double nature of the sound is essential to mark, initially because it is tied up with Blanchot's decision to link the narration—through the title—with Freud's concept of the stereotypical primal fantasy, a child's witnessing sexual intercourse between her parents. In it, some accidental noise plays a key role. As Freud remarks, "Indeed, it is doubtful whether we can rightly call the noise 'accidental.' . . . Such noises are on the contrary an indispensable part of the fantasy of listening [*Belauschungsphansien*], and they reproduce either the sounds which betray parental intercourse or those by which the listening child fears to betray itself."[12] There is then a double sound allied with a double betrayal: the parents' sonorous activity reveals the secret of origin (through the logic of *Nachträglichkeit*), the child, its secret fascination concerning its own origin.[13] The audible-inaudible event has its source in the imaginary and when brought to the world splits, into not a "real" and a phantom sound but two ghost sounds that concatenate in proximity to each other. One fascinates the spellbound child who is transfixed by what is heard as it dispossesses her of agency and volition. The other frightens in how it could reveal her hideout, from where she takes in the illicit and excessive enjoyment of the scene witnessed. The encounter with the remainder condenses the two into the enigma of the other's sound and the *jouissance* linked to it. The child's fantasy construction follows in suite.

Freud's position on the formation of fantasy is worth noting. He writes to Fliess that they "are related to things heard in the same way as dreams are related to things seen. For in dreams we hear nothing, but only see."[14] Sonic and not visual experiences provide the material for the confabulation of fantasy. The fantasy of origin, the primal scene, is at the same time the origin of fantasy, the original fantasy. The sound of a heart that beats no more and the transgressive listening that detects it collaborate to tell a story of birth. In a fabulous account, one is told how the adult (narrator, "Blanchot") came into being, surviving the deadness of what does not survive.[15] Furthermore, while the fantasy functions as a provisional account of the enigmatic sound (voice of life), it elides the spacing, time lag, or deferral inherent in listening to the voice and comprehending it. Covering over the traumatization produced by the voice's surpassing the knowing grasp, the story constructs the subject out of *différance*—the time between listening to the non-beat of the heart and making sense of it. Story is a moderation (mode, modification) of excess. Freud repeatedly asserts that the voice, inner and outer, self and other, is always understood *nachträglich*, later, retroactively. Listening precedes the arrival of meaning making; in between, language and the text take their places. Derrida extends the line of thinking to the signature of the one who puts it in writing.[16] He will further use the claim to his advantage in attacking Husserl's fundamental position in phenomenology.[17] In the original Freudian version, comprehension is repeatedly put off, extending the time of fantasizing, the ending of which comes as an unfulfillable promise.

The psychoanalytic account emphasizes the risk of a "real" understanding of the vocalic enigma, one that would supplant the fantasy with an impartial view of the (absent) origin of life. Analogous to the child who is unwitting witness to a parental sex act and whose fantasy subsequently infects all "true" (scientific, investigative, empirical) versions of the event, so too with the child in the recit. What objectively takes place beyond the window above the garden will have been understood subsequently in the wake of the traumatic audition. Objectivity will remain hostage to excess, which has already set the stage, props, and script, so that reality bears marks of implausibility. Objectivity puts on the costume of delirium, the fool's motley or the mystic's ecstasy. The border between rationality and madness—naming the possible, responding to the impossible—is more thoroughly effaced; isn't it the erasure that invites virtuality to the table? Consider the hyperbolic expressions used to describe the boy's undergoing a "ravaging joy" that is witnessed by a "flood of tears." It gives evidence of living "henceforth in the secret," a life whose core preserves in the logic of the crypt an auditory experience of death. That the subjectivity engraved on the stilled heart is constituted by the desire to listen, to fantasize (*Belauschungsphansien*) and fictionalize, and to be possessed by a transgressive enjoyment. The boy will refuse to be consoled by reason, the language of the signifier; eschewing it, he "says nothing." To affirm the fictional nature of the account over "truth," he "will weep no more."

In the text, there is the child's voice that retains its muteness to defend the secret, and there is the voice of the heart, concealed in the expiration of time: two voices. The writer who works with the neuter works with the double voice. The double voice, the voice of the double, voice doubled (equals four, each of the two having its echo). The voice of the double is its specific (in an alchemical sense) and plays a role in the double's drama, where it is judge and accuser, companion, adversary, and friend. Yet it lacks a name and an identity; "Wouldn't it be more convenient if I could name you?" asks the narrator-protagonist of *The One Who Was Standing Apart from Me* to his double, who equivocates in reply (TOW, 279). As long as the choice is between speak or kill, the double voice will lack proper designation. It will resound as a question (whose voice?) that disrupts the ongoing resonation of the first voice. As if it possessed a greater eminence, like the law in Kafka, the companion voice permits no escape from hearing. That also is the trial and terror of its interruptive power: "This was, in a way, the most terrible thing about it: one can't really disappear when one must die in two separate worlds" (ibid.). It is the dead time of the heart, its absent pulse, that holds sway over the doubleness of voice. Friendship is enunciated from within that time, the temporality of the *entre-temps*, or immemorial time, as Blanchot writes of his friend, Georges Bataille, "the interval, the pure interval, that, from me to this other who is a friend, measures all that is between us, the interruption of being" (F, 291).

This might mean: suspension of nomenclature. No more nominalization, no more world, but it would be incorrect to assume that friendship imposes a rule of silence, mute adoration, or mistrust of the other. The double of voice is emitted and met with desire, which joins through the spacing of deferral. To give voice, to listen; to inscribe, to give ear—a circuit under the auspices of a desire that evokes friendship. Neither a concern of passion nor a destiny, but a superabundance of the vocalic force of spacing "in itself" that exercises the stoppage in order to . . . vociferate. Blanchot: "What there would be between man and man, if there were nothing but the interval represented by the word 'between'—an empty space all the more empty as it cannot be confused with pure nothingness—is an infinite separation, but offering itself as a relation in the exigency that is speech" (IC, 68). Friendship arises in the interval when a second voice responds to a first to bring the voiced event to fruition; affirmation is greeted by being affirmed. Voice happens after the fact, *après coup*, when the voice's taking place is deferred through the other's listening and returning the ball. If it weren't too simple, one could say that exigency, excessive desire, rouses from muteness the voice that fills a space of relation and in carrying back and forth (re-lating) produces friendship for its twosomeness. It is, however, simplification to say that voice is ready-made laden with desire and requires no provocation to resound. Its gift must be gotten, even if forgotten.

Writing takes dictation from the other and inscribes it by means of some durable technology, so that, upon being read, a text will have been called into being. The voice put in writing "is what leads us to sense a relation entirely other, a relation of the third kind" (IC, 73). A relation to alterity makes infinite the connection between terms and absolves absolutely the relation of the terms. To write is to propose an infinitely open relation with another as reader who, in the freedom of reading, accesses the inaccessible presence of the one who writes. The reader's ear listens to the other's voice "from the crypt," and responds in her own voice with a subvocal "yes"—even if forgotten. Both terms, writer and reader, relate to voice's alterity and the voicing of language, but differently. The other stands in an asymmetrical relation to each, and they together stand in a doubly asymmetrical relation to one another.

The double's voice, the other, enigmatic voice whose uninvited appearance changes the landscape of sense, is not a nothing or a particle (vocable) thereof. As with the voicing of a heart that beats no more, it is a singular. It is not one speaker's voice, remixed and played over after some help from the soundboard. It is *almost* the I's voice but says things in a way that the I would not—the subject's voice displaced by the least minimal difference, one differential tick. Or perhaps it would belong to the I, given the disposition to assimilate an unrecognizable voice that comes out of her own mouth, that is, to reduce alterity to the same. The question, Is there an other voice or only the ring of one's own?, is sometimes answered, by, as Blanchot writes, "the impression that this reduplication was not the frame of the memory but the opening of space" (TOW, 271). But it is certain that the other voice is plural. A multiple of doubles, a "plural speech" that refracts the vocalic intransigence into a spectrum of signifiers, concatenating together as if a bunch of phantoms.

The display of desire is acted out in the Narcissus myth by the figure of Echo, to which I turn later. For now, it is important to understand that Echo is fascinated by fascination. It is with Narcissus's fascination that she desires to join, to participate in the repetitive surrender, the dispossessing self of self, effaced to the point of pure desiring. But she is always already late, too late. The moment of the voice—the invocation from the "infinite separation"—the event *given* voice as well as the event *giving* voice, is no longer. It has passed before she can marshal hers. Because this is true for her, she has no voice of her own, only a voice borrowed, deficient in time, in great need of borrowed time, in the sense that its time is the before of the after. She belongs to a deficit economy which requires life on credit. One noteworthy feature in the estrangement of fascination is that Echo comes before (temporally, logically, hierarchically) her own voice. She creates her own anteriority which is readable only in retrospect. This will be part of her tragic nature. The other part comes by compliance. By means of a stratagem, she is able to woo Narcissus, whom she loves but who loves only the image he gazes at. She provides a voice for the auditory image of his voice, of himself in the event of giving voice. Thus, she satisfies sonically the condition that the watery surface satisfies ocularly.

Excursus on the Dummy

The dummy is not dumb but dumber. The homonymy, which follows an obvious etymological trajectory, is performed in one of the two senses by the final unvoiced "b." A doll or puppet, the dummy is not stupid, but like Lucky in Act 2 it is voiceless.[18] It has had its voice-making apparatus removed or never had one in the first place or speaks like "a heart that beats no more." After all, the dummy in mind is inanimate, and though the expression "the voice of the sea" or "the voice of color" displays a slippage of meaning, the dummy does not need loose or poetic usage to be granted voice. Through ventriloquy, it gets one.

Ventriloquism with the dummy calls sovereignty and rationality into question. Is the dummy the limit-experience of reason, or is reason the limit-experience of the dummy (presented as smarter than its human partner)? It asks, Who is in charge, whose voice is it anyway? The voice speaks in well-formed propositions, but from where do they issue? Are they mechanical reproductions or does the source embody conditions for the possibility of a rational being (the Kantian question)? Ventriloquism operates as an inverse of Echo's voice, which is an (affected) effect of the voice of recitation. To recite is to duplicate vocally a prior enunciation; there is the symmetrical case of duplicating a subsequent enunciation, what will have been but has not yet been said, which will not be considered. In a strong sense, all vociferation is recitation. "There is nothing new said under the sun." Echo's voice differs from pure recitation in one important respect: her voice is given to and at the service of desire. She desires the presence of and union with her beloved Narcissus, who feels only annoyance at the sound of her voice. Provoking none of the desired receptivity on his part, it leaves him disturbed by its uncanniness. It sounds to his ear like some version of his own, dubbed by alterity. The mimetic effect could translate as mockery, mimicry, parody, or travesty—all tainted with indiscretion. Blanchot adds that "this voice is narcissistic precisely in the sense that he does not love it—in the sense that it gives in nothing *other* to love" (WD, 127).

Echo repeats Narcissus's voice in words that come from his own mouth—by divine decree forbidden for him to hear—but in her own voice. She publicizes the voice, though because she is inexpert, it is only the final phrase that is enunciated. It is, however, *his* voice, the voice that has incorporated an uncanniness since it lacks an auditory signature, a resonance that would sign for him and render it uniquely his own. She voices his voice in her voice and thereby gives his own voice to him, grants him his signature which the vociferation hitherto possessed only in potential form. Thus, Echo is the arche-reader, the one who reads what has been put in writing, needed by the work "in order to assert itself as a thing without an author and also without a reader" (SL, 193). Like a catalyst that remains unchanged throughout a transformation, Echo participates in language by effectuating it, conferring on it an efficacy, a *Sinngebung* that is singular, yet strangely different from her own singularity. That participation menaces her uniqueness in voice—it is not recognized by Narcissus—and of course fails in the desired purpose. It grants its gift while confirming the closed nature of narcissistic love.

Ventriloquy or ventriloquism is the thrown voice, the voice thrown (*geworfen*) to create the appearance of coming from the mouth of the dummy. The craft of the ventriloquist is to produce a voice that seems to originate from a place that it does not, to simulate an origin, the voice box of an other. This is a performative counterfactual, doing *as if*, which could pass for the general formalism of mimetic work. *Geworfenheit*, with its rich Heideggerian overtones (Dasein is the thrown of the throw), brings to mind that the delivery of the dummy voice instantiates an existence for an inanimate thing (the doll or puppet). *That it is* to the extent that the one who listens presumes the thing speaks; it possesses the facticity of language. Insofar as accomplished by the ventriloquist, the simulation of Being, the dissimulation of the ontological difference, disturbs the everyday voice with its vulgarity. The thrown voice exposes the subject to what is saturated with itself and opens to an acceptance of it as real instead of a *trompe d'oreille*. It covers over how speaking operates like the dummy voice, ventriloquized from a source that is other. It elides the role of alterity in the constitution of the voice that audibly or non-audibly speaks.

As the dummy speaks without a voice of its own, it listens with a deaf ear turned toward the world. What does it hear? One understands when one listens with the dummy's ears. One then knows one's own voice as other; or conversely, only when one hears one's own voice as other does one listen with the dummy's ears attuned to the iterative generativity of conversation.

This is true of inner (non-acoustic, mute, "reading") voice as well as outer, when a listening ear is turned toward the source of the vociferation, the center of its emission. In the case of writing, the inner voice enunciates for the one who writes and has its sonority consumed in the shared attraction that binds together the double.

Yet to hear one's own voice as phantomatic other, to be affected by the altered vociferation that one calls one's own and recalls the question of "ownmost," is to glimpse the maw of the abyss. One's voice (outer, inner) is where one is, ontologically speaking. If it is a resonance of the voice of being, the "that there is," then it is the authentic vociferation of one's ownmost potentiality of being (*Seinkonnen*), one's "I am." The problem arises when voice can be ventriloquized because in that case an other can simulate one's voice; or worse, another can put one's voice in hers. Furthermore, the other need not be a human or animate vociferation, but natural phenomenon or a well-devised mechanical one ("It was the wind playing/that sounded my own"). One would have to remain skeptical whether the truth of one's own voice hasn't been exchanged by the supplementarity of the dummy. The possibility of conspiracy should not be discounted, with the technology of non-living voice reproduction. In the loss of authentication, ready no longer to identify the voice as one's own, one concomitantly loses the power to distinguish the other's voice as other.

The dilemma is closely linked to another question, namely, Is there something misleading in voice of any kind, the *vox* of voice—dissimulating itself so as to keep the secret? The secret is not easily dismissed by claiming that there is none: "The secret is that there is no secret." The noble lie minimizes the cost of seeking the secret out, face to face with the secrecy interior to the search and the seeker. The secret kept by the voice in the crypt of voice is the vocalic encryption of the absence of origin (the voice doesn't come from one's own larynx), which operates by eliding the voice so as to make the origin appear desirable, capable of being desired as well as desiring. The chronic rewriting of absence into excessive enjoyment further obscures the fictive character of a personal voice. The crypt, moreover, is consequent to incorporation without assimilation, interiorizing that which cannot be made over in the material of identity, the other voice. It isolates or quarantines a portion of vocality, contact with which is menacing to the subject.

The secret of voice manifested with an apparent omnidirectionality can arise when one is spoken to by some "voiceless" thing, a dummy, which turns into a site that has "called" voice to it and become a hot spot for ventriloquy. This is the so-called acousmatical voice, a voice that comes from somewhere caused by something "I know not what."[19] Other cultures could read it as oracular, divine, messianic, magical, diabolic, or mad. Here two lines of thought cut across one another, leaving marks in each without coinciding. There is the ear *for* the other (asymmetrical with the ear *of* the other) that hears in the ventriloquized event the challenge to centering. Along with it and reminiscent of narcissism, there is the echo without origin. This is a duplicate of a voice that voices itself before it is voiced by a subject's vociferation. It is an *après coup* or an anterior-of-the-posterior echo: hearing a voice before the event of emission. The echo that precedes the voicing and comes before it is capable of producing a shock in the listener, the dawn of comprehension.

The first line passes through the ear for the other where Heidegger locates the call (*Ruf*) of conscience. The source "remains in a striking indefiniteness," without "name, status, origin, and repute," and the lack of familiarity is traumatic.[20] Signaling the breakup of the everyday identity of the subject, the need to understand exposes the desire implicit in resoluteness (*Entschlossenheit*). Only in desiring it does Dasein hear the acousmatical call for what it is, its own inner authority, conscience. The desire for a vocalic object where there is none, properly speaking, is to want to find the ventriloquized voice from where it projects the sound. In both cases, an ethereal version, a lure, is found; in the flight from itself, the inessential self-erasure of the thing heard, the question of who listens disturbs the confidence of listening.

It could be said of the silent heartbeat, reticent about its source(lessness), that it resounds acousmatically across a time that is yet to come. Cessation of the pulse—death—is an event that will have taken place in the time the reader has constituted the signature of the recit. An imminence still pending, a death deferred to an indefinite date in the future comes to call in the reader's present; to read is always in the present tense.[21] The pulsation on mute then is an event defined by the ending that comes beforehand. As a listening recipient of the mute heart, the reader understands subsequently what preceded her vicarious arrival on the scene. One could go farther and, bearing in mind that the heart is homonymous for feelings and desires, the reader's comprehension of what the narration wants to say (*vouloir dire*) needs to be in place prior to reading. She needs to have read before beginning to read. This paradox is inherent in the hermeneutic circle, aporetic if linear time is assumed.

Thus, the dummy that mouths words without speaking is a screen for the voice that brings the ear to the alterity that lurks in vocality. The shock of inanimate "speech"—the smoke and mirrors of it—produces the condition by which the excess of the signifier, the other voice, can be incorporated and language acquired. The dummy's demand to be heard attracts the listening, passing to the interior while bypassing the protection. Vocal singularity there repeats itself as it disseminates sameness. Fascination with the dummy voice in turn demonstrates an indiscretion, an unconcern, an overexposure to surplus value. The demand is excessive, as Heidegger notes with the voice of conscience, "that it wants to be *heard only as such*."[22] A demand different from any particular demand or desire, hence, an unconditional demand, not capable of fulfillment. Is there a reconciliation with "bad conscience"? Perhaps a desire to desire the demand of excess and nothing else, to want in a heartfelt way to take in the call. At the same time, the demand of the dummy ("Listen." "Do as I say.") goes the other way, the demand directed to the dummy. This Heidegger only intimates. The listener places her demand on the ventriloquized voice in that she holds authority over its and the ventriloquist's fate. Intent absorption in the words, or a deaf ear (return to *Verfallen*), both possibility and impossibility, are entwined in the tympanic register of the listener.

On Echo

In the myth, Echo loves Narcissus and desires union with him. Lacking body, she has voice and the power to repeat the last word or words that he speaks: this is the limit of her enunciative ability. She produces a voice voiced bodilessly, a voice vociferated by an other that poses (in) the voice of Echo, a redub of Echo's voice, given to be but not hers. Considering her incorporeality, she exemplifies the ventriloquized voice though she is neither dummy, marionette, nor puppet but an animate, rational being (though mythic). Hers is a unique voice, projected vocally into her virtual voice box from a source outside, where it resounds just like hers would—if it possessed functional vocal chords, as if the ectoplasmic larynx had taken a language arts course. Narcissus too is said to be mute, at least in the sense of lacking the conditions of vocal speech, whose circuit always passes through the other and returns to the one who enunciates. When Narcissus speaks, Echo responds: "Is there someone near me?" "Me . . ." It could be said, as Blanchot does, that as the first lacks voice, the second lacks language because he is without contact with the other, because the disembodied voice provides only a "mimetic, rhyming alliteration of a semblance of language" (WD, 127). But in the maddening semblance (*Schein*) that offers "the repetitive sound of a voice which always says to him the self-same thing, and this is a self-sameness which he cannot attribute to himself," there remains the uncanny transport of vociferation: voicing that dissimulates its source (ibid.). There Narcissus encounters an alterity that opens linguisticality for him. He is thereby enabled to be among those who have a language; he "participates without membership" in the community of speakers.

    One must imagine Echo's voice as the project of desire. It is her desire that produces the rebound definitive of the echo-effect in general. The basic form of the echo, we saw, is when an inbound voice strikes a refractory surface or "wall" that causes it to bounce back. Since it starts only when the first voice is finished, there is a mirroring, but without the field reversal (left for right) that occurs with vision. Desire operates like a wall in that it repeats and redirects the original voicing back to its source. Her desire for union plays out in the mingling of her repetition with his enunciation, a phonic event that is a kind of marriage. One would need acute hearing to discern the replay or echo of her echo as the consummated blend of the two voices continues to travel forth and back. There, in that braid or swirl, mimesis suffers a slippage that leaves it increasingly far from being imitative. It becomes senseless noise, related by an increasing distance to linguistic production. It reveals the outside of voice, the haunt that all voice tries to obliterate in vocal compliance with the rules of good speech. The charge of echo-effect is voice overladen with itself, signification overridden by the material (maternal) excess, the clatter of its own glottals and fricatives, the logos over-sublated to the point of entropy.

Blanchot's brief remarks indicate that, regardless of its poverty, Echo's voice carries an audible signature all her own, her own "self-sameness." Thus, it cannot be alterity's voice, the otherwise than voice, because that voice is without signature, provenance, or origin. It is other to itself as well as "other to every other," that is, other to otherness. A step beyond the limit-experience of voice, it is transgressive and menaces her voice and Narcissus's with its aphonic resurrection of dead voice ("a heart that beats no more"), voice with an amplitude gone flat, whose tempo has run out and whose rhythm decayed, but which refuses to abstain from vociferation. Echo's voice, for another reason, is a case study all its own. Hers alone, it is at the same time put in(to) her voice by what is other, desire. Her sole need to vociferate is to ensure a contact with her beloved who cannot otherwise penetrate her invisibility. Her audible capability is her only hope of manifesting and because of its inherent weakness, it too fails her. Narcissus's words reinitiate the play of desire—staging the conjunction of the two voices, their choral effect, a resonance or dissonance that could alert him of her presence—and she utters them, longingly, quaveringly, in the "self-same" tonality, modulation, assonance, alliteration, and rhythm as his. Desire has paired the two vocalities that differ only in apparent location, which, according to the echo-effect diminishes volume and pitch on the second. Although the signifier of each is always identical, they cannot combine dialectically (as they wed alchemically). They do not converse or partake in discourse, hence forbidding a reciprocal understanding. Conversation is ruled out by the playback, which operates like a reversal. The voices remain non-commutative and intransitive; they pass by each other without completing the circuit.

This is the absent generosity that Echo feels. Ordinarily, voice is given. It is a gift to the one that vociferates who then turns it to pass it to the other. The debt owed to the donor is cancelled by the expenditure to the second recipient, leading to a balanced economy. Echo suffers the costliness of vociferation that is usually excused by the forth and back of conversation, its *da* and *fort*. Because she is unable to make a contribution to the signifier, its meaning grows increasingly impoverished as it accumulates the unvocalized fragments of Narcissus's speech. Their "unemployable negation" conveys a speaking from the outside that is an inexpungible part of her audible signature. Moved by desire, her repetitions also carry the murmurous jabber that escapes narcissistic palaver. Producing the opposite of what she wishes, they menace the ear of him she loves. Thus, she experiences a double absence: a speaking that she cannot assign and that wounds with the secret poison of incoherence. It is her purgatory.

Yet the hidden is the sacred and, therefore, Echo is generous without measure. This is true of desire in general: the excess of its economy intimates the movement of sacrifice. Its narcissistic fixation on the object has the effect of freeing up the sacred by giving the sacred to itself, "where the sacred itself, night in its unapproachable profundity, is given back . . . to the inessential, which is not the profane but less than any such category" (SL, 175). Because of her excessive desire to converse with her beloved, she remains insouciant to the freedom, which allows it to be the supreme gift, the gift that permits the sacred, its work and enunciation, to appear within the narcissistic frame of desire. The voice of Echo in its innocent love unbinds the sacred from the ritual of voicing meaning, the *Sinngebung* of everyday conversation, and gives the possibility of transmitting night's essence. The otherness that resounds there necessarily carries a trace of the eternal recurrence, the depth of voicing achieved through the remembrance of "ancient time," time without a presence.[23] The re-voiced otherness "marks the surplus that every mark of identity produces, without the mark of this surplus suspending identity, and without this surplus ever being—marked, free of the mark, acquitted by it" (SNB, 40).

The relative lateness of the addition of Echo to the Narcissus myth belies the depth to which Echo is implicated in the dynamic of desire. Stripped of her figuration and proper name, echo is the very installation of desire. Resounding, desire makes an appearance as a repetition of itself. It never stops playing one and the same sequence of scenes in the fantasy of life that it lives. Each repetition is an echo of the one prior and this is where echo comes in—as a love to repeat, a desire for iteration, an attraction to the next thing that is not different from the current one ("the sky, the *same* sky"). One time finds its enjoyment, *jouissance*, in an other time that is upcoming, pending, not yet, deferred. In that way, satisfaction is never actual, but fleeting, spectral, always virtual. It suffices without sufficiency. Echo then is the resonance, the audio soundtrack, of this love of the other that must live in the absence of consummation. It wants union with the object of desire and provides a sonic dimension for the disclosure of it, which nonetheless remains obscure, "staticky." Furthermore, a paradoxical closure results from echoic repetition, a self-echo or feedback loop, echo echoing echo ad infinitum—echo becomes the name of an action, a verb, as well as of a thing. With the ever-present feedback of desire's echoic repetition, the recursion of desire's desiring, echo manifests as the sound of time's own iteration. Conceptually, it is iteration in the process of creating an audio track of itself, lip-synching itself.

One could take another step, considering that echo is the event that vocatively gives the primal word, the only enunciating, that recurs endlessly. This states the meaning that Echo represents, the attraction to the signifier, the desire to repeat it to infinity—even if the finite repetition is incomplete and faulty. The signifier itself is figured as the self-relation that Narcissus enjoys, in a closure that never closes since it is lacking an other. The signifier is turned toward a repetition of itself that it regards erroneously to be a signifier other than itself. It is this fundamental (mis)orientation that Heidegger would understand as errancy's root. Since it cannot be repaired, since Narcissus cannot turn from the reflection that is his or see it as another's, the errancy is an essential feature of the linguistic structure, the play of self-love that is built into the signifier. The errant orientation is not rectified or corrected by the voice of the other and thus language is constituted for the subject with this inherent misappropriation. The subject of voice has a constitution that structurally misconstrues its identity. Only such a voice is capable of lying.

Echo's echo, the murmurous sigh that surpasses all vocality without negating it, is the resounding of eternity as incessant. Blanchot signs it as the sirens' song, which is the disaster when it happens to sound, voice, and the auditory in general: "ordinary and at the same time secret, a simple, everyday song sung in an unreal way by strange powers."[24] In his work, it also is glossed as one version of the *il y a* made vocal, representative of ruined voice, voice dysfunctional and inoperative. Such vociferation has the effect of ruining other voices and raising the question of authenticity. Echo's gift is a double gift. First, it is voice in recognition of itself, sovereign voice that has itself repeated as if by another voice, like it but not its own. Echo herself is not incapable of hearing her failure to respond to Narcissus's articulation. She can hear the divergence of her version from his utterance. She knows what a fully adequate iteration would be but cannot will one; thus, she plays the role of the one who knows. Second, she gives voice ruined, ruined voice, inarticulate, making monotonous animal sounds that defy interpretation since they are essentially non-hermeneutical. The ruination of voice *is* echo, what happens when pressing the sustain pedal on the piano too long. As echoes of a secondary and tertiary nature build and overrun all boundaries of separation, lines that would impede crossing, voice then is diverted from the signifier—meaning-making—and becomes the voice of an idiot.[25] Echo's voice comes by way of pure excess as it struggles to produce a discrete (and discreet) place for itself in conversation, and fails. This is the nymph's tragedy. And achievement, her "invention" of the neuter voice, for it is that—as Blanchot puts it: "as if the neuter spoke only in an echo, meanwhile perpetuating the other by the repetition that difference, always included in the other, even in the form of the bad infinite, calls forth endlessly: the balancing of a man's head given over to eternal oscillation" (SNB, 77).

Could one say that Echo's problem is in the precipitation of rhythm—or a presentation of the problem without allowing access to it? Blanchot has one of his conversants express it thus: "In this turn that is rhythm, speech is turned toward that which turns aside and itself turns aside" (IC, 31).[26] Narcissus is turned toward Echo's voice which is in rebound from his; the echo in general has turned the originating voice around 180 degrees and is about to turn from itself in its turn. Rhythm is equivalent to the frequency of iteration of the turn, the languidness or rapidity with which the enunciating is repeated in the echo-effect. Voice in the neuter, the neuter or narrative voice, owes its immediacy to a specific rhythm, as if the voice that dictates to the one transcribing speaks in a tempo all its own. The patient respect that the one who puts it in writing has for the inner voicing is a measure of the authenticity of transcription; and, as Orpheus knows, impatience is the link with desire.

But Echo gives a double gift, a double beat. The second takes up the "extreme danger" that Blanchot ascribes to rhythm. It has to do with the reason that an army breaks off its march when crossing a bridge: the sympathetic vibrations may destroy the thing. Echo's second gift manifests the failure of conversation, that the turn of voice from one to the other is disabled and cannot successfully pass over the interval between the two. Although she addresses him, hearing his own words repeated leaves Narcissus confused about ascribing the utterance to a natural (what else is there?) event. But there is more to it than an act of mimesis. The extreme of torsion with its variable rate of turning of the turn (its rotation) undoes the phoneme, and audibility in general. The production of sound by the vocal apparatus is radically disharmonized, the *phone* destabilized and rendered inoperative. Dialectical vociferation returns to its nondiscursive basis, phonemic production subverted, and mere babble takes to the airwaves. Echo's second gift is access to the other time, the "most ancient," immemorial, but no more past than future; such time is an interval, an *entretemps*, between everyday time ("vulgar" time) and time of the imaginary. It is the gift of the sirens too, whose "enigmatic song [is] always at a distance, designating this distance as a space to be crossed and designating the place to which it leads as the point where singing will cease to be a lure."[27] Crossing to where time "runs the other way" and space ceases to contain things leaves the voice box traumatized and voice a series of failed sonic experiments.

Because the second gift belongs to an economy without debit or credit (an aneconomy), the interval accompanies every voicing. It is the permanent possibility or omnipresent overtone of garble or burble. It is the supplement that menaces meaning with some nonsequential phonemic product and eventually replaces it, an Orwellian doublespeak that offers only the semblance of linguisticality. This does not mean the gift is audible or manifest. Think of the disaster gone vocal: the ruination leaves all voice intact, putting in question whether it is "the advent of what does not happen, of what would come without arriving, outside being, and as though by drifting away" (WD, 5). Never in contact but at a distance, the voice of the non-present leaves no acoustical effect on "vulgar" voice and its perpetration of meaning. The threat remains a secret actualization of the arrhythmia of being. The parasitic contamination of discourse (one could say, by a sacred tempo) proceeds with no elaboration of voice, oral, whispered, "silent," speaking silence. A distant tintinnabulation, it resounds in background listening and gives testimony without attestation to the unbridgeable interval it leaps. This sonic decay is an aural halo that englobes each phoneme from the interior. In it is concentrated the sacrificial nature of all speech.[28] A strange guarantor of the act of renunciation that every sovereign voice makes when giving voice to its situation.

Holy Voice-Work

The neuter voice exhibits a brand of devotion special to it. Its compass of endless deferment, deferring repeatedly to what is to come as it surrenders what has passed, unrepentantly constitutes a commitment to worship. The sacred object is delay, *différance*. In context, the other time or otherwise than time marks the occasion when the body of attainment is sacrificed, when that worship extends to the God of postponement, the God who comes only ever after, and is not yet and no longer. Such a God, a *deus absconditus* who is perfectly bereft and empty of audibility, remains absent but for his being. That he is never present to voice since presence is abdicated presents a problem for divine fiat, address, and interpellation. Holy voicing would be a (mistaken) ascription of vociferation to the *il y a*.[29]

The neuter may be considered the post-Romantic voice of the divine *par excellence*. Blanchot's respect for Hölderlin (and Novalis and Schelling) is as immense as his concern for voice subsequent to the double betrayal, enacted by God and by humankind—when the relation of creation was refused by both. Similarly, when Hölderlin asks, "What will become now of art, now that the gods and even their absence are gone, and now that man's presence offers no support?" one could replace "art" with "voice" (SL, 233).[30] Moreover, if that loss is an opening to the multiple at the expense of unity, neuter voice becomes a weapon against the transcendental One—and its allies, the other, lesser transcendentals of being, goodness, and truth. It champions difference, deferment, plurality, and diversity.[31] Important to note is that the adversary is neither worship nor devotion (nor less, God, who neither exists nor does not) but a positive attitude toward the transcendental signified. It is the origin of the "sickly desire" that seeks self-identity and, remaining oblivious to the disaster, infects all desire with its sickness.[32] Could one go on and say that Narcissus's desire, to be one with the reflection, names that disease? That the narcissistic drive for unity suppresses the binary? That the worship under examination is tantamount to purification of desire (the child being killed)?

A purified desire: one no longer subject to the law. Seeking unification with its object, such desire is oriented toward an impossible attainment that would render satisfaction necessarily transgressive. The sickness, in Hölderlin's eyes, is the contradiction wrought by unity—that cannot be sublated and is the flaw of reason. Desire for an impossible unity, the impossibility of the one identical self-same, lies for him at the root of human suffering. What is purification but a through and through active oblivion, Blanchot's insouciance, a forgetting that "forgets the law"?[33] This is the inspired release from intentionality which posits the lawfulness of consciousness as well as of *Sorge*, care, which breeds guilt. According to a phenomenologically styled *epoché*, releasement does not arise from the transcendental essences that yield meaning, but the inessential and insignificant throwaways that lead to a surprising purity and authenticity. The realm of errancy functions as a strange attractor to the attention; *die sorglose Nacht*. It draws it forth in fascination, neutralizing desire—not so much reducing it to zero as rendering it desirous of excess. Purification takes place by way of *jouissance*.

Suspension of the law of desire comes as an *epoché*. The *epoché* puts the power of the law out of play, so as by reduction to purify its influence. In contrast to a phenomenological *epoché*, which is an act of consciousness, inspiration is neither self-given nor a gift of the world. If its origin were a here or there, there would be a trace of the source—but there isn't since the excess is only a trace of a trace. It remains after subtracting auto-affection and the other's gift from the totality. The remainder remains beyond production or designation, an absence without being. In nullifying the law, confining its sphere of influence to itself, desire is freed . . . unto what? For one thing, to the double danger of forgetting its lawful work and of squandering its resources in a ruined economy. The question of the positive aspect of freedom remains just that, a question. That is why everything is risked in the liberation of desire.[34] In what is determined by this "first liberation," the source of divinity is sought through an intensified gaze—the force of fascination squared—that neutralizes care and accepts the unlawful incessancy. What happens then is unknown. In this desert, the authority of voice may yet resound.

The threatening intimacy of authority voiced ruptures the mindful wait of intentional consciousness as well as the restraint of "bad conscience." Desire beyond the law remains as tensed as the impatience of the former but lacks the guardedness of the latter. It has become aimless unconcern. Desire then is able to give way to a disastrous passivity that lacks power to affirm (or negate) an object. In the boiling forth of the force, in its release to patience without measure, the field of expectation—both the project (*Entwurf*) and anticipation (*Vorlaufen*)—is clarified and made transparent to itself. Here, a basis of understanding is possible. The slate is not so much wiped clean of desire as saturated with it. Or: desire ceases to be viewed as a lack but as an excess. From the work of overabundance, desire sends forth the spark, the flare of brilliance, that ignites the night: the happy and synchronous *Ursprung* of art.[35] There all promised is authorized, and that which voices authority is language as origin, "the pure springing of the origin, where speaking precedes not one or another utterance but its possibility—where speaking always precedes itself" (SL, 181). The danger of this voice to interiority and the integrity of self is strange and unusual. It is the vocalization of the word idled by an insurmountable inoperability, with which nothing can be done, said, or vocalized. Loss of voice, speech impediment, aphasia, paralysis of expression, demobilized thought, "I can't find the word": the symptoms are deficiency and fault. In fact, where deferment suspends linguistic play by "nonintentional consciousness"—anxiety before mortality—the encounter with holy voice is found. God speaks while Job is dumbstruck. He speaks in the spacing.

The intimacy of spacing—it lets there be separate phonemes, sounds, and resonations—is an affront to the sovereign subject. That is its discretion. It tells nothing and allows everything. Even that isn't true, since it has a telling influence and impact. Its aridity, however, threatens one's voice the way hot, dry desert air does, with a choking purity. The threat to power and production, the demand to renounce time management, the charge to become immobilized: the dispossession underlines the peculiar freedom that spacing would work. Outside of protocol, agreed-upon forms, and rhetorical expression, the voice of spacing with its whirling nocturnality assaults language, coming as if from the "terrifyingly ancient" (*l'effrayablement ancien*), and then there is inspiration. One's breath is breathed in with the errant word. If able to linger with the banished thought, one is in contact with the being of what is given voice, words. If able, one meets the absolute demand of voice, that which assigns to giving voice a responsibility that cannot be accomplished and a guilt for taking part in what cannot be said.

"Nothing can be heard in the spacing." Of course, *différance* isn't audible or inaudible. It neither exists nor doesn't. There is no primal word, as Derrida says, *contra* Heidegger. But within the spacing, voice waits for a first transcriber that (who) would represent a "permanent possibility" of language's taking place. Its wait meets a refusal that is multiform, a disastrous sleep that coincides with the first meaning for forgetting: "It does not happen" (WD, 5). Marginal, between marks, backgrounded, the voice that cannot be discerned from the wake that holds it, despite a careful attention, comes in a carefree hiatus. It appears, Blanchot writes, as "the long night of insomnia" from which there is no exit save to accept inspired desire, the excess that is holy voice (SL, 184; italics omitted). God's may be in the spacing but in the breakup of the One there sounds a diabolical voice—which is why multi- or polyvocality offers no solace. Furthermore, mastery is the easier choice. That way, truth attracts and not the errancy of a trackless terrain, as the double failure of Orpheus teaches, the twin neglect of the call of the law and of the agon against the summons of lawlessness. Voice in that turn is returned to the world, to everydayness, where its twofold oblivion of death and liberation serves its sovereign aspiration.

Spacing, the space between, neither-nor, the neuter. The God of the neuter is in spacing's inordinately weak force of omnipresence. It is necessarily prior to the first distinction, before the waters above separate from the waters below. Before that, in the homonymy of "before," *différance*, a force that splits, "the spirit that hovers" to double all things. It distinguishes the same from the different as it asks what anteriority is the enabling factor.

The holy of voice utters the phoneme for desire-in-excess, where desire allies with the force of spacing, its animation or anima. Underlying the "metaphysics" of virtuality, this thought relates the soul and the stars, since desire is sidereal in etymology. The turbulence of pure being, the *il y a*, the *khora* as image of desire, is turned toward audibility in the murmurous recoil of sound from apprehension. Deferred, such voice is always already ahead of itself, doubled as it strives to detain and contain within itself the muteness of the thing. Its twin invaginations overlap, the first a silent one, the second, on the verge of arriving on time, to interfere with each other—a cacophonous event, aggravated by the auto-replay effect. Nonetheless, in its hesitancy, the holy of voice is pregnant with delay. Only an Orphic patience, hyperbolically "more passive than passivity," can bear the fruit of hearing, its ear in wait inclined toward that night. The birth, in the deferred interval between inscription and decoding, regulates the repetition of inner speaking. It "keeps silence."

Between the conception and "birth" in double desire is a replay of the alchemical reading of the Narcissus myth. In the first desire, lack or need, killing the child-Narcissus is tantamount to terminating the erotic attraction to his image, to image *tout court*. By ritual death (no less deadly than mortal death), Narcissus incorporates the image (of himself, seen as other) and prepares a crypt for both. In the dark of encryption, its fertile, patient space works the transformation of hearing (*Hören*), enabling the work of delay. Mortal substance, if it is that, gives way to immortal stuff, the material of one subject to a dying without end: *material prima*. Under this condition of immortality, desire is imbued with excessive life, the excess of being over consciousness. It is the surplus of desire that wounds the risen Narcissus, now a Christ figure ("dead-immortal"), that moves under an excessive suffering peculiar to survival: in front of the terror of the other night. *Subissement* is Blanchot's neologism for it, "the absolute passivity of total abjection" (WD, 15).[36] Here, eros reigns still and forever, but with nonchalance in the carefree sacrifice of what most matters. Narcissus transformed ceases to want objects and positions—end posts of various kinds—and desires only to seek a pathway through the labyrinth of temporal delay although it holds no central chamber or minotaur. He seeks the trust of living on, neither accepting nor rejecting the encounter with superabundance, alert to the spacing contained therein. Could one alternatively say: narcissistic desire, which Narcissus comes by naturally, is no different from excessive desire, since immortality is the gift of the disaster. Disaster banishes death along with other endings. Thus, Narcissus transformed is the same Narcissus as he who enters the crypt, except for one thing. He is able to say, "I am alive. No, you are dead" (I, 9).

5

Voice *Eo Ipso*

Desire of writing, writing of desire. Desire of knowledge, knowledge of desire. Let us not believe that we have said anything at all with these reversals.

—Maurice Blanchot, *The Writing of the Disaster*

Toward the Counterlife

Narcissus peers at the image of himself: Isn't this the figuration of a desire that declares itself universal? Which, according to some thinkers, exhausts all desire, and, according to others, serves to divvy up the field. Thereafter the concept follows a Platonic mold. Socrates, who argues in the *Symposium* that desire lives for a missing something *x* and dies upon attainment of it, assigns as its meaning a deficit that must be recouped. It is a receptacle that must be filled. Lack, want, deficiency, insufficiency, absence: the chain runs on. To the extent that satisfaction exists, desire is mortal, and by an inversion, is the essence of mortality. Only non-desire—meaning a desire that forfeits its object—would qualify for immortality, a holy or angelic desire.[1] True or not, the figuration is as inadequate as the positing of a single form of narcissism.[2] Narcissus, as seen, is blind at the point of narcissistic desire. His eye is rendered inoperative by the seduction of the blind spot, the place where sight is unable to coincide with the origin of vision or to recuperate itself. Attracted, his eye goes through the image (that would be of him) unto what resides within it, the image of itself, which is a nothing cut and pasted on nothing (the *khora*). There, desire inverts, turns passive, and wants to be taken by a force over which it exercises no power. In this way, desire that is narcissism incorporates a desire that is non-narcissistic. Since it is the condition of an undigested incorporation that produces the crypt, the other desire dwells encrypted in "vulgar" desire. It seeks what remains in excess of the object, and with acquisition impossible, such desire is undying. Within Narcissus's love of the reflection lies the power to have and to hold; within the love itself, its *punctum caecum* (for all love is blind), lies the disabling of that power.[3] That excessiveness, through which the road to wisdom may lie, leaves his search for union stalled; it is the improper side of his desire.

Narcissus attempts to embrace or be embraced by the image. Both gestures represent the same stretching toward the void of desire, reacting to the negative economy by restoring balance. The exercise at the same time covers over the concupiscence of the eye as if to reveal a mirror without an image. To the extent that Narcissus recognizes the blinded condition and how it welcomes desire's alterity, surplus desire, then his movement is more than a narcissistic reappropriation that would destroy the other in advance, namely, the killing of the killing. Along with Orpheus, he becomes a figure of the outside. The superabundance bound inescapably to what he wants is impossible to get.[4] And this gives a description of his experience (*Erleben*) of desire as an aporia: where the possible remains impossible, where success fails, where failure succeeds.[5] Suppose that Ovid's forgetfulness in retelling the myth—that Narcissus can't recognize himself in the image—is a device for recording the aporetic vision. "He sees without seeing."

The impediments to Narcissus's desire reveal the perversity of desire in the limitation of enjoyment. As long as desire drives toward an impossible attainment, its truth is contradiction. This condition is maintained by the alternation of approach and retraction, *fort* and *da*. It will practice ritual worship of deferment by postponing the realization of the blind spot. What is at stake, moreover, lies in the paradoxical nature of excessive desire: it marks the self's relation to itself and is thereby responsible for a desire that is wholly narcissistic. The surplus of desire functions as a mirror or sounding board that redirects the reflected image (video, audio) to rebound to its origination and be apprehended. This can be put otherwise. Similar to the dynamics of ocularity, desire relates first to the other that is anterior to the constitution of a self-relation. Desire of the other is originary to a desire that belongs to the self. Just as to gaze upon himself, as Narcissus secretly wants, requires the gaze of the other upon him, so too what he wants requires what the other wants of him. The circuit contains a trajectory called into being by the other desire, desire in excess, that which wants to be wanted by Narcissus. An "animate" factor in the equation, the surplus exerts a longing that actuates his hunger for the image. It lives on in his endless quest for union. The relation between the two desires, furthermore, is asymmetrical. Derrida remarks, "It is only starting from the other, from a kind of self-renunciation, that narcissism grows, and grows always in losing itself, and this contradiction is at once its limit and its condition."[6] The impersonal, non-narcissistic other of desire calls Narcissus to his place and the panoply of his wants and needs take their place in the structure of the self entrusted to the excess.

That Narcissus's longing for conjunction with the other is a gift of the other desire means that his wants and wishes (*Wünsche*) are destined by the surplus. They appear aleatory, gratuitous, and inessential. But the surplus doesn't look more essential, more significant. It is bereft of all importance. To the extent that the desires are appropriated by a self-generated identity ("Narcissus," "Echo's beloved"), he fails to take account of the thing of desire, its nocturnal origination ("without beginning or end"). An Orphic insouciance or unconcern, Blanchot's version of *ataraxia*, does not resolve the impossibility he encounters.[7] Nor does it restore the broken hegemony of the I or dispel the aporia of desire. But it does indicate the way to triumph with failure, to trump loss and win the game. Orpheus is the case in point. Although he seeks to neutralize his escape (reduce collateral damage) from the force of the other desire by mastering its excess, by making it of another time "measured otherwise," he cannot succeed (SL, 173). But it borders on giving birth to the work, the work of writing. *Pari passu* for Narcissus and the work of desire. Here is the interweaving of the two, desire and writing.

To succumb to the other desire—that ruins the longing for the beloved—is unavoidable. In the surrender lies a freedom that bears no signature of Stoic imperturbability, a strategy that would preserve mastery of the I. The law of desire forbids the enjoyment (cleverly circumnavigating the thing that counterfactually satisfies) that the excess gratuitously gives and withholds. Because the illicit is inherently enjoyable, "desire's measureless movement" is endlessly pursued. The gift that inspires with the high tonality of being also traumatizes. Inspiration, therefore, wrecks a life plan, the structured and relatively stable organization of what one wants. For writing, desire for the work is offset by the forbidden gift "breathed in" and any attempt to produce a record of that resonant emission, a work, period, is replaced by the consolation prize of the day journal.[8] Even Orpheus cannot escape ruination, for the supreme sacrifice (the most desired thing) yields only the uncertainty of the work. Has glad accident produced one? To surrender the desired object, even with the supplementary recognition of its unattainability, promises nothing, no work in the face of excessiveness. There, desire undergoes an inversion, becoming no longer what one wants but rather *what one cannot help not wanting*. The intensification of passivity (obsession, compulsion, craving) coincides with enjoyment.

In fact, Orpheus is unable to forgo the prohibition, the gift that is transgressive, an access to the outside. The inspiration that fructifies the writing of desire is therein squandered. That is its allotted destiny, that to which it is delivered (*überantwortet*). What would have been the work (in the future perfect conditional) is sacrificed for a different writing put in play by desire for writing and productive solely of hodgepodge texts, distortions of narcissism necessarily ill-informed by force of impossibility, "the vertigo of spacing." Desire has carried voice off into an airless desert where the breath for vociferation is unavailable. This can be said otherwise: voice without breath is the installation of a secret language, whose nonvocality appeals to the promise of epiphany. Isn't the locus here of the Orphic genius, that would sacrifice the absolute concern . . . for less than nothing, a shrug of the shoulders, wink of the eye, gratuitously? As if what counted was the insignificant, inconsequential nature of the gesture, as if the giving back passed virtually unnoticed, as unnoticed virtuality.

Why the work is so hard to understand derives from the self-withdrawing gift, the cash value of which cannot be tendered. Neither it nor the surrender of it can be bought. Fascination, the extreme of passivity and freedom, puts it in play; freedom from fascination "secures" the work, brings it to the point of inscription and ensures a place in a culture's history. The turn that exposes fascination as a detour educes a background figure, always hidden, but patently there, the resemblance of the thing ("pure" resemblance) that assaults the desire to write.[9] As soon as the subject is lured from its interiority, the outside empties into the enclave and seals it off. There, in the presence of absence, a quasi-form, intransigent and anonymous, occupies itself with destroying the vestiges of identity and taking up residence, and assumes the double's voice. Then there are two that dwell in nearness (*Nähe*), one that would be sovereign, the other that stubbornly refuses categories of mastery. In contrast to the prolixity of the interior, the other speaks in the silken voice of a "mouth without moisture," a language without a subject, a personal pronoun without a person, that follows a God without syntax, a godless law—this other that is the same. The closeness of the double is then different by the least minimal difference to the infinite separation of the outside, as the attraction to the first is the same as that to the second.[10] Attraction to the hidden companion (sacred in concealment, as is Eurydice) would constitute dissimulation. That is, the double only appears to be a presence (present to the presence of the I), while it repels as strongly as it attracts and while it requires a guardedness against absorption into limitless indistinction. Thus, the companion enacts a strange demand to write as it concomitantly calls for disregard of its appearance.

What the desire to write wants to write is . . . the desire to write. Thus, the double is built in right there. The one writing wants to inscribe the desire to write, to write in the force of desire as it produces the text, so that the document (if that) registers and perpetuates the impulse of its own genesis. It wants to inscribe the origin. Softer than its giving voice to an ineffectual death that would bring nothing to an end, *sotto voce* is the writing of the rebirthing, the re-beginning that is Narcissus's transformation. To write is to repeatedly generate the desire to write, to listen to the voice of the other as it levies a death sentence on the writing. Conjoining the generation with the corruption, writing follows a pathless path between the always already and the never yet.

The desire to write would then coincide with the impulse to bond with the double in a way that differs from a link with presence. This sounds a lot like "the human relation," as Blanchot explicates it in an exchange in *The Infinite Conversation*:

> [T]he human relation, as it affirms itself in its primacy, is terrible. . . . It is most terrible because it is tempered by no intermediary. For in this view there is between man and man neither god, nor value, nor nature. It is naked relation, without myth, devoid of religion, free of sentiment, bereft of justification, and giving rise neither to pleasure [*jouissance*] nor to knowledge [*connaissance*], a neutral relation, or the very neutrality of relation. (IC, 191)

Some of the terror derives from the massive irreversibility of the double. Does it offer the guidance of a master? A lawfulness that at once escapes from law? A hypnotic voice ("Trust in me") that undoes the vigil that surrounds inscription? Some of it echoes Bataille's thought that philosophy begins in fear, not (as for Plato) in wonder. Furthermore, to venture into the relation and its *effrayablement ancienne* is to engage friendship. Friendship is the field where nothing is certain and everything is without destiny, the terrain rutted with ambiguity, where attempts to root out clarification are vain and without purpose (UC, 95–96). It is a "relation of the third kind" where both terms ("I" and "the other") absolve themselves of relatedness without meeting with success or failure. Friendship, the human relation, arises in response to a primal fear that concerns nothing in particular.[11] When the human relation links with the double, the desire to write is capable of producing the work, which, akin to friendship, "is very old, frightfully ancient, lost in the night of time" (SL, 229).

More fully compounded, the desire to write is the desire "to write within the secret of the ancient fear" (SNB, 57). The attraction is the human relation with the companion that is not an interlocutor or even a speaking subject: the outside. The secret "no-secret," alluded to in "A Primal

Scene?" blends perfectly with what shows itself, and manifests (if that is the word) as the companion in *The One Who Was Standing Apart from Me* notes, "the renunciation of mystery, the ultimate insignificance of lightness" (TOW, 298). Writing consonant with such desire runs up against the limit that language reaches. Limit not as a positive demarcation, but an empty delimitation that the companion declares is "'outside' all speech, apparently more secret and more interior than the speech of the innermost heart, but here the outside is empty, the secret is without depth, what is repeated is the emptiness of repetition, it doesn't speak and yet it has always been said already" (TOW, 322). The hollow, which corresponds with language's giving withdrawal from everyday voice and a general erosion of intentionality, clears a neutral space. Writing is submergence along the length that separates (by connecting) the one writing from (with) the companion, the I from the narrative *il*. The place between the two lets each manifest while dispossessing both through its law as it gleams momentarily in its sparkling disappearance. The intensity is fearsome.

The "secret" concerns language. Once stripped of everyday instrumentality (communication, guidance, direction), its utility as cultural memory and guarantor of a future, and its sovereignty in onto-theological discourse, language is void of power, that is to say, of making meaning. Even that isn't right. Reduced to a streaming murmurousness that tremblingly strikes the ear, it gains the ability to dissemble, make believe, pretend, and dissimulate. Sheltering voice from the *tremendum* is accomplished by a depthless forgetting, the frail fall into endless, pointless waiting. The wait should not be confused with coming to a stop; it is the endurance of a restless movement that effaces memory and resolve. It is a forgetting, as seen, that is not allied with distraction or the closing of a vigil but a tensed attentiveness.[12] So intractably contained within, the attention deletes each new impression as it refuses to be (re)drawn from absorption in its own feverish wakefulness. Continuity and resemblance erode. Since anything radically new that is not the repetition of a preexisting form is rejected, attention is focused on the olden beyond measure, the ineffaceably ancient, language at the origin.

But the outside of origin, that to which language would like to give voice, does not congeal to a positive locus or privileged position. A labile place of lack, like the shiftiness of the companion, walks language to its premature demise and dissolution. Hence the tendency to think death together with the origin, as if an interchange of one for the other in a brilliant explosion of momentary contact were originary. Since both are ineffectual and unempowered, and death carries off no thing to the grave, language as *Sinngebung* is unbounded and without limit. It becomes vaporous at the edges that randomly crisscross the interior, death repeatedly recommencing the origin while the origin takes on death's endlessness. What *is* language

then? —the docile retreat of voice, too weak to distinguish the slightest difference with its haloing of each thing with a sonorous amplitude.[13] Death's
dawn-like disappearance, the night tide of originating vanity, both in the
unnerving hush of a voice perpetually unable to clear its throat: this is the
being of language.

It is also the infinite of speaking, "an infinite demand that imposes
itself with an irrepressible force" with which the zeal for writing is seized
(IC, 135). Only at the limit—the condition of the death camps—where
the human relation is given in absolute form is it actualized. The form in
which voice then appears is not the monologue but conversation, a turning
together toward that away from which one and the other are both turned.[14]
It can be speaker and interlocutor, man and double, man on man, person
with machine. It could be all. The pivot is the voice—inaudible, unbidden,
provoked—around which the conversation pivots.[15] That voice is primal. It
is anterior to both the initial fold of voice and voice before it could have
given itself language, the point where perceptions outrun an ability to exhale
and share the eventness of things. It is voice choking on itself, too full
to function properly, apoplectic expulsion of sound-making that correlates
with nothing else—the Nazi lieutenant's choking or Lucky at the end of
his monologue in Act 1. Or, perhaps voice giving voice only to smallness,
disgust, boredom, and regret—low things. Or, suffocated voice . . .

The voice with which writing desires to write is not conversational
in the usual sense. Voice overcome with traumatic encounter wreaks havoc
on the onto-theological order, on what *is*. Its dispossessive strain is greater.
It intensifies the refusal within itself to give voice to unreality and irreality.
"To converse," Blanchot writes, "is also to turn language away from itself,
maintaining it outside of all unity, outside even the unity of that which is.
To converse is to divert language from itself by letting it differ and defer,
answering with an always already to a never yet" (WD, 34–35). The exilic
voice declaims from outside the conversants' circle that is brought to writing—off the mark at domestication. It reintroduces quasi-transcendentally
the disunifying force that imperceptibly draws the conversation through the
turnings. Walking the rim of abyssal violence, it extracts its exigency from
what, for Blanchot, is the ultimate choice:

> —One would have to say, then, that man facing man like this
> has no choice but to speak or to kill.

> —It is perhaps, in fact, the summary brutality of this alternative
> that would best help us approach such an instant: should the
> self ever come under this command—speech or death—it will
> be because it is in the *presence of autrui*. (IC, 61)

The voice that conspires with *différance* "earlier" than ontology doesn't distinguish between murder (of *autrui*, the other person) and letting live. At the same time, its weakness establishes the *either . . . or* and sustains it as a diversion of death. Voice is the terrifying negation from out of the interval between speech and radical violence, weighting each in a relation of vicissitude. A noncorrespondence between the conversants persists as voice traverses the impassable shambles, not reducing or effacing it nor mitigating the threat of the knife or the pistol.

"To speak or to kill" recollects the sanction of the human relation. Since it "passes by way of the recognition of the common strangeness" of the friends, it is subject to contestation (F, 291). To fiercely question a presumption of relation preserves the infinite separation and absolute dissymmetry of conversation whose strange attractor is never given voice but preempts it. As if the voice of one in its congested condition (imagine a case of chronic phlegm) could never be known with sufficient intimacy to put the other at ease. As if torture were always on the table.[16] And voice, like the Nazi lieutenant in *Instant* who "choked in a bizarre language," "resonated like a low-pitched sound in several registers at once, always below the lowest vibrations, those which one still liked to muffle" (I, 3; SNB, 78).

To return to desire, if writing the desire is in collusion with ancient fear (fear of reality turned upside down), the desire itself—exigency, striving, longing—must be madness or nihilism or both. That "writing is the desired, undesired torment which endures everything, even impatience" links writing with violence and indiscretion (WD, 42). To attend to the outside as it self-withdrawingly gives voice and to translate it into the neuter is an act of violent containment. "What speaks when the voice speaks?" Blanchot asks. "It situates itself nowhere, neither in nature nor in culture, but manifests itself in a space of redoubling of echo and resonance where it is not someone, but rather this *unknown* space—its discordant accord, its vibration—that speaks without speaking" (IC, 258). Because of desire, a sleepless vigil on errancy (the *il y a*) is retired in a sonic *vox fiat*, provoking the play between wakefulness and slumber. What motivates this particular desire? Desire in general would implicate some erotic insistence, the capture of a reserve worth spending or the spending thereof. Although suppression of it is a theme popular with thinkers (Kant, Hegel, Marx), Blanchot is leery of the temptation. Desire for life's missing element is a station along a way to the limit-experience. Recall in "A Primal Scene?" how the young boy "grows weary" with boredom a moment before the sky opens. Wanting to write promises knowledge, intelligence, recognition: a multiform satisfaction that makes a life worth living. That the promise is empty, its fulfillment impossible, would seem to border on nihilism: nothing to be done because nothing sought can ever be achieved. This is passive nihilism. A more active, Nietzschean form ties it to the nonexistence of goals, including 'the impossibility of being done with it and of finding a way out even in that end that is nothingness" (IC, 149). Nihilism becomes a redundancy, the impossibility of nihilism. However easily it can be put aside, and however easy it is to say what is undesired in writing (formlessness, brutality, chaos, indifference), what is the erotic pressure?

Recall Nietzsche of *The Gay Science*, who writes of the necessity "to create a thirst, a hunger, a taste for hidden and forbidden powers"—as if to forge the impulses of longing out of the dissatisfaction inherent in writing itself.[17] This is another case of performativity, the anteriority of the posterior that creates the very thing it describes. He continues:

> Did Prometheus have to fancy, first that he had stolen the light and then pay for that—before he finally discovered that he had created the light by coveting the light and that not only man but also the god was the work of his own hands and had been mere clay in his hands? All mere images of the maker—no less than fancy, the theft, the Caucasus, the vulture, and the whole tragic *Prometheia* of all seekers after knowledge.[18]

A reckless generosity is in play with Prometheus, and *play* is the important term. It underlines the empirical nature of desire whose risk includes the pathos of erotic failure, sudden disappearance of longing, role of illusion and fantasy, and incapacity to translate desire into a rational calculus (all themes in Nietzsche's writing). Inasmuch as experimentation differs from obeying protocols and milking outcomes, it opens desire to the fantasy that creates it, its object-cause. To desire the non-satisfaction of the desire to write (as does Proust) is not the way; but to play with such a desire, to hunger or have a taste for it, opens the impulse to question. "It" is something like the happy chance, at the limit, the *felix culpa* that comes when it comes. To make it play is not a power but a Heraclitean charm or plain good luck, luck, Blanchot emphasizes, that "is in search of writing. . . . But play? Yes, play, even if you cannot. To play is to desire, to desire without desire, and already to desire to play" (SNB, 28).

Desire's lack of formulaic clarity underlines the ongoing agon that puts writing the desire at stake. This has to be clearly marked. There is the lure of the object of desire, dangerous and obscure. The play of writing does not pit presence (or the conservation of presence) against the "ancient fear." Blanchot would add that it isn't done in the present, to make present or present itself—as though a presentation—less does it represent—as though transcription were representation. The play has an inherent subtlety. Its pivot is the return of the power to return, another Nietzschean twist, an anterior recommencement that can play with the multiple presupposed by (eternal) return. The rewrite, therefore, precedes the writing, on occasion suspending it before it happens or actualizing its self-erasure. Rallying the very possibility of beginning again, rewriting keeps separate from initiatives of production and claims no writing at all, past, present, or future, as its own. It is neutral in the mode in which it repeats inscriptively what doesn't occur and delimits the writing to a time unmeasured by unity of presence. In this sense, desire to write involves surplus, a relation of excess that is persistently unable to define that of which it is excessive, but nonetheless is repetitive in relation to it.[19] It puts in play a return which has, "far from putting an end to it, marked the exile, the beginning in its rebeginning of the exodus. To come again would be to come to ex-center oneself anew, to wander" (SNB, 33).

What is "first" or archi-writing that remains apart from desire-non-desire? Under the force of *différance*, it must mark and therefore be separate from what marks it; it must be already folded and doubled. Being nothing and at the same time different from it, the mark—wherever the disjunction is read—demands a new rupture, new violence. This is the advent of the human relation, the law, and the neutral voice. Blanchot glosses the "first" writing as the "written Torah" and the second, the "oral Torah." The voicing of "oral Torah" and vocality in general derives from "written Torah," the holy word outside, put in writing there but awaiting a discourse to welcome the neutrality of inaugural inarticulation. Although a repeat of an initial marking of absence, and no less written than "written Torah," "oral Torah" is necessary for conversation and "common legibility," which is to say, grammatical law. "Oral Torah" and writing everywhere preserve the interruption wrought by the initial mark. To the extent that writing preserves a relation (without relation, of the third kind) to "first" writing, the vocation serves by conveying news of the disaster, the neutering of desire. It thereby gains nothing in truth, authenticity, or authority—hyperbolic claims that belong to prelapsarian time. The "first" writing is "otherness itself, a severity and austerity that never grant authority, the burning of a parching breeze, infinitely more rigorous than any law."[20] In relation (without relation, of the third kind) to it, responsibility appears; it "comes as though from an unknown language which we speak only counter to our heart and to life, and unjustifiably" (WD, 26).

Voicing counter to what one feels and how one lives, responsibility has been stripped of its ethical heritage, that with which Levinas might have endowed it. In fact, Levinasian ethics have been turned upside down: "[I]n the relation of *the Other to me*, everything seems to reverse itself" (WD, 19). For Levinas, face to face with an other dispossesses the subject of all power save that of serving as hostage to the other's state of need. "The Other who dominates me in his transcendence is thus the stranger, the widow, and the orphan, to whom I am obligated."[21] Does radical alienation from one's possibilities support a relation or is it simple "inquisitorial persecution"? Replying negatively to the former, Blanchot proposes responsiveness is to the impossible, inarticulatable "first" language as well as to its double, the rupture transitively marked in "second" language. "To *name* the possible, to *respond* to the impossible" (IC, 65). This is no proto-ethics (meta-ethics) since with regard to otherness, no appeal to experience is legitimate—as with the disaster that "always takes place after having taken place, [therefore] there cannot possibly be any experience of it" (WD, 28). In both cases, one is confronted with an *après coup* logic that elevates thought above experience (*Erfahrung*). Praxis must remain an open question. Blanchot says, "I can no longer appeal to any ethics, any experience, any practice whatever—save that of some counter-living, which is to say, an un-practice, or (perhaps) a word of writing" (WD, 26). A counterlife: that would be an ephemeral entry into a time of archetypal fear that destroys utterly the very identity of living without in the least affecting survival. In the advent of that life, responsibility arrives—elsewhere.

Yet sober, the counterlife, life cognizant of the disaster, is not somber or tragic. Disaster, cataclysm, catastrophe, explosion, apocalypse: the chain of violence could be lengthened. Perhaps one meets disastrous traces only within the compass of reading, where the disaster "would liberate us from everything if it could just have a relation with someone; we would know it in light of language and at the twilight of a language with a *gai savoir*" (WD, 5). Recall that forgetting suspends sedimented layers of guilt. A freedom from the accusation of the other (for one's indebtedness) would pursue a light unconcern that the neuter voice anticipates, Blanchotian *ataraxia*. But liberation does not give itself to recognition since a language with its catacombs of meaning withdraws itself as soon as given. It is retained by the excess of signification (the cut or symbolic castration), an inaccessible gift of voice, "the unknown name for that in thought itself which dissuades us from thinking of it, leaving us, through its proximity, alone" (WD, 5). Thus, counterliving breaks from the heaviness of intentional life and as it walks in the valley of ancient fear, remains calm. Under this condition, the one who writes takes in hand an undisclosed infinitude of language and lets it fall immobilized into grammatical law, yet outside: participation without belonging. It is the "un-practice" of responsibility that tracks down the author and traps her in the space left vacant by the withdrawal of meaning.

Could one say that living the counterlife is virtual life? It would be a life that contests the primacy of recognition (ideal or idealized), with its enclosed circle of unity, identity, and the symbolic order. Contestation would then be directed toward the remains of Cartesianism with its determinate structure and concrete experience. No longer posited in a time-space grid, events neither realize a past potentiality nor stay indeterminate in the present. They already have occurred or are yet to arrive—suspended quasi-transcendentally between a priori and a posteriori, simultaneously an immemorial past and future to come. They also would follow, as per Derrida, a logic of heterogeneous auto-supplementarity (the other in the same), as if the second comes first and the first, second. Destinations would predate embarkations, on a model of "the book of life." The "as if," moreover, would signify an unconditional impossibility, stronger than bare counter-conditionality. Since in counterlife, one can respond to such virtuality but not name it, the coming to pass of the future could not be known until after the "cause" shows itself. Without the power of resolute anticipation, experience takes on another meaning.[22]

In the counterlife, the event itself is afflicted with *différance*, that is, marked, and in terms of signification, "The sign represents the present in its absence. It takes the place of the present."[23] The thing of the event—its being what it is—is irretrievably hidden in the self-withdrawal of presence, and the event is otherness itself. The event becomes the "effect of language (*fabula*)."[24] That which calls for responsibility on the writer's part, the event, appears disjunctively and duplicitously. It is itself *or* an apparitional, phantasmic, and spectral, ghost or *revenant*, of itself. The inaccessible interior of the event, now doubled, lures in its concealment because from its hiding place, it announces the one writing to herself. Older than the order of knowledge, it fascinates—the way age does. It quietens the recognition apparatus (Kant's categorials), neutralizing active and passive voices, and dispossessing the attention in its wakeful vigil. In the neuter condition of fascination, the event turns inside out and outside in as it internally accommodates its other, repeatedly substituting the other for itself and vice versa. Infiltrating the reality of life, it produces phantomatic effects that are indistinguishable from the order of things. Which is it, event real or event ghosted?

The counterlife lies at the limit of intentional consciousness, or, put otherwise, it is the limit that enables appropriation, *Jemeingkeit*, the mine-making apparatus of everydayness. Its story iterates the fictional "as if" that confabulates meaning, produces the evental plot, and repetitively substitutes it for the event's unapproachable interior, a kind of literary de-distancing that fails to nullify the relational distance. In life, an event flees from itself, succumbs to the advent of the double, and then subtracts itself from its sameness or self-identity. Meaning-making is the transporting, distributing, and disseminating of fragments of nonidentity that break from the opaque interior space and weave an identity that the event tells of itself. Within the chaotic eddying that is arche-writing or "written Torah," the fragments can be other than words, to wit, syllables or letters or inchoate scratches on rock. The

resurrection or reconstitution of them as (empirical) writing—correspond-
ing to phenomenology's vacant intentionality—their binding and unbinding,
marks the vigil of transcription. The writer depends on "a good ear" that
hears the voice dictated by the vociferation, a voice that can conform to the
quasi-transcendental ledger and, despite the alterity (inaudible, strong accent,
marbles in the mouth), come up with the proper-improper assonance, tempo,
alliteration, spacing, and so forth. Impossible task?

Is the virtual life, the counterlife, in fact a fictive literary life, Anna
Karenina walking across the pages of the novel? Certainly, the virtual is not
opposed to the poles of reality-unreality; that is the distinction of realism.
The counterlife event takes place when describing looks like naming and
naming resembles description, when activity and receptivity are without
distinction, and when the event has already occurred and yet is still to come.
It produces words without events, miraculous poetic happenings that disclose
another aspect of virtuality: the virtual rejects a discrete border between
animate and inanimate, existential and categorial. The evental nature of
the word then emerges in a subject's conscious intentionality so that a word
in its ideality can live and attest to this or that. Recall Thomas who reads
and hears words as events, "giving his substance to them, establishing their
relationships, offering his being to the word 'be'" (TO, 68). If ontological
privilege is (poetically) transferable to the signifier, then virtual life depends
on an acuity of listening, taking in the origin of the world in the world. At
this point, Blanchot's conversants put it thus:

—And this goes for the pure movement of writing.

—And with what clarity and in what a simple manner the voice
offers itself to the one who holds himself or herself with the
space of such a book, ready to hear; how distinct the rumor is
in the indistinct. Reduced to the essential, but rejecting only
words that are useless to listening, with a simplicity that at times
divides and redoubles itself, the voice speaks eternally. (IC, 329)

At another stage, the counterlife (but not counterfeit!) derives from
Blanchot's deregistering Husserl's thinking on intentionality. The intentionality thesis posits a vector from consciousness toward the event it illuminates. The light of consciousness discloses the being delivered over to it and
lets it be perceived as such. But if the event is not irreducibly conscious,
if it maintains an interiority immune to worldly perception, then by inversion it is capable of a perception too. As seen, the two directednesses do
not intersect and are not symmetrical. The outcome is the skewing of the
gaze (toward events, toward itself) of consciousness; it is always warped,

bifurcated, and indirect. It comes up short in detecting the formless nonidentity that forbids recognition; it cannot breach the "protective membrane."

On Imaging

The axis of inquiry of Blanchot is the imaginary. In the disbanding of the event's cognitive delimitation together with the bracketing of the phenomenological correlation, the nimbus of virtuality makes an appearance. The event guards the hidden, inaccessible secret, the ideal transparency, behind designation, what one does not desire to name or desire to not name, to honor concealment because one would mourn the name. To call the event by its definite description is to linger on the edge of night, between time (the *entre-temps*) and time ("vulgar") and to invite dissimulation of it or of some event other than the one named. The event takes on the spirit of a haunt that inserts itself inappropriately into disparate situations and takes one by surprise when made object of its imperceptible perception (gaze, hearing). Not only one but a multiple, an "inoperative" community of individuals socially linked by the event's impersonal concern; the Facebook of the thing. Concomitantly, the event's perceptual act is not recognizable because it does not cross paths with one's own and cannot be reassembled.

When discursive language and the symbolic order are disqualified from display of reality, Blanchot turns to the image. Each image relies on the entire imaginary field to show itself, and shows itself unmediated. The last fact is obvious since mediation is a unique and rightful power of language. In the reserve of mediation is death and deception: it replaces a living entity with a lifeless signifier. By contrast, the image is straightforward and direct, even in deception. But it is hard to read.[25] It borders on oracular and messianic signification and tends to put forward a scriptural voice. In its distance from the symbolic order that draws its *ergon* from negation, the imaginary founds itself on eros, erotic libidinousness. Eros speaks in images and at an early stage of philosophy called forth some of Plato's finest. All images are indebted to erotic backing and draw currency from the reserve of life-force. What flashes up is the relation with death, the excess that does not survive. The erotic itself inhabits a night "alongside of the night as anonymous rustling of the *il y a*" and suffers an affinity, even a confusion, with that other night.[26] In the erotic is radical equivocation. As Levinas locates it, exhibition (exorbitant disclosure) clashes with clandestinity, to yield profanation. Meaning-making, *Sinngebung*, is made a travesty as it is displaced from the straightforwardness of discourse; "[W]hat it discovers does not present itself as *signification* and illuminates no horizon."[27] Which is to say, the erotic does not partake of but is parasitic on the signifier-signified relation as well as linguisticality in general. Hence, Blanchot can note it by a "movement outside the true" (SL, 77).

The relation of the image with death is foremost. A cadaver, a life-less body, a human body depleted of its animating life, sets the stage for that interplay. Death leaves behind an imaginary form that fascinates more than the original in the way it haunts: not only the original—rather, the rest of the world left behind. Blanchot notes that "someone who has just died is first of all very close to the condition of a thing," but the thing's condition, being essentially hidden, exerts an uncanny, strange, displaced influence (SL, 257). What has left the mortal remains does not deposit a mirror image or a supplement that would imperil the former life with replacement or substitution. The mortal remains—that must include us as living remnants—then holds the fascination of an image. As the cadaver draws vision outside the visible world to where vision is no longer empow-ered by intentionality, toward a remainder that is enjoyable, it meets lapses unto utter passivity, understood as a receptivity beyond measure. Then, it is the plaything of a magnetism that overrides local desires in its extravagant hunger for contact. The force that makes the night equivocal is the erotic, the *il y a*, the "primary process" of Freud.

An image is grammatically an image *of*, as if syntax itself were aware of the need for further supplement. What it is *of* would appear to come first, for example, this photograph is an image of my dog. An image of the deceased, the cadaver flees the world of truth and utility to acquire something extraordinary, ungraspable spacing. One could equivocate, with Blanchot, that it is an image of itself (does an image have ipseity?) or it is an image of nothing. To dampen the amplitude of vacillation, its restless trajectory ambles between what the image apparently posits and an abso-lute lack of imposition. Where it lies on the bier is elsewhere to where the cadaver lies. As if it had been dispersed into the surrounds and left behind "an obscure and vain fullness" (SL, 259). What is at work, moreover, in the extreme incomprehensibility of the cadaver's image is a kind of universality. This means two things: that the image seems to obliterate the truth specific to each and every place, affecting a relation to death; and that it indicates the need for the neuter voice to fill the vacuum left by the old words.

When it is said that an image is *of* nothing, to hear the doubled meaning is important. It signifies that since the nothing is absolutely lacking in properties, attributes, and modifications—essentially self-emptying—the appropriative *of* cannot get purchase. Instead, the word inverts to indicate expropriation, a dispossessive movement that absolves it from matters of relation. "Nothing begets nothing." Or: the image is *of* the nothing that matters, on which everything depends (by way of enigma) for being what it is, the "unemployable nothing," *das Nichts*. Then the image assumes the importance of a frame—the *Als Struktur* is disclosed as such—since it images the nothing so as to withdraw it infinitesimally from itself and invite perception to it, and human relation. It does so, moreover, to contest the glory of meaning-making, truth, and utility by means of "a resemblance that has nothing to resemble" (SL, 260). Resemblance as a relation relieved of its terms enframes self-referentiality and is recursively abyssal, yielding *en abîme*. That an image resembles itself sounds tautologous, but its latent heterogeneity shows where the crack to the outside lies.

The irredoubtable doubling—effect of *différance*—displays the image as a self-disruptive and disseminating process in which it retraces itself as other. Its composition is congruent with its decomposition so that as it lovingly embraces its form (visible, audible, gustatory), it releases itself phoenix-like to its creative self-demolition. Unlike a linguistically favored term, the image has no protection against the destabilizing difference responsible for the eternal slippage of the imaginary from phenomenology's grasp. It is condemned to give meaning the slip. The image that makes and unmakes itself in a region opaque to the phenomenological clearing (*Lichtung*) is exhibited, betrayed, thematized, and forsaken by exposition: profaned. The image "itself" (does it possess ipseity?) escapes the more swiftly because, given its quasi-transcendental appearance as a unity, it does not keep its self-identity throughout its infinite self-giving, and the flabby receptivity of the linguistic system that raises itself above the excess cannot endure it. Inverting the statement, the doubling or self-iteration of the image is the quasi-transcendental condition of both possibility and impossibility for meaning.

The phenomenal world is forgetful of the image because the image, rather than inhabiting the *Umwelt*, haunts memory and desire as it withdraws itself from circulation. With the self-retreat, phenomenalization tends to efface what is already *sous rature* by leaving out of account the eccentric operation of the image and reducing the latter to a placeless entity within the world-scheme. Art work—or more specifically writing—retraces how the image loses self-identity and evades recognition, how since the "ancient fear" it has cut itself immemorially free from the world in favor of a superabundant alterity that challenges the opposition of the same to the other. The writer who signs the work while under the spell of idealism, appropriating the image for the sake, say, of copyright, may not be aware how the text itself has etched a countersign that doubles (or splits) her signature, rendering it what it is not.[28] Examining a piece of writing, it remains unclear whether the writer changes the image into her signature or allows the image to (counter)sign for itself—or whether both alternatives simultaneously apply. Furthermore, whenever putting the image in writing encounters the materiality of the process (paper, pencil, keyboard, audible vociferation), the countersignature derails the guidance toward linguistic comprehension that the image would furnish. Mastery and loss of mastery are married (alchemically) to the signature's divisibility, which disfigures appropriation (symbolic castration) by the image's inscription. The image's signature confirms and denies the writer's, and this aporia is definitive of the work of writing. In ambush of Orpheus, that signing eventually turns him in the direction of Eurydice, his loss, and his failure.

Death enters into the acutely sensitive negotiation between image and the work of writing as it labors to retrace and remark the former's self-resemblance (its self-remaking trajectory "from nothing to nothing") that ghosts a free receptivity to the imaginary.[29] Although success may be aided by the repeatability of the image's signature (supplement to the writer's), defeat of a retracing likely stems from both obliviousness to the image's detachment from itself and recalcitrance of the split to be contained and made linear. This is not to be confused with the repetition of a fixed object or abstract entity; the source of confusion being the tours and detours along which the image returns to itself as other while it absconds with the instrument of inscription. Its interchange with writing turns the exterior into a vessel or crypt for her own interiority in that the image brims with a receptivity that overrides the signatory's appropriative tendencies. It may be that the archi-trace of the image foretells the stylistic, literary, and poetic flourishes it is given, but the outcome is never predetermined. Without an impulse to work, the image's opening out or inflating in—its expropriation—makes the event of writing possible. The writer's signature falls into the tomb of text. Since her signature blindly (deafly) replaces a living, breathing presence, now signed as absent, expropriation means the death of death, Blanchot's (or "Blanchot's") "encounter of death with death" (I, 5). As he shows, what occurs is not resurrection or immortality but a living on, a survival of a subject's interiority now encrypted in the writing that absorbs it. It de facto sequences the *fort* and *da* of signing and countersigning wherein the writer moves deeper into virtuality and spectral existence.[30]

What is the scene of writing? The countersignature of the image—its affirmation of the writer's—leaves a place for the one who comes to read the text. The interweaving of the two functions as a reflective surface to mirror the writer's signature back to the reader. Similarly, in linear perspective painting, the spectator "sees" the painter in back of the deceptive screen that acts as the canvas. It is as though the work has expropriated and absorbed the singular event staged by the painter and now projects it willy-nilly to whoever regards it. Only a trace of both artwork and artist remains, in wait to awaken the spectator to the alterity come there to roost. The trace can be said to "figure" the blindness (deafness) on the part of the painter or writer in the signing-countersigning of the image. The blurriness of the figuration repeats the obscure attraction of the indeterminate image, and that inexactitude repeats the liberation from any goal the work might be said to serve: a teleological suspension of the aesthetic. This is the "blessing before the knowing" ordained by the infinite receptivity on the image's part as it takes in the one to whom it is offered, a blessing that is repeated when the reader (viewer) takes in the work that traces it. This is the blessing that guides by "wounding" the blessed and that withdraws the guidance as soon as a knowing mastery recommences.

To speak of the image in this way is to recall its bracketing effect, wholly distinct from the phenomenological *epoche*. Its suspension of spatiality transforms (under the power of *différance*) the spacing between image and percipient. For Husserl, the reduction takes the exteriority of "the things themselves" and puts imposed meanings (drawn from sedimented habits of perception) out of play in order to come to the essence of exteriority, its eidetic signification. The reduction of the image for Blanchot operates otherwise. It does not yield a self-identical object in correlation with a transcendental ego. Among other things, it calls into question Heidegger's reading of the *epoche* in terms of thrown projection (*Entwurf*). Even while resembling itself, the image is nonidentical; it is ecstatic (outside itself) and exterior to the interiority of the subject it absorbs in its beholding. Upon being reduced, the image becomes that against which the subject's perception is thrown (*entgegenwerfen*), in other words, its reflectivity. No longer hidden, the action of the fling is disclosed as that which constitutes the space between without yet belonging to it. The flinging back and forth, image to recipient to image again, summons the work, as the failure Orpheus knew (turning from the look into the nothing beyond the image) is endured.

With respect to the work, the Blanchotian *epoche* puts subjective memory out of play. This does not signal a presencing that allows an impression to disclose an interiority bereft of all guardedness. The suspension instead alludes to the key role of "objective" memory, the remembrance of the exterior, what he calls "forgetfulness without memory . . . To remember forgetfully: again, the outside" (WD, 3). One is drawn to something that has forever evaded the present and provides no purchase on representing it, where representation depends on a system of signs. One is drawn to what takes precedence over and re-members the subject's own memory and welcomes it and the interiority in which it abides—a kind of spacing that permits the storage of specific memory-traces. Self-erasing and -disappearing in present experience, such memory may recall the inaugural "throw" that delivers Dasein's own life over it, the initializing that is covered over (*verdeckt*) by resoluteness of specific projections. It may recall the totality of "throws" that engenders the host of others who belong to the *Mitwelt*, a recollected of the fatedness of the socius, social being.

In another sense, the uncovering of a memory of the exterior—of passivity, submission (*subissement*), and receptivity—remembers a "realm that is so to speak absolute" (SL, 32). Absoluteness of impossibility and absoluteness of law belong to the image insofar as it participates in the immemorial. It is the law that holds charge over the writer's retracing, the violence of which is suffered by the image (already a ruin of "first" violence), the writer, and the material substratum, for instance, paper.[31] The retracing, moreover, names the ruin and collateral damage of the writerly intervention. But the retracing—image transfixed by the work—has no record of the most severe violation: suspension of the *epoche*. Reduction of the reduction is apparent in the disappearance of that which bears the image's inexpressible ordeal, namely, the paper or photoactive monitor screen, that presents what is never present (and never absent) but virtually persists. To put out of play the meaning attributed to the image is to aggravate its hermetic inclination and render it more nonrelational, as if it retreated to its sealed condition (recall Blanchot's mention of Eurydice's "sealed face") (SL, 172). To highlight the alterity is to remember that it does not belong to sense and sensitivity, that it has been in a container inaccessible to perception.

There is a further development in Blanchot's take on thrownness, "a movement that involves infinite degrees" (SL, 261). The putting in writing of the image derives from an indifferent force that the image "throws off," that effects the one writing to "throw" words on a page—no holds barred, to emphasize the risk that what is written might be a "throwaway" and must needs be "thrown out." Is the writer irretrievably tied to or "thrown in" with the image? That the venture remains Heraclitean and aleatory from the onset, as Heidegger writes in *What Are Poets For?* There is, however, a complexity to it. While relation with the image is bound for ruin inasmuch as the image's non-self-identity destines it for dissemination of its effects and wastage of the project—by which the writer "fraily falls" with the image—the image's self-remarking repetition assures a nonarrival at any predetermined end, disallowing any means of accomplishment whatsoever—permitting the writer to fall away from it. The matter of release is aporetic. The aporia is precisely the pivot that Orpheus finds impossible to negotiate as he turns back toward Eurydice and then away from her. He is both thrown in with her (fatefully intertwined) and thrown back to his lot (the day-world, his song).

The aporia indicates a rupture in the ground, a falling through *en abîme*, an abyss. To be precise, the abyssal character is double. Belonging to the "incessant and interminable" past, splitting the present into a now and not-now, the image subtends "vulgar" time, everyday temporality. To put the image in writing, to represent it, encounters the demand of the outside and its terrors of incommensurability: the sublime. To fall into this first abyss is to undergo the deep catharsis of a Sophoclean tragedy. The second belongs to the image itself that rewrites or remarks itself in the process of giving itself back, withdrawing, or executing its own reduction. Although the first abyss disseminates its effects across the phenomenal image, the second is confined to the image and remains exclusively with the imaginary. To fall into it places no demand on the writer's objectification but disappears with each appearance generated by its abyssal iterations. One neither falls into nor out of it. This is true because of the image's infinite exteriority (an excess that is the same as and other than a lack) that hollows out the recipient's interiority, then occupies it as an empty and vain interior that holds nothing inside itself.

The point between falling in with (into) the abyss and falling out with the image is where Narcissus meets impossibility. As the water's reflection plays with his misidentification, substituting its own nonidentity (the concrete figure without figure), and parasitizing his interior with its otherness, he protests and grows impatient. Here the two abysses bypass each other, remain nonintersecting and askew, at the same time that each contributes to the image's misalignment with his representation. Each fall, each lapse into indeterminate being and the pull back from fascination, causes the other to tremble. He suffers frustration and, unable to continue with the reduction that lets the image be image, messes up the throw—his project with the mirror-image—and, addressing it as insufficient, throws something away. That tossing out, as though of a piece of waste, is the pathos of artistic creation. The *punctum* is also apparent in Orpheus's double fall, at "its point of extreme uncertainty" (SL, 174). The inevitable outcome of his contest with impatience discloses how the fall into representation (the throw that gives him his song) must struggle with the falling out with the image (Eurydice lost again) if the work is to appear. The double bind (the exorbitant tension or torsion) does not excuse him from responsibility but renders its discharge impossible. Blanchot would say that in the impossibility "are situated the essence of writing, the snag in the experience, and inspiration's leap" (SL, 176).

It is also true that in Narcissus's or Orpheus's thought of the event of the image, he cannot recognize himself. The image's virtuality, its undelimited volume, correlates the thought with what undoes its identity, and phenomenally the figure becomes disfigured and dispensed to the proper and improper. Thought is unable to glyph the spacing fissure of the world that appears simultaneously in the world and in his interior. In the textual transcription of the thought, the paralysis is counterpart to the fragments, debris, and dendrites, while the text functions as the virtual receptacle of the image. They are re-collected and resynthesized as they are disseminated throughout. Although resynthesis might suggest a gathering of particles unto a single time, the image is recalcitrant to synchrony, partaking of both the temporal and the extratemporal (*entre-temps*). In this way, the "always already" blends with the "not as yet" to make highly uncertain the arrival of the thought at the place of recognition. To be in contact with the image, to (always) cross the threshold one can never cross—to de-distance it—that is the desire of Narcissus and Orpheus. Only in the desert of that desire (or the desirelessness of the holy), pared from attachment to the logos and the world, could he have reproduced the self-remarking image without possessing it or altering it under appropriative demands. Impossible!

For Love of the Beloved

Who loves the beloved and who (what) is the object of the subject's love? As a supplement to the erotic, it is helpful to reconsider the myths of Narcissus and Orpheus—fraternal demigods forever separated—with an eye (ear) toward love. The short answer is, for each, an image. A watery reflection or a "nocturnal obscurity . . . with closed body and sealed face," respectively, animates the passion of the heart (SL, 172). Understood as the remainder of meaning that fails to be taken up by the linguistic cut, that excludes that which is linguistically unsuitable, the excess of the thing that fails to be folded into the world, the waste, the image attracts an impartial, objectless, nonobjectifying love in each. This is because the beloved's resistance—love cannot persuade it to be an object of intentionality—and because the love itself is aimless—insofar as its nonintentional "object" deflects the arrow of consciousness. In imitation of courtly *amor,* such love involves a detached magnetism that wanders without destination (imagine Orpheus's upward path after he loses Eurydice a second time) and without true source. It is nonetheless obsessive and endless, perpetually in denial of the fact that its nonfulfillment and superfluity perpetrate its persistence.

If the subject of love is not a subject, what does the absence of an object of love betoken? But the subject (Orpheus, Narcissus) would resist any claim against its atomic simplicity, sameness, and full presence—it would cling to the onto-theological position of absolute unity. Does not the image of the beloved (Eurydice, Narcissus himself) excite the lover's unitary memory and confirm the entrenched belief in sovereign identity? First of all, the storehouse memory needs to be separated from the spacing that constituting it effaces itself as soon as its effects (specific traces) appear. *Différance* precedes the marks of remembrance the way that the possibility of differential memorization precedes actual retained experience. *Différance* belongs to the "unconscious." That the subject is already separate from and other to itself means in the interiority of the lover, inscriptions made in memory, on the archi-writing itself, are not etched from outside it but are products of the spacing's marking itself. Spacing is "auto-hetero-affective." The lover is same as and yet alien to herself. The glimpse of the abyssal condition won by Orpheus but lost to Narcissus distinguishes the two heroes.

Related and unrelated to himself, "Narcissus" is a name for something whose interior describes a border between death and life, absence and presence, and . . . hate and love. Narcissus both loves and hates himself, the animator, and hates and loves the image so attractive to his eyes, the animated. But the fate of his love depends on the *anima*'s loosening of attachment to the denomination and the thing named. Without release, he remains in denial of his hate-love, ineffectual as a lover, and tied to a death that gnaws at his desire. Everything he wants turns to ashes. Love comes alive on the occasion of the psyche's memory that is *über*-subjective, impersonal, and collective. In the rupture (rapture, *rature*), it celebrates the relation without relation, the nonrelationality of relation, and the attraction to love before falling in love. The subject is recalled to what must be timeless and unavowable, and like that which ties one to the other, "must have no part in any kind of duration" (UC, 32). Furthermore, Narcissus must take care "not to reduce it, not to reconcile it, even by comprehending it, that is, not to seek to consider it as the 'faltering' mode of a still unitary relation" (IC, 68).

To resist reduction to unity, which is to succumb to onto-theological habitude, Narcissus needs to stop resisting that memory that remarks (remembers) itself as other. In part, it is a memory-trace of his mother (the nymph Leiriope), of his birth, and of an originary detachment and connection. The unique etching, cut, or "scar" permits him to remember himself as a single event, though one that is always doubled, repeated, and disseminated over the course of a life. Functioning as a call, it signals consciousness of the immemorial's radical independence and self-remarking, a version of the irreparable wound that he suffered upon birth. To the extent Narcissus refuses it, he imagines himself absolved of the natural order of love, an imagination that conceives him to be a self-sufficient, autonomous source of law. Since refusal is unable to block the originary, destitute, and "maternal" self-tracing, he both allows and rejects (*fort* and *da*) the auto-erotic replacement of his "natural" hetero-eroticism. Besides, the refusal is matched by the memory it would resist. As the canvas resists the pressure of the brush, the immemorial substrate receives and bears what his experience traces in it. By way of a self-maieutic inversion, Narcissus's masturbatory activity then mimetically follows his mother's giving birth to him, the other memory's anteriorly laying down traces of his erotic passion before they occur.[32] The ghostly umbilicus of self-desire, unfolded and stretched to linearity, represents the writing of his story, had he cared to tell.

If Narcissus were able to step out of the story's idealizing frame, then he would see his interiority that bears the scar of the mother, exteriority, and the ruins of the disaster. He would be susceptible to the work of mourning, that which Derrida calls "love."[33] It would direct consciousness to the empty magnetism, impenetrable to eros that circumscribes and then returns to haunt after extinguishing itself in "unrequited" love. It would be to interiorize the consummation that signifies the death of love as well as the memorabilia associated with it, and to attend the *yahrzeit* candle incandescent in its grief. It would grant the mourning its afterlife, its right to survive the denial, recrimination, and repression that keep free of his life, that keep at bay the emptiness disseminated across his passion and prevent an immeasurable absence from expropriating the object of desire. The revamped narcissistic love would welcome the unconscious into which some things fall, wrinkle and furrow it, creating the creases in which consciousness may grow. Its work of mourning would coincide with a celebration of the disaster.

That love is not a single subject (the object, not a unitary object) recalls the Platonic saw that all lovers are suppliants, cognizant of needing to lower themselves before the power whose effects they honor. As a rite, supplication is a dyadic relation, the supplicant and the one being supplicated, "invisible and out of play but present in an almost immediate presence" (IC, 93). For Narcissus (or Orpheus), this would be the deity, Zeus or Aphrodite. Kneeling by the pool, Narcissus retracts his body into a ritual posture to exalt the object of his prayer and signify his beggarly condition. In addition to the worship implied, he indicates both an absolute powerlessness and its claim to another law, a law other than that of the land and one reserved for the disempowered, impoverished stranger. Blanchot cites Aeschylus: that "the law protecting those whom force would crush merges with the law that holds the world in equilibrium and whose symbol is the scales of Zeus" (IC, 94). Subject to the law of the outside, Narcissus in his weakness entreats the god that his ardor be reciprocated. Although fixed in immobility, he is suppliant, literally, "he who comes," that is, yet to come, without home, nomadic, of unknown origin. By law, then, Narcissus's plea, from which the god must not turn, is troubling because one doesn't know where it will lead. That is to say, Narcissus's love expressed in humility's posture is doubled: abundant self-gratification puts in shadow the sacred weakness that separates him from the earthly domain of mete and measure.

The duplicity and separation call the attention to it. As suppliant, Narcissus is aware of the untraversable space between him and the world of light, hope, and justice. There is no guarantee that supplication will be honored. When he speaks (as Ovid has it), the voice enters a middle space or no man's land where nothing is possible or impossible other than the giving of voice. If Zeus were to reply, it would correspond to one of his monikers: *omphaios*, the master of voices—though it could not be certain that it is he who speaks. Voice itself has arranged a space to deliver a shattering blow to end all common measure. It is voice itself that binds in separation. Fervent, forceful, and purified by misfortune, it is voice itself that writes the play in this null place—a drama that could bring joy or the lightning bolt. "Do you love me?" —". . . love me. . . ." Speak or kill.

Such voice tends to sharpen the obscurity of Narcissus's, or the human, situation. It accentuates the hidden divisions of the world, its irreconcilable contraries, affirmations that nullify each other, and demands that are self-negating. It brings together the parties, suppliant and power possessor, to listen to the other, to the otherness of the conversant, as voice echoes to and fro across the hiatus. To be in the human situation is to be afflicted with diversion, the matter of curiosity (*Neugier*) that Heidegger, who follows Augustine's notion of *concupiscentia*, attaches to everydayness.[34] Not surprisingly, the affliction has to do with voice, specifically the impassible distance between speaking to oneself and hearing it, listening to the voice given on mute, the interior voice. The infinite traversal is neglected by Husserl in his famous analysis of the "inner voice," the voice that keeps silence, and which is recovered by Derrida in *Speech and Phenomena*. Husserl reflects on a moment of self-reproach when he hears himself "to himself," "You've gone wrong." He describes the event as auto-affective and exemplary of the perfect correlation of *noema* and *noesis*, the co-origination of subject and object that precludes all exteriority. This inner loop is the founding prescription of transcendental idealism. Once the delay between the vocal enunciating and the auditory comprehension of the enunciation is reinserted, and the opaque inner spatiality of *différance* reaffirmed, the split subject is no longer privy in the same way to inner commentary. Its privileged presence has been subtracted. Narcissus must suffer the opacity of his interior voice as it utters (to whom?) its ardent wishes. He is cut off, by an infinitesimal difference and infinite delay, from understanding what he says he wants and how he entreats the god.

An enlightened Narcissus would recognize that self-address, the soul apparently voicing to itself its own admonition or recommendation, is part of a conversation with the other in him. The double, his companion who stands apart, makes use of the otherness of language and mutely directs itself vociferously at him. What is given voice and so marked must over the course of an interval be decoded—and this way of putting it shows the strict parallel with writing. What is written must be deciphered in reading. That is, the voice put in writing must wait out the interval (short, long) after which the voice reading comes to comprehension, even as guidance has been taken away. The blurred border between inscription and dictation reaffirms the silent spacing necessarily anterior to empirical vocalization, mute, inscriptive, or public. With that *pas au-delà,* in the absent possibility of crossing, the voice that patiently aims at Narcissus, despite his preoccupations, and manages to get across its message. Or does not, since the message is no-message, is nothing, and in this way, the other voice keeps its secret power to derail and limit the legibility. But this is no failure since in breaching interiority, his ear turned toward the muteness (toward which it had always already turned), he finds that alterity aphonically addresses him. His receptivity would be a step toward affirming the law-giving force of the call or recall. It would be a recognition that outside itself, the law is yet more powerful than when it is *eo ipso* the law. "Thoughts that come on doves' feet guide the world," Nietzsche writes. "It is the stillest words that bring on the storm."

Assume Narcissus converses mutely with himself (already a modification of the myth and his tragic lack of self-relation), he would notice that inner discourse introduces a distance from itself. In the lacuna from which his voice longingly whispers is also that of the other's, immune to passion. The recovery of narcissistic voice passes by way of an inaudible, aphonic community. It has reduced the phenomenological reduction that had posited a transcendental I without a stake in the desires and projects of any communard. But the multiple voices cannot be made out *as voices*; they are like the sound the ear finds in a seashell. What it means to enunciate is a kept secret, a jumble of enunciations with amplitudes leveled, interwoven, and made undecipherable to human ears. The multiple is not compelled to give accounts deposited in words yielding the breathtaking expanse of experience. The multiple repeats itself mimetically, but since that voice overflows any divisions within it, its mimesis is internal to itself. Mimesis ceases to be an easy love of copying, effortlessly pressing the "start" button on the Xerox machine or the easy cohort of verification of identities. Strangely, while its facsimile of silence differs from silence by only the least minimal differential, the multitude voice remains indeterminately the same, that is, other. The voice that utters as it withdraws in the very course of giving, gives withdrawingly. Narcissus can't get in touch with it because the voice remains absolutely out of touch with everything, including itself. It has successfully eluded the grasp of self-sameness (indeed, of empirical accident), and in its impurity, embodies the sacred untouchable.

Yet, he can be touched by the voice or something in the voice. It touches unilaterally, in an asymmetrical way that bypasses aural capability. The effect of extending his ear to its omnipresence is to abandon his listening to that which it withdrawingly gives, its asonority. He cannot reach the voice but it reaches toward him, forever short of arriving. Aided by the mediation of the desire to love himself, the voice, however, does touch itself, self-remarking as other, and at the same time preserves its isolation, its remove from a process of coding-decoding. The voice slips between the touching-out of touch or the touching-touched because the two never coincide, recalling the breakup of intentionality and its correlation of *noema* and *noesis*. It plays hide-and-seek (*fort* and *da*)—but, notice, *plays*—with Narcissus's consciousness and although in the agon, it flirts with victory, there is uncertainty which would spell triumph.

In the radical ambiguity of contact—the haptic character of voice in general—Narcissus is at a loss to say whether being touched emotionally is an effect of alterity's vocality or his delusion, or both. The indistinct utterances seem like cosmoses, arrangements packed in relations of extreme tension, not indifferent to their places, that aim at a secret difference. Each arrangement is closed and unique, surrounded by a silence that buffers the dangerous content. The mode of speaking—in archaic tradition—yielded word games, anagrams, riddles, puns, and verbal jugglery: that which was pleasing to the gods. Heraclitus, whose moniker was the Enigmatic, used language in a way that reinvests in voice the power of mystery. Narcissus's being at a loss respects the hidden simple and sacred nature of address. The exterior vocables vociferate within because they have opened the portal to interiority and awakened Narcissus to the contestation of their meaning. That he fails to disambiguate them honors their profundity and leaves intact the linguistic play, for the gods' pleasure.

The effort to decipher the voice that speaks only in silence is misguided until Narcissus acknowledges that he himself is implicated. He is not transcendent to the inscription voiced. He abides anachronistically in the crypt of the incomprehensible text, in the waste material that makes it up since it is composed of the remains, inutile, extra, and valueless. Although in the secret sacred place, its officials prevent him from breaking the seal of the *Sinngebung* and trap him in the precinct then hollow and vacated by the voice. That space is replete with its (counter)signature, affecting the everydayness with *Unheimlichkeit*, and ruining his curiosity. And yet, since the inclusion invites making sense of it, he is detained below in the catacombs of meaning. There he discovers that to objectify the reading, to break into its illegibility, runs into the inverted intentionality of the voiced inscription. It is he who is object of that "meaning" that it would make of him: one under accusation of profanation.

Profanation renders the unreadable voice readable.[35] It attempts to make the shared or communal voice single and singular. Were Narcissus not (by divine decree) immune to self-reading, he would read without reading the audible signature of his own. The voice before him would cock an ear, announce him to himself, watch over the conspiracy of his most secret present, and examine his heart.[36] It would constitute his subjecthood.

His consciousness would be preceded by a kind of conscious comportment that is prior to that of a transcendental ego. Although included in the choral (*khora-l*) multiple, his voice would meet an unwavering vigil of the voice that immemorially defeats the impulse of reading, blocking passage to self-understanding (already denied Narcissus). Subversion (hand in hand with the success) does not, moreover, predicate an external force but one that radiates from a most sacred precinct. It takes aim at the source of animation, the heart, that it has in some sense engendered through its way of circulating in the spacing of *différance* that precedes the constancy of space. The hauntology of voice derives from turning intentionality inside out, making of it a perversion. Narcissus's voice no longer appears before the faculty of intuition where it would be seized and its "naturalistic" inherencies put out of play. Profanation and perversity, inevitabilities for sure, recast this very moment as the nonintersection of two dissymmetrical intentional vectors, one a priori and the other the a posteriori effect of his directedness. What guards itself from manifestation is *that* voice's lapse from Husserlian phenomenological rigor, its "awareness" that interiorly enfolds that of Narcissus, and keeps him prisoner.

The point of lapse, where the specification of the *epoche* breaks down and is perverted by the surge of alterity, is the absented chiasmus where the two intentionalities would intersect but don't. The failed crossing is due to the fact that *that* voice's aim is not a mimetic reproduction of human consciousness. It is not reparable by a higher synthesis or metalevel that would reassemble and integrate each, but instead the two flutter past one another, indecisively back and forth between reality and fiction. If it is produced, the fiction elides the nonencounter, making it as if no rupture had taken place. The mimetics, moreover, do not impute a derivative role to that which the voice aims at Narcissus. Overturning the venerable idealist distinction between a priori and a posteriori, the voicing of exteriority in-forms human consciousness at the origin. It is creative, generative, engendering, recalling that mimetics has dimensions far more profound than that of a carbon copy. In fact, it figures the irritant of desire, relaying to Narcissus the fact that his devotion and stalwartness to the beloved image are inadequate. Its intentionality impels him to cast about for how to commit himself ever more deeply, to embrace it, to assume it to the utmost. All the time he struggles to tear the image from unreadability and the other night, to open his heart's space exclusively to it, to demystify its enigma, to make visible its invisible gaze. It does not work . . . it is unworked in the image's inessential unworkability.

Conclusion

In the moment of writing down what is desired to be put in writing, an originary point is encountered. There where the impulse to write meets its destiny, an event takes place. It may or may not be productively inscriptive. It may or may not produce words on a page or screen. The meeting marks a failed intersection, a kind of counter-encounter: what might have been the chiasmus of the intentionality of the one writing and that of that which she would write. Since the imperceptible arrow of "consciousness" from the thing is necessarily askew from that of the writer, there can be no gathering of revelatory light, no synchrony that holds the two in a single present moment. Yet there is, for Blanchot, "a disclosure that discloses before any *fiat lux*, disclosing the obscure through the detour that is the essence of obscurity" (IC, 31). The vehicle is the voice, the sounding of language, either audibly or inaudibly, that registers the "turn that turns toward that from which it turns away" (ibid.).[1]

The event of writing cannot clarify what it seeks to write or the desire that impels it. That event records the voice given by the night's disseminating its disastrous influence on everyday consciousness. The nonintersection of vectors exerts a strange action on the writer, a kind of release (*déclenchement*) of aim on her part that obliges her conscious endeavor to take form under the care and concern of the object. A space of absence ("*l'espace litteraire*") is offered in which the singularity of inscription, text, and the book takes place. One must not infer, however, that the release, an effect of opacity, comes from the writer's being perceived from the outside. From the deep interior, from the secret heart of the writer—what would most belong to the present—the thing takes her in so that the pulse of perception, the living rhythm, is brought to animation. Otherwise than, yet at no distance from, the one it heeds, that which would inscribe the writing circulates with what writing would inscribe, both in proximity and immune to de-distancing and other weaponry of recognition. The two are separated only by the least minimal difference, *différance*. The noncongruence produces the illusion of the "scene of writing." The "clean miss" defines the non-present in the moment as well as the experience of nonexperience. The illusion is that the writerly voice is absolutely interchangeable with the other vociferation, a position that assumes that the writer exercises sovereign control over the encounter.

The illusion is more felt in reading, a supposed inversion of the writing event. But no. There is a "profound struggle" between reader and writer, not for critical analysis or extraction of meaning, but, "to allow the book to *be*: written—this time all by itself, without the intermediary of the writer, without anyone's writing it" (SL, 193). The reader (you, esteemed reader) reaches back into the text, into its fold, to touch what occludes entry into the pure presence of the act. A free act, the effort relieves the inscription of its heavy anguish and grave sobriety and pares it of the "always formidable experience" that necessarily informs it. Being read, however, the text reads in return, listening to the unspeaking heart of the one reading. Although respectful of holy concealment, the peculiar address of the counter-reading affects the circulation or exchange between it and the reader. Listening to while reading the mute voice of the text, the reader responds to the dephasing of the present by what does not give itself fully to the vocalic intentionality, namely, the object's perverse counterdesire that remarks the desire of her own. *That* desire does not obey laws of the human condition; nor does it imitate the law of the law that governs meaning-giving. Nor is there a metalevel in which discourse might unify, relate, or regulate the two. Nonetheless, in its austerity, the desire of that which propels writing into existence and shapes the human consciousness primarily and (it must be said) irresponsibly gets read. It cannot be said that the writer writes because she is passively written on but that she is passive because in front of an immeasurable force that stuns the writerly impulse and turns it on its pivot, she is charged to give an account of the incommensurable.

That account must be performative and mimetic. Derrida's proposals in *Dissemination* advance a new logic for the case where one mimes nothing, where there is nothing to mime, where nothing is the preferred target of the mime. To inscribe what is desired to be written de-scribes a space of endeavor and neutralization in which the object's voice is a critical component in establishing a work. *That* voice mutely guides the labor, delivering the writer to (and from) her suffering unto a remarkable gestation of her own "self." It precedes and succeeds the impulse that is named desire as well as the split between desire and non-desire and attainment and nonattainment of desire. One could say that it critically figures desire itself, or at least the deficit between an adequate performance and one that misses the mark. *That* voice is not susceptible to compromise and forever recalls the attention to the gap. In the performance of recall, Blanchot wishes to designate a space of betrayal, a double betrayal. The synchrony that once bound together the two vocalities has been obliterated by a joint decision by the voice "from the whirlwind" and that of the writer's desire, both the divine and the human. In the new diachrony, the writer "must become the guardian of this absence, losing neither it nor himself in it" (SL, 274). Time's absence, being's absence, desire's absence: these comprise what is readily called experience, the other experience. They are the very constituents of subjectivity and interiority, the heart's core. If the writer has a vocation, if the writer's voice is called to dictate anything at all by way of a work, it must be to mark the prerogative of the passage in which they give voice to that which she is to inscribe. "Voice is a hidden treasure wanting to be known."

Notes

Introduction

1. Philippe Lacoue-Labarthe adopts a similar premise in his short, percep-
tive article "The Contestation of Death," trans. Philip Anderson, in *The Power of
Contestation*, ed. Kevin Hart and Geoffrey H. Hartman (Baltimore: Johns Hopkins
University Press, 2004), 141–55.

2. Georges Bataille, *Inner Experience*, trans. Leslie Anne Boldt (Albany: State
University of New York Press, 1988), 7.

Chapter 1. Narcissus

1. OB, 35.

2. The reference is to Serge Leclaire's classic study, *A Child Is Being Killed:
On Primary Narcissism and the Death Drive*, trans. Marie-Claude Hays (Stanford:
Stanford University Press, 1998), esp. 1–16.

3. The thought concerns the body of alchemical literature surrounding the
mysterium coniunctionis. For example, see Edward Edinger, *The Mysterium Lectures:
A Journey through C.G. Jung's Mysterium Coniunctionis* (Toronto: Inner City Books,
1995). Also see Stanislas Klossowski de Rola, *Alchemy: The Secret Art* (London:
Thames and Hudson, 1973); and C. G. Jung, *The Visions Seminars*, 2 volumes (Zurich:
Spring Publications, 1976).

4. "The primary narcissistic representation fully deserves to be called *infans*.
It does not and never will speak. Precisely to the extent that one begins to kill it
can one begin to speak" (Leclaire, *A Child*, 10).

5. If he were to succeed in being killed . . . is his repeated failure any more
tragic than Orpheus's single one? Probably not, but it is worth noting that the

multiple operates differently from the singleton. It at least captures the temporal movement that Orpheus's lacks. Poetically announced, the Orphic symbol, the lyre, is eternalized in the stars whereas Narcissus's is the flower whose appearance each springtime announces the annulus of the sun. The figure is implanted in the narrative told each time the child beholds its reflection in the world and seeks to embrace it. It figures the Lacanian mirror-stage.

6. Especially, "Freud's Legacy," in PC, 292–337.

7. Blanchot amplifies this: "[I]t is thus neutral in the decisive sense that it cannot be central, does not create a center, does not speak from out of a center, but, on the contrary, at the limit, would prevent the work from having one; withdrawing from it every privileged point of interest (even afocal), and also not allow it to exist as a completed whole, once and forever achieved" (IC, 386).

8. Furthermore, "[T]here must be a crossing in order for there to be a limit, but only the limit, in as much as uncrossable, summons to cross, affirms the desire (the false step) that has always already, through an unforeseeable movement, crossed the line" (SNB, 24).

9. *Thomas the Obscure* echoes the same thought: "Between this corpse, the same as a living person *but without life*, and this unnamable, the same as a *dead person but without death*, I could not see a single line of kinship" (TO, 96).

10. There is a complex relation between Blanchot's inversion of Heideggerian care (*Sorge*) in insouciance or unconcern and the Stoic imperturbability. The particular nullification of ethical value is in need of an investigation that lies beyond the present study.

11. There is also the refusal of refusal, the double negative. One of the characters of *Awaiting Oblivion* says, "I sometimes have the impression that you recall only so that you can forget: so that you can keep the power of forgetting perceptible. It is rather forgetting that you would like to remember" (AO, 54).

12. Compare the account in SNB: "[S]omething accomplishes itself there, in every absence and by default, which does not accomplish itself, something that would be the 'pace/not/beyond' that is not part of duration, that repeats itself endlessly and that separates us" (SNB, 105).

13. Blanchot is clear on how suicide promises what it cannot deliver: "Dying sometimes gives us (wrongly, no doubt), not the feeling of abandoning ourselves to the disaster, but the feeling that if we were to die, we would escape it. Whence the illusion that suicide liberates (but consciousness of the illusion does not dissipate it or allow us to avoid it)" (WD, 2–3).

14. "To fail without fail: this is a sign of passivity" (WD, 11).

15. Compare: "Transgression transgresses by passion, patience and passivity" (SNB, 119). Also see John Gregg's commanding analysis of transgression in *Maurice Blanchot and the Literature of Transgression* (Princeton, Princeton University Press, 1994), esp. ch. 1.

16. The weakness of the logos is what the narrator of TOW finds when reading words: "And no doubt what they may ask of me has no relation to the idea of writing; it is rather they who want to be inscribed in me as though to allow me to read on myself, as on my gravestone, the word of the end, and it is true that, during these nocturnal moments, I have the feeling of being able to read myself that way,

read in a dangerous way, well beyond myself, to the point where I am no longer there, but someone is there" (TOW, 323).

17. Derrida in *Parages* asks, "Would it signify, once more overlapped in itself, one of those syllables or phonic elements that, before the civilized order of language, on the side of phantasm or drive?" (P, 47).

18. *Vorsicht* in Heidegger belongs to the ontic interpretation of being-in-the-world: "[I]nterpretation is grounded in a *foresight* that 'approaches' what has been taken in fore-having with a definite interpretation in view" (BT, H150).

19. Hence, authenticity, the "proper" stance of Dasein, is a negation of a negative, the emptying of the identifications that constitute being-in-the-world. The kenosis of Dasein is identical with the gesture of transcendence, being.

20. Blanchot writes of the pronoun "I" in this way: "The self is not a self but the same of myself, not some personal, impersonal identity, sure and vacillating, but the law or rule that conventionally assures the ideal identity of terms or notions. The self is therefore an abbreviation that one could call canonical" (SNB, 4).

21. "Being-in-the-world is in itself *tempting*" (BT, 177). Heidegger's view could be fruitfully compared with Freud's attribution of libidinous drives to the ego. In "On Narcissism," he observes, "[T]he auto-erotic instincts are primordial; so there must be something added to auto-eroticism—some new operation in the mind—in order that narcissism may come into being." In *Great Books of the Western World, volume 54 Freud.* (Chicago: Encyclopedia Britannica, 1947), 400.

22. For Freud, this turn institutes a lowered self-regard, an interior dysfunctionality: "Love in itself, in the form of longing and deprivation, lowers the self-regard; whereas to be loved, to have love returned, and to possess the beloved object, exalts it again" (ibid., 410).

23. The other is "neither another self for me, nor another existence, neither a modality or a moment of universal existence, nor a superexistence, a god or a non-god, but rather the unknown in its infinite distance" (IC, 77).

24. BT, 167.

25. As if passage to the outside summoned by "a mysterious command, which came from me, and which is the voice that is always being reborn in me, and it is vigilant too" removes one from truth-conditions altogether. DS, 80.

26. Compare: "This lassitude, this desire is the madness which is never current, but the interval of unreason, the 'he'll have gone mad by tomorrow'—madness which one mustn't use to elevate or to deepen or to lighten thought with it" (WD, 8). Compare: "Madness would thus be a word in perpetual incongruence with itself and interrogative throughout, such that it would put into question its possibility and, through it, the possibility of the language that would admit it, thus would put interrogation itself into question, inasmuch as it belongs to the play of language" (SNB, 45).

27. Compare: "Forgetting, the acquiescence to forgetting in the remembrance that forgets nothing" (AO, 33). Memory's leaving off of the null point then blanks on a forgetting that liberates.

28. The importance of dread as a category for Blanchot, as for Kierkegaard (though differently), needs to be emphasized, for example, "Awareness is dreadful, and yet dread does not depend on awareness. Dread without awareness can indeed

depend on another form of awareness, that which isolates it, this absolute solitude that comes from awareness and traces a circle around it, the loss of awareness that it entails and that does not diminish it, that is, on the contrary always more dreadful, the immobility to which it reduces us because it can only be suffered and never suffered enough in a passivity that cannot even promise us the inertia of a dead thing" (SNB, 114).

29. Recall what Blanchot says in his first essay on Levinas: "[T]he thought that thinks more than it thinks is Desire. Such a desire is not the sublimated form of need, any more than the prelude to love. Need is a lack that awaits fulfillment; need is satisfied. Love wants union. The desire that one might call metaphysical is a desire for what we are not in want of, a desire that cannot be satisfied and that does not desire union with what it desires." He continues: "the very desire for what must remain inaccessible and foreign—a desire of the other as other, a desire that is austere, disinterested, without satisfaction, with nostalgia, unreturned, without return" (IC, 53).

30. *Confessions*, 10:34.

31. Ibid.

32. Ibid., 10:35; compare Heidegger, BT, 171.

33. "Impeded speech that found its equivalent in silent ease, inexorable, leaving room only for the continuous murmur of the river crossing the room between immobile hills. Ease as of a thing already written and nevertheless always still to be written and always not writing itself" (SNB, 82).

34. Which is an invocation of Blanchot's recit of the same title; compare: "It is true that this friend had disappeared. Since when, he could not say; they had for so long been used to speaking to each other from afar, from near, through the rumors of the city, or even through the repetition of an ancient language, always read to give them a place in its game" (SNB, 78).

35. For Blanchot, such a book is identified with the Bible: "The Bible not only offers us the preeminent model of the book, a forever unparalleled example, it also encompasses all books, no matter how alien they are to biblical revelation, knowledge, poetry, prophecy, and proverbs, because it holds in it the spirit of the book" (IC, 427).

36. The journal functions as a safety valve or touchstone for the writer; it "represents the series of reference points that a writer establishes as a way of recognizing himself, when he anticipates the dangerous metamorphosis he is vulnerable to" (SL, 29).

37. Leslie Hill's helpful discussion of the repositioning of presence, the neutralization of its ontological powers (advocated by Heidegger) shows how it is at the heart of Blanchot's refutation of *Being and Time*. See *Maurice Blanchot and Fragmentary Writing: A Change of Epoch* (New York: Continuum, 2012), 142–53.

38. Leclaire, *A Child*, 13.

39. "Everyday man is the most atheist of men" (IC, 245).

40. Levinas, in an early review of Blanchot's work, speaks of a "nomadic memory": "From the depths of sedentary existence a nomadic memory arises. Nomadism is not an approach to the sedentary state. It is an irreducible relation to the earth: a sojourn devoid of *place*" (PN, 136).

41. "For in the everyday we are neither born nor do we die: hence the weight and the enigmatic force of everyday truth" (IC, 245).

42. Derrida notices that "what puts in movement, approaches, gathers together proximity and in proximity, outside it, the far, is *force,* or rather *the difference of force,* the force always different and thus always excess in relation to itself, disproportionate [*demesurante*]" (P, 22). Levinas would add, "Here again forgetting restores diachrony to time. A diachrony with neither pretention nor retention" (PN, 146).

43. "Thus the minute of living on is retained as a minute of truth beyond truth: almost nothing, a suspended moment, a 'start,' the time it takes to take someone's pulse and to turn over the hourglass" (Derrida, P, 146).

44. "That sovereign forgetting that liberates language from its servitude with respect to the structure in which the *said* maintains itself" (PN, 143).

45. Blanchot recalls Hegel in a similar context: "The result was perhaps, absurdly, that the experience which initiates the movement of the dialectic—the experience which none experiences, the experience of death—stopped it right away and that the entire subsequent process retained a sort of memory of this halt, as if of an aporia which always had still to be accounted for" (WD, 68).

46. The narrator of *Awaiting Oblivion* says, "The present that forgetting would make: presence free of any present, with no relation to being, turned away from every possibility and impossibility" (AO, 54).

47. Michel Foucault, *Maurice Blanchot: The Thought from Outside,* in *Foucault/Blanchot,* trans. Jeffrey Mehlman and Brian Massumi (New York: Zone Books, 1990), 34.

48. Derrida, P, 140.

49. BT, xxix.

50. To read *The Genealogy of Morals* as the anterior response to *Being and Time* is to take the ridgepole of the former as a study of repression of memory, i.e., forgetting. One of the characters of *Awaiting Oblivion* says, "Being is yet another word for forgetting" (AO, 35).

51. Compare: "We assume that forgetfulness works in the manner of the negative to restore itself in memory—in a living, revivified memory. This is so. It can be otherwise" (WD, 85).

52. The delirium is connected with the fetishism of things, the surplus value accorded them by the general economy of capital. See Michael Marder, *The Event of the Thing* (Toronto: University of Toronto Press, 2011), ch. 1.

53. Compare: "Forgetfulness designates what is beyond possibility, the unforgettable Other; it indicates that which, past or future, does not circumscribe: patience in its passive mode" (WD, 117). More explicitly, Blanchot defines nonarrival as dying: "Dying (the non-arrival of what comes about), the prohibited mocking the prohibition" (SNB, 95).

54. Blanchot conceives it as "a sort of hidden elaboration *of* the hidden which would keep separate from the manifest and which, identifying itself with this very separation (nonidentity) and maintaining itself as not-manifest, would nevertheless serve nothing but manifestation" (WD, 85).

55. Although the term remains equivocal, Blanchot gives strong support to a sense of forgetting that opens both ways, toward the solid reality of things and

toward the empty indistinct presence into which the world crumbles. As he says, "First to forget. To remember only there where one remembers nothing. To forget: to remember everything as though by way of forgetting. There is a profoundly forgotten point from which every memory radiates. Everything is exalted in memory starting from something forgotten, an infinitesimal detail, a minuscule fissure into which it passes in its entirety. If I must eventually forget, if I must remember you only in forgetting you, if it is said that he who will remember will be profoundly forgotten by himself and by that memory which he will not distinguish from his forgetting, if . . ." (LM, 85–86).

56. Blanchot says little about myth in general: "The Greek myths do not, generally, say anything; they are seductive because of a concealed, oracular wisdom which elicits the infinite process of divining. What we call meaning, or indeed sign, is foreign to them: they signal without signifying; they show or they hide, but they always are clear, for they always speak the transparent mystery, the mystery of transparence" (WD, 126–27).

57. "Myth would seem to be the radicalization of a hypothesis, the hypothesis whereby thought, going right to the limit, has always included what desimplifies, disjoins, and undoes it, what destroys at its strongest point the possibility of its maintaining itself even through fiction narrative (a return to sheer telling)" (WD, 86). But this is only apparent. Myth surreptitiously preserves the line between truth and untruth.

58. " 'There is no explosion except a book.'—Mallarme" (WD, 124).

Chapter 2. The Mirror

1. Autobiography or autothanalogy is Lacoue-Labarthe's hypothesis in "The Contestation of Death." Leslie Hill offers a brief critical aside on the mimetics of the text and how it recites the scores of declensions from Freud's original speculation. Hill, *Maurice Blanchot and Fragmentary Writing* (New York: Continuum, 2012) 333–40.

2. A similar list drawn up for the question mark of the title ("A *recit?*") can be made for *The Madness of the Day*, first published in the journal *Empedocles*.

3. Exclamation: "Nothing dialectical in this '*pas*' " (Derrida, P, 20).

4. The place of Merleau-Ponty as a forbearer to the analysis of vision is brilliantly explored by Leonard Lawlor, *Thinking Through French Philosophy: The Being of the Question* (Bloomington: Indiana University Press, 2003), esp. ch. 3.

5. Yet, the tragedy is ambiguous: "[W]hat Narcissus sees is the essence of the secret: a schism which in fact is no schism, and which would give him a divided self without any I, while also depriving him of all relation to others" (WD, 134).

6. Compare: "Dread puts to sleep with a sleep in which it stays awake to keep us entirely in dread: put to sleep for dread" (SNB, 130). Blanchot's account can be compared with Heidegger's and the salient role of *Angst* in constituting remembrance and sovereignty.

7. "To keep the secret is evidently to tell it as nonsecret, inasmuch as it is not tellable" (WD, 133).

8. The form of superimposition, exemplary of supplementation, is important to Blanchot. Compare the italicized narrative in *The Step Not Beyond*: "On the threshold, coming from the outside perhaps, the two young names like two figures

behind the glass about whom we could not say for sure whether they are inside or outside, since no one, except the two figures, who expect everything from us, could say where we are" (SNB, 100; italics omitted).

9. The errancy Blanchot associates with glass is evident when the protagonist of *The Madness of the Day* has his vision impaired by glass when a madman attacks him. The demand for an account (*recit*) by doctors and the police expresses the narrative need to relate seeing and glass.

10. "I read it also as a new thought of the citation according to the eternal return, the repetition of the *yes* that begins only by doubling itself—yes, yes—by citing itself one more time" (Derrida, P, 14).

11. Insistence without assertion of existence. The neuter "would establish the center of gravity of speech elsewhere, there where speaking would neither affirm being nor need negation in order to suspend the work of being that is ordinarily accomplished in every form of expression" (IC, 387).

12. Lacan's long excursus on "I see myself seeing myself" can be read as an exegesis of Narcissus's position and the identification of the I with consciousness. See "Of the Gaze," in *The Four Fundamental Concepts of Psychoanalysis*, ed. Jacques-Alain Miller, trans. Alan Sheridan (New York: Norton, 1981), 67–122.

13. Blanchot's severest criticism of Levinas focuses on the otherness of the other: "[T]he other becomes rather the Overlord, indeed the Persecutor, he who overwhelms, encumbers, undoes me, he who puts me in his debt no less than he attacks me by making me answer for his crimes" (WD, 19).

14. Levinas, OB, 146. That subjectivity, Levinas continues, "is one absolved from every relationship, every game, literally without a situation, without a dwelling place, expelled from everywhere and from itself, one saying to the other 'I' or 'here I am'" (OB, 146).

15. See Bataille, "From Existentialism to the Primacy of Economy," trans. Jill Robbins, in *Altered Reading: Levinas and Literature* (Chicago: University of Chicago Press, 1999), 155–80.

16. Compare the relation between death and dying: "It is dying, the error of dying without completion, that makes the dead one suspect and death unverifiable, withdrawing from it in advance the benefit of an *event*" (SNB, 93). But also: "Between this corpse, the same as a living person *but without life*, and this unnameable, the same as a *dead person but without death*, I could not see a single line of kinship" (TO, 110).

17. To the extent that written ventriloquism happens, it would need to be added to the list of impersonations.

18. In a Bergsonian moment, Blanchot writes, "Fragmentation is the spacing, the separation effected by a temporalization which can only be understood—fallaciously—as the absence of time" (WD, 60).

19. The idea is found in a late poem of Hölderlin, cited by Blanchot who comments, "the sky in its empty clarity and in this manifest void the face of God's remoteness." Hölderlin: "Is God unknown? Is he open like the sky? I rather believe so" (SL, 176).

20. Blanchot comments on Eckhart's thought: "The beyond is inside us in a way that separates us forever from ourselves, and our nobility rests in this secret that causes us to reject ourselves absolutely in order to find ourselves absolutely" (FP, 26).

21. Compare: "But what responds to the appeal of literary reading is not a door falling or becoming transparent or even becoming a little thinner; rather it is a rougher kind of stone, more tightly sealed, crushing—a vast deluge of stone that shakes the earth and the sky" (SL, 195).

22. See Hans-Jost Frey's careful analysis of reading for Blanchot, "The Last Man and the Reader," in *Yale French Studies* 93: *The Place of Maurice Blanchot*, ed. Thomas Pepper (New Haven: Yale University Press, 1998), 252–79.

23. Kevin Hart's extensive meditation on the "counterspiritual life" makes a similar point. Hart also locates Blanchot's sense of the sacred in "the revelation, consequent upon an ontological attunement, that the distance between being and image is always and already within being itself." *The Dark Gaze: Maurice Blanchot and the Sacred* (Chicago: University of Chicago Press, 2004), 224.

24. Derrida examines the challenge of Kierkegaard's Abraham on Mount Moriah: "[R]esponsibility . . . demands on the one hand an accounting, a general answering-for-oneself with respect to the general and before the generality, hence the idea of substitution, and, on the other hand, uniqueness, absolute singularity, hence nonsubsitution, nonrepetition, silence, and secrecy" (GD, 61).

25. The female character of *Awaiting Oblivion* who as it were dictates the writing says, "In order to hear me, it would not be necessary to hear me, but rather to give me to be heard" (AO, 24).

26. Blanchot continues: "[T]he writer never reads his work. It is, to him, illegible, a secret, before which he does not stay" (SL, 23).

27. Blanchot: "But the language of writing *momentarily*, in the extenuatedness it presupposes—in its repetitive difference, its patient effraction—opens or offers itself in the direction of the other, through very perplexity. It is divided in two that we live-speak, but since the other is always other, we can neither console nor comfort ourselves with the binary choice. And the relation of one to the other ceaselessly comes apart; it undoes every model and every code; it is the nonrelation from which we are not excused" (WD, 79).

28. Heidegger defines the apophatic function as "to let what shows itself be seen from itself, just as it shows itself from itself" (BT, 32, H34).

29. The dream is connected with empiricism built on an uncritical concept of experience (*Erfahrung* or *Erleben*) and its assumption of a transcendental signified.

30. There is this statement: "The self is therefore an abbreviation that one could call canonical, a formula that regulates and, if you like, blesses, in the first person, the pretension of the Same to primary" (SNB, 4). And this: "[I]t is not identity that the Self in myself brings me. This self is merely a formal necessity; it simply serves to allow the infinite relation of Self to Other. Whence the temptation (the sole temptation) to become a subject again, instead of being exposed to subjectivity without any subject, the nudity of dying space" (WD, 53).

31. "I will try in vain to represent him to myself, he who I was not and who, without wanting to began to write, writing (and knowing it then) in such a way that the pure product of doing nothing was introduced into the world and into his world" (SNB, 2).

32. The radical ambiguity in the authorial position does not exclude the possibility of plurality. The voice writing can be at the insistence of a community, even

an "inoperable community." Subjectivity without a subject can be the vociferation of an order of participation in which singularity and individual identity have been effaced.

33. This is another way of saying a watchword of Blanchot's, "To *name* the possible, to *respond* to the impossible" (IC, 65).

34. To bear in mind throughout that "[s]peaking is not seeing," i.e., "Speaking frees thought from the optical imperative that in the Western tradition for thousands of years, has subjugated our approach to things, and induced us to think under the guaranty of light or under the threat of its absence" (IC, 27).

35. Derrida comments on the passage from AO: "[T]hat's *pas* under the name of *forgetting* such as he [Blanchot] uses it, such as it can no longer be thought, thought 'starting from' a thought-of-being. If 'being is yet another word [*nom*] for forgetting' [AO, 35], it names a forgetting of forgetting which it violently places in a crypt" (P, 85).

36. The two interlocutors of *Awaiting Oblivion* exchange on this: "I sometimes have the impression that you remember only so that you can forget; so that you can keep the power of forgetting perceptible. It is rather forgetting that you would like to remember." —"Perhaps. I remember when I am two steps away from forgetting. It is a strange impression" (AO, 14).

37. Recall Levinas's version of synaesthesia, his notion of the "listening eye" that can hear the resonance of the verb *to be* (OB, 370).

38. See note 25.

39. "I say this encounter is terrible, for here there is no longer either measure or limit. . . . One would have to say . . . that man facing man like this has no choice but to speak or to kill" (IC, 60).

40. Derrida notes that "*mimesis* no longer allows itself to be arraigned, to be compelled to give accounts and reasons, to subject itself to a verification of identity within such a frame" (G, 93–94, right).

41. "The event that they forget: the event of forgetting. . . . The ability to forget endlessly in the event that is forgotten" (AO, 77–78).

42. "in the impatience and imprudence of desire which forgets the law: *that is inspiration*" (SL, 173).

Chapter 3. Death as Instance

1. Similarly, inspiration obliterates itself with the gesture by which desire forgets its law. This parallels writing, i.e., "Writing marks and leaves traces but the traces do not depend on the mark and, at the limit, are not in relation to it. The traces do not refer to the moment of the mark, they are without origin, but not without end in the very permanence that seems to perpetuate them" (SNB, 54).

2. OB, 163–64; EE, 65.

3. The full citation from the final footnote of "The Essential Solitude" reads: "[I]n literature, doesn't language itself become entirely image, not a language containing images or putting reality into figures, but its own image, the image of language—and not a language full of imagery—or an imaginary language, a language no one speaks . . ." (SL, 34n).

4. This is one of several important chiasma with Levinas, who sees forgetting as a necessary condition for the ethical. "The forgetting of transcendence is not produced as an accident in a separated being; the possibility of this forgetting is necessary for separation" (TI, 181).

5. Blanchot continues to provide the counterview to Heideggerian resoluteness. Compare "The disaster, depriving us of that refuge which is the thought of death" (WD, 3). Death gives possibility, namely in the gesture of bearing witness to the existence that is mine. Then also, "[I]n death, one can find an illusory refuge: the grave is as far as gravity can pull, it marks the end of the fall; the mortuary is the loophole in the impasse" (WD, 48).

6. Silence lacks the efficaciousness of the *Ruf* of conscience. Compare: "Silence cannot be kept . . . it demands a wait which has nothing to await, a language which presupposing itself as the totality of discourse, would spend itself all at once, disjoin and fragment endlessly" (WD, 29).

7. Thomas S. Davis gives a compelling argument that connects the second or counter voice with Blanchot's vision of the political. See his "Neutral War," in *Clandestine Encounters: Philosophy in the Narratives of Maurice Blanchot*, ed. Kevin Hart (Notre Dame: University of Notre Dame Press, 2010), 304–26.

8. This is one way to make sense of Blanchot's statement: "a language that is also addressed to the shadow of events, not to their reality, because of the fact that the words that express them are not signs, but images, images of words and words in which things become images" (SL, 34n).

9. To clarify the thought: "In the work of mourning, it is not grief that works: grief keeps watch" (WD, 51).

10. If the "death of death" is conceived as freeing an attention fixed by anticipatory resoluteness, then the labile and fractious attentiveness can be dedicated to the event of writing. Leslie Hill comes to a similar conclusion in his extensive argument: "[T]he fragmentary is inseparable from an affirmative attention to the singular event of its own writing." Hill, *Maurice Blanchot and Fragmentary Writing* (New York: Continuum, 2012) 124.

11. The way Elrond reads Elven moonscript in Rivendell in *The Hobbit*.

12. Cf. "[T]he possibility of literary fiction haunts so-called truthful, responsible, serious, real testimony as its proper possibility" (D, 72).

13. Kevin Hart emphasizes Blanchot's concept of non-experience or experience without experience; see *The Dark Gaze*, 127. Blanchot writes: "Non-experience is offered in the most common suffering, and first of all in physical suffering" (IC, 44).

14. "A testimony is always given in the first person" (D, 38).

15. Levinas, "Nonintentional consciousness" (EN, 129); he also describes it as a "presence that fears presence, stripped bare of all attributes. A nakedness that is not that of unveiling or the exposure of truth" (ibid.).

16. It is important to bear in mind that *bezeugen* as a homonym carries the meaning of engendering, being born. To an etymologically sensitive thinker such as Heidegger, the internal semantic connection resonates throughout the later discussion of Dasein and is ultimately the grounds for sanctifying the notion of conscience (*Gewissen*).

17. "no one/testifies for the/witness."

18. BT, 272; H, 284–85.

19. Derrida notes, "The 'without' in the 'X without X' signifies this spectral necessity, which overflows the opposition between reality and fiction. This spectral necessity . . . allows what does not arrive to arrive, what one believes does not arrive to succeed in arriving Virtually, with a virtuality that can no longer be opposed to actual factuality" (DE, 92).

20. Is this not another passage where lines of Blanchot's thought cross those of Kierkegaard, who writes, "[T]o die means that it is all over, while to die death itself means to live to experience dying. And if one can live to experience this for a single moment, then one lives to experience it forever" (*The Sickness Unto Death*, trans. Alastair Hannay [London: Penguin, 1989], 48)?

21. D, 92.

22. Heidegger, PLT, 60; "Truth is un-truth."

23. For Levinas, relation without relation designates the psychism or self, "thought of as a relation with the unrepresentable. As a relation with a past on the hither side of every present and every representation, not belonging to the order of presence" ("Truth of Disclosure and Truth of Testimony," in BPW, 101).

24. This action of the magical is essential to Blanchot's understanding of linguisticality and underlies the broad discussion of resemblance, image, and the imaginary. Here, he says "what makes the 'miracle' of reading—which perhaps enlightens us concerning the meaning of all thaumaturgy" (SL, 195).

25. While it may be true that writing cannot be radically separate from reading, the one who reads can affirm without enduring the torment of putting the work in writing. Blanchot appears to hold the view of total distinctness between writing and reading, though John Gregg in *Maurice Blanchot and the Literature of Transgression* (Princeton: Princeton University Press, 1994) argues that he himself violates it. Of keener interest is Hans-Jost Frey's assertion that the difficult read of a Blanchot text stems from the absence of hidden meanings. Such meanings typically present an obstacle to the reader, requiring her to think critically, analyze, and interpolate to get to the bottom of things. That there are no concealments itself then becomes the obstacle to the habituated mode of reading the text. See Frey, "The Last Man and the Reader," 252–79.

26. Yet nonviolence is impossible inasmuch as language (as Derrida shows) is violence. Compare: "Violence is at work in language, and, more decidedly, in the speech of writing, in as much as language conceals itself from work: this action of concealing itself again belongs to violence" (SNB, 44).

27. The alchemical death of Narcissus that follows his marriage to the image passes through "prime matter," conceived as material purified of coarse properties (that appear to the senses) and returned to an original, refined state. There the substance is able to take on a new form, that of the mortal-immortal being, the "body of Christ." See Edward F. Edinger, op. cit.

28. Hans-Jost Frey makes this point: "Here reading can no longer be conceived as understanding. . . . The will to understand peters out when one is distracted." "The Last Man and the Reader," 263.

29. "[A]nd this transport is the same as the one which lifts the work to being and makes of the welcome the sheer delight whereby the work proclaims itself" (SL, 196).

30. It is important to bear in mind that awakening is the fall to the *il y a*, bare being. Compare: "To awaken his attention: there was nothing to that; he was always awakened to the point that all that seemed to remain of him was the emptiness of a vigilant wait, the distracted absence, nonetheless, of inattention" (SNB, 230).

31. This is Frey's point: "[T]he reader must disregard everything, or see through everything, that establishes the work in the world of the visible, and listen to what, in the work, can only be perceived as an echo of the unmasterable pre-worldly" ("The Last Man and the Reader," 278).

32. To continue the citation: "Mortal inattention to which we are not free— or able—to consent, or even to let ourselves go (to give ourselves—up); the inattentive, intensely attractive, utterly negligent passion which, while the star shines, marks—under a well-disposed sky and upon the earth that sustains us—the push toward, and the access to the eternal Outside" (WD, 55).

33. Thus, chance and luck enter into the writing: "To write is to seek luck, and luck is the search for writing, if it is only luck by the mark that, in advance, invisibly, responds to the line of demarcation—the interval of irregularity where luck-bad luck, game-law, are *separated* by the nil or infinite caesura and at the same time *exchanged*, but without a relation of reciprocity, of symmetry, nor even of a standard" (SNB, 28).

34. Or: "What is God? Unknown, yet rich with particularities is the view which the sky offers of him" (SL, 176).

35. Compare Hent de Vries's acute thought: "The instant of death . . . is also and at once an *instant death*, the death of death, death to death, death without death, a being always already one step beyond death, a 'being,' if one can still say so, that is other than the being-toward-death and other than the being toward the death that is *mine*." De Vries's analysis touches on several of the points of the present study. " '*Lapsus Absolu*': Notes on Maurice Blanchot's *The Instant of My Death*," *Yale French Studies* 93, 30–59; 43.

36. To which is appended "transgression, this lightness of immortal dying," i.e., indifference to the limit or law, imperturbability toward prohibition (SNB, 111).

37. Helene Cixous comes to a more cynical conclusion concerning the evasion of responsibility; see *Reading: The Poetics of Blanchot, Joyce, Kafka, Kleist, Lispector, and Tsvetayeva*, trans. Verena Andermatt Conly (Minneapolis: University of Minnesota Press, 1991), ch. 3, esp. 95–109.

38. The materiality of the gaze, its "imaginary matter," is what Thomas Carl Wall addresses as a key to Blanchot's theory of writing: "Imaginary matter—matter that is its own image and that only appears in poetry (but remains unseen, unobserved unperceived, silent)—is matter *as such*, in its *ipseity* or origin." But it is questionable whether *materia prima* has ipseity. Thomas Carl Wall, *Radical Passivity: Levinas, Blanchot, and Agamben* (Albany: State University of New York Press, 1999), 69.

39. Foucault also notes: "This forgetting, however, should not be confused with the scatteredness of distraction or the slumber of vigilance; it is a wakefulness so alert, so lucid, so new that it is a good-bye to night and a pure opening onto a day to come." *Maurice Blanchot: The Thought from Outside*, 56.

40. Compare: "Dying (the non-arrival of what comes about), the prohibited mocking the prohibition, there where it would be in some way forbidden to die and thus where dying, without ever coming to a resolute act of transgression, would disperse in its indecision (dying being essentially indecisive) the moment infinitely divided by it due to which, if this moment reassembled itself, it would be necessary to die outside the law and always clandestinely" (SNB, 95).

41. *Memoirs for Paul de Man*, rev. ed., trans. Cecile Lindsay, Jonathan Culler, Eduardo Cadava, and Peggy Kamuf (New York: Columbia University Press, 1989), 34. Compare: "[E]ver since psychoanalysis came to mark this discourse, the image commonly used to characterize mourning is that of an interiorization (an idealizing incorporation, introjection, consumption of the other)" (WM, 159).

42. Blanchot notes, "But if so-called subjectivity is the other *in place* of me, it is no more subjective than objective; the other is without interiority. Anonymity is the same, and outside is the thought of the other . . . just as the neutrality and passivity of dying would be his life" (WD, 28).

43. Levinas, "Bad Conscience and the Inexorable," in *Face to Face with Levinas*, ed. Richard A. Cohen (Albany: State University of New York Press, 1986), 39.

44. Compare: "Dread, the subterranean world where waking, sleep, cease to be alternatives, where sleep does not put dread to sleep, where, waking, one awakes from dread to dread: as if dread had its day, had its night, its galaxies, its ends of the world" (SNB, 120).

45. "Power over the imaginary provided that the imaginary be understood as that which evades power" (WD, 9).

Chapter 4. Echo

1. Levinas picks the thought up in his analysis of *The Madness of the Day* when he speaks of "the approach to that writing in its significance without signifiers—that is, in its musicality" (PN, 157).

2. Compare WD, 112: "Let us recall Hölderlin: 'All is rhythm,' he is supposed to have said to Bettina." Then also: "What is rhythm? The danger of rhythm's enigma" (WD, 5).

3. The auditory image is not an inscription of a sonic metaphor ("The bell was a loud clang") but the force of an unsounded vibratory pattern capable of affecting human perception all the while remaining imperceptible.

4. Blanchot: it is "foreign to man, and very low, awakening in him that extreme delight in falling which he cannot satisfy in the normal conditions of his life" (*The Station Hill Blanchot Reader*, "Song of the Sirens," 443). Compare Vivian Liska's luminous observation: "In this entwinement, reality and the imaginary fold in upon each other, undoing their distinction as they head toward a *dehors* that knows neither an interior space nor one that would oppose it." "Literature as Contestation in Blanchot and Adorno," in *The Power of Contestation: Perspectives on Maurice Blanchot*, 89.

5. One could speak of shame, the primary affect, that results from the exposure of a hidden intimacy of the exterior, what one ought not to have heard, what is none of one's business, and what compromises one's status. Compare Blanchot on Kafka on shame, "that shame survives, which is to say, the infinite itself, a mockery of life as life's beyond" (WD, 53).

6. BT, 266. Freud, following Schelling, speaks of the uncanny as something that "ought to have remained . . . secret and hidden but has come to light." Sigmund Freud, *The Project for a Scientific Psychology*, trans. James Strachey, in *The Standard Edition*, vol. 1 (London: Hogarth, 1966), 345.

7. The logic parallels that of the work of mourning. In both cases, the empty place is taken in to make memory (*habitus*, obedience to the law) possible, and with memory, remembrance of the dead (mourning) and speaking of death (language). "Speaking is impossible, but so too would be silence or absence or a refusal to share one's sadness" (WM, 72).

8. Psychoanalytically, it is rooted in Freud's primary process.

9. On viewing the conjunction of the presence and absence of living voice as the alchemical marriage, compare: " 'Which of the two?'—'Neither one nor the other, the other, the other,' as if the neuter spoke only in an echo, meanwhile perpetuating the other by the repetition that difference, always included in the other, even in the form of the bad infinite, calls forth endlessly" (SNB, 77). The neuter as the novelty of being without being.

10. Levinas makes a relevant observation: "The silent world is a world that comes to us from the Other, be he an evil genius. Its equivocation is insinuated in a mockery. Thus silence is not a simple absence of speech; speech lies in the depths of silence like a laughter perfidiously held back" (TI, 91).

11. Gary Peters makes a similar point in his perspicuous essay, "The Rhythm of Alterity: Levinas and Aesthetics," *Radical Philosophy* 82 (March/April 1997): 9–16.

12. *Penguin Freud Library*, vol. 10, 154.

13. *Nachträglichkeit*, the anteriority of the posterior: "The fantasies arise from things *heard* but only understood *later*." Freud, *The Origins of Psychoanalysis*, *Letter to Wilhelm Fliess* (New York: Basic Books, 1977), 196.

14. Ibid., 197–98.

15. More precisely, Freud allows a kind of universal life, where life is attributable to everything including the "so-called inorganic, dead matter . . . deprived of breath." See Derrida, *H.C. for Life, That Is to Say . . .* , trans. Laurent Milesi and Stefan Herbrechter (Stanford: Stanford University Press, 2006), 114.

16. See "[T]he signature becomes effective—performed and performing—not at the moment it apparently takes place, but only later when ears will have managed to receive the message" (EO, 50).

17. See SP, ch. 6, "The Voice that Keeps Silence," 70–87; e.g., "An objective 'worldly' science surely can teach us nothing about the essence of the voice. But the unity of sound and voice, which allows the voice to be produced in the world as pure auto-affection is the sole case to escape the distinction between what is worldly and what is transcendental; by the same token, it makes that distinction possible" (79).

18. The reference is, of course, to Samuel Beckett, *Waiting for Godot* (London: Faber and Faber, 1956).

19. According to Diogenes Laertius, students of Pythagoras, the Acousmatics, were required to listen from behind a curtain to his lectures without seeing him for a probationary period of five years.

20. BT, 264.

21. Compare: "Dying (the non-arrival of what comes about), the prohibited mocking the prohibition there where it would be, in some way, forbidden to die and thus where dying without ever coming to a resolute act of transgression would disperse in its indecision (dying being essentially indecisive) the moment infinitely divided by it due to which, if this moment reassembled itself, it would be necessary to die outside the law and always clandestinely" (SNB, 95).

22. BT, 264.

23. Cf. "The thought of the *everything comes again* thinks time in destroying it, but by this destruction that seems to reduce it to two temporal instances, thinks it as infinite, infinity of rupture or interruption substituting an infinite absence for present eternity" (SNB, 23).

24. In *The Station Hill Blanchot Reader*, 443.

25. This is how Blanchot draws forth the idea of double relation from Bataille: "It is perhaps given to us to 'live' each of the events that is ours by way of a double relation. We live it one time as something we comprehend, grasp, bear, and master . . . we live it another time as something that escapes all employ and all end, and more, as that which escapes our very capacity to undergo it, but whose trial we cannot escape. . . . The experience of non-experience" (IC, 207).

26. He continues: "In this turn that turns toward that from which it turns away, there is an original torsion in which is concentrated the difference whose entanglement every mode of speaking, up to and including dialectic, seeks to slacken, to put to use, to clarify: speech/silence, word/thing, affirmation/negation—all the enigmas that speak behind every language that is spoken live in these" (IC, 31–32).

27. *The Station Hill Blanchot Reader*, 449. Liska has reservations about the reference to immemorial time; "The disruption he [Blanchot] invokes ends up in a spherical time, the most closed and continuous of constructions—an abyss eternally circling around itself" (100).

28. Although Blanchot writes, "the disaster as withdrawal outside the sidereal abode, and as refusal of nature's sacredness," the refusal itself comes impossibility, as an impossibility to refuse keeping the secret of nature (WD, 133; italics omitted). The disaster is the *epoche* that reenacts the sacred, maintains it in another time, tempo, and rhythm, and preserves the originary from incorporation into the logos.

29. Thus Levinas's confusion over the God-word and that of the *il y a*: "The rumbling of the *there is* is the nonsense in which essence turns, and in which thus turns the justice issued out of significance. There is ambiguity of sense and nonsense in being, sense turning into nonsense. It cannot be taken lightly" (OB, 163).

30. Blanchot goes on to say that "Hölderlin conceives profoundly that this absence of the gods is not a purely negative form of relation. That is why it is terrible" (SL, 275).

31. Blanchot remarks, "What would happen if the One could be defeated? How could it be defeated? Perhaps by speaking, by a certain kind of utterance. Such is probably the combat of the disaster" (WD, 140). Here, the enunciating is subvocal, inaudible, and on mute, the way the one writing speaks and is spoken to.

32. "Hölderlin: 'Whence comes, then, among men the sickly desire that there be only the one, and that there be nothing but is part of the one?'" (ibid.).

33. As Blanchot remarks, "*That* is *inspiration*." And asks, "Is inspiration, then, that critical moment when the essence of night becomes the inessential, and the first night's welcoming intimacy becomes the deceptive trap, the *other* night?" (SL, 173).

34. Not the liberation *from* desire, *ataraxia*, but the liberation of desire from its law, from the trajectory that lawfully pursues the object and whose drive lawfully avoids the selfsame object. Such desire is "aimless."

35. About this "glad accident," Blanchot writes, "There hid behind this facility an extreme demand, and . . . the insecurity of the inaccessible, the infinite experience of that which cannot even be sought, a probing of what never is in evidence, the exacting demands of a search which is no search at all and of a presence which is never granted" (SL, 177–78).

36. Which is "an attempt to name the inert immobility of certain states said to be psychotic, the *patior* in passion, servile obedience, the nocturnal receptivity of mystics—dispossession, that is, the self wrested from itself, the detachment whereby one is detached from detachment, or again the fall (neither chosen nor accepted) outside the self" (WD, 15).

Chapter 5. Voice *Eo Ipso*

1. Rene Char: a "realized love of desire that has remained desire" (IC, 47).

2. Cf. Derrida: "There is not narcissism and non-narcissism; there are narcissisms that are more or less comprehensive, generous, open, extended. What is called non-narcissism is but the economy of a much more welcoming, hospitable narcissism, one that is much more open to the experience of the other as other." In *Points . . . Interviews, 1974–1994*, ed. Elisabeth Weber, trans. Peggy Kamuf et al. (Stanford: Stanford University Press, 1995), 199.

3. In his eulogy for Roland Barthes, Derrida notes, "It is indeed necessary . . . to recognize, and this is not a concession, that the *punctum* is not what it is" (WM, 57).

4. Compare Blanchot's citation of Simone Weil: "Desire is impossible" (IC, 47).

5. Could one also say that it is a formula for the desire for experience, the appropriative *Ursprung*, where experience disallows a return to self but heteronomously speaks the other, allowing Narcissus to evade the monotony of inner discourse?

6. Derrida, "Portrait d'un philosophe: Jacques Derrida," in *Philosophie, Philosophie* (Revue des Etudiants de Philosophie Universite Paris VIII, Vincennes a Saint-Denis, 1997): 17. Translated by Pleshette DeArmitt in "The Impossible Incorporation of Narcissus: Mourning and Narcissism in Derrida," *Philosophy Today* 44, no. 1 (Winter 2001): 88.

7. The question of the derivation of Blanchot's unconcern from the Stoic *ataraxia* lies beyond the scope of the present study.

8. The writer "feels an extreme reluctance to relinquish himself in favor of that neutral power, formless, without a destiny, which lies behind everything that is written, and his reluctance and apprehension are revealed by the concern, common to so many authors, to keep what he calls his *Journal*" (SL, 28–29).

9. It is revealing that the double remains submerged in Blanchot's account of Orphic inspiration, as if by sleight of hand the outside had become welcoming and hospitable to the writer's intention, and that to write from the essential solitude is to be bereft of companionship. This is the unfulfilled wish of the narrator of *The One Who Was Standing Apart from Me*, whose feeling toward the other is highly ambivalent.

10. The narrator of *The One Who Was Standing Apart from Me* describes the encounter with the double as "a joyful pleasure, a strange cheerfulness, the impression that this reduplication was not the frame of the memory but the opening of space" (TOW, 271).

11. For instance, the narrator of *The One Who Was Standing Apart from Me* says: "Yes, I recalled his reply, the violence of his repudiation, by which he had apparently tried to break me, but I could not 'take it badly,' I could only acknowledge that he was right, I who alone was still right, and exactly what had happened? Surely this went farther back, surely, when this had been said, something quite different had come to light through this remark, had sought a way out, something older, dreadfully old [*d'effroyablement ancienne*], which had perhaps even taken place at all times, and at all times I was tied to the spot" (TOW, 282).

12. Levinas views it as insomnia: "Its very occurrence consists in an impossibility, an opposition to possibilities of sleep, relaxation, drowsiness, absence" (EE, 62).

13. Compare Agamben's treatment of the halo effect, in *The Coming Community*, trans. Michael Hardt (Minnesota: University of Minnesota Press, 1993), ch. 13. "The halo is this supplement added to perfection—something like the vibration of that which is perfect, the glow at its edges" (54).

14. The interval, where voice passes from one to the other, is paramount. "The power of speaking interrupts itself, and this interruption plans a role . . . so enigmatic that it can be interpreted as bearing the very enigma of language: pause between sentences, pause from one interlocutor to another, and pause of attention, the hearing that doubles the force of locution" (IC, 75).

15. Compare: "What is present in this presence of speech . . . is there beyond reach (of the one who says it as much as the one who hears it). It is between us, it holds itself between, and conversation is approached on the basis of this between-two: an irreducible distance that must be preserved if on relation with the unknown that is speech's unique gift" (IC, 212). God is in the spacing.

16. Blanchot's remarkable words on torture: "This violence, perfected or camouflaged by technique, wants one to speak, wants speech. Which speech? Not the speech of violence—unspeaking, false through and through, logically the only one it can hope to obtain—but a true speech, free and pure of all violence. . . . [A]nd thus it calls again into question the truth of our language understood as dialogue, and of dialogue understood as a space of force exercised without violence and struggling against force" (IC, 43).

17. *Joyful Wisdom*, trans. Thomas Common (New York: Frederick Ungar, 1960), 234.

18. Ibid.

19. Compare: "The attraction of (pure) exteriority—the place where, since the outside 'precedes' any interior, writing does not deposit itself in the manner of

a spiritual or ideal presence subsequently inscribing itself and then leaving a mark, a mark or a sedimentary deposit that would allow one to track it down in order for words to restore it—on the basis of that mark as deficiency—to its ideal presence or ideality, its fullness, its integrity as presence" ("The Absence of the Book," in *The Station Hill Blanchot Reader*, 475–76).

20. Ibid., 483.

21. TI, 215.

22. Derrida: "The event is another name for that which, *in the thing that happens*, we can neither reduce nor deny (or simply deny). It is another name for experience itself, which is always experience of the other." *Ecographies of Television: Filmed Interviews*, with Bernard Stiegler (Oxford: Polity, 2002), 11.

23. Derrida, MP, 9.

24. Derrida, SM, 102.

25. "What fascinates us robs us of our power to give sense. It abandons its 'sensory' nature, abandons the world, draws back from the world, and draws us along" (SL, 32).

26. Levinas, TI, 258.

27. Ibid., 260.

28. Compare Derrida: "*Point of speculum*: here I am blind to my style, deaf to what is most spontaneous in my voice" (MP, 296).

29. Derrida has two thoughts here: First, "What is called poetry or literature, art itself . . . in other words, a certain experience of language, of the mark or of the trait *as such*—is perhaps only an intense familiarity with the ineluctable originarity of the specter." *Sovereignties in Question: The Poetics of Paul Celan*, trans. Thomas Dutoit and Outi Pasanen (New York: Fordham University Press, 2005), 57. Second, death arrives "as soon as the draftsman considers himself, fascinated, fixed on the image, yet disappearing before his own eyes into the abyss" (MB, 68).

30. Derrida notes the sequence as it takes place in painting: "Just as I was about to draw, I no longer *saw* the thing. For it immediately flees, drops out of sight, and almost nothing of it remains; it disappears before my eyes, which in truth no longer perceive anything but the mocking arrogance of this disappearing apparition" (MB, 36). *Pari passu* for other modalities of sense perception.

31. Derrida's thoughts on paper: "Paper is already 'reduced' or 'withdrawn,' 'sidelined.' . . . But can we speak here about paper *itself*, about the 'thing itself' called 'paper'—or only figures for it? Hasn't 'withdrawal' always been the mode of being, the process, the very movement of what we call 'paper'? Isn't the essential feature of paper the withdrawal or sidelining of what is rubbed out and withdraws *beneath* what a so-called support is deemed to back, receive, or welcome?" *Paper Machine*, trans. Tachel Bowlby (Stanford: Stanford University Press, 2005), 50.

32. One could go on and say, with Michael Marder's convincing analysis that the mimetics embody the interchangeability "of writing and masturbation," as Derrida argues in the case of Jean-Jacques Rousseau. See *Of Grammatology*, trans. Gayatri Chakravorty Spivak (Baltimore: The Johns Hopkins University Press, 1974), 78.

33. "A narcissistic melancholy, a memory—in mourning of love itself. How to love anything other than the possibility of ruin?" (MB, 68).

34. BT, 165/H, 171. Blanchot's inversion of Heidegger is to put insouciance forward, that one no longer driven by care and desire finds a light detachment to guide projects.

35. Recall Levinas: "The simultaneity of the clandestine and the exposed precisely defines *profanation.*" He continues with the following observation: "It appears in equivocation. But it is profanation that permits equivocation—essentially erotic—and not the reverse" (TI, 257). This is eros present in Narcissus's entry into the vault of meaning.

36. Compare Derrida, D, 340.

Conclusion

1. Blanchot continues the thought: "[T]here is an original torsion in which is concentrated the difference whose entanglement every mode of speaking, up to and including dialectic, seeks to slacken, to put to use, to clarify: speech/silence, word/thing, affirmation/negation—all the enigmas that speak behind every language that is spoken live in these" (IC, 31–32).

Selected Bibliography

Agamben, Giorgio. *The Coming Community*. Translated by Michael Hardt. Minneapolis: University of Minnesota Press, 1993.

Bataille, Georges. *Inner Experience*. Translated by Stuart Kendall. Albany: State University of New York Press, 2014.

Bruns, Gerald L. *Maurice Blanchot: The Refusal of Philosophy*. Baltimore: The Johns Hopkins University Press, 1997.

Cixous, Helene. *Readings: The Poetics of Blanchot, Joyce, Kafka, Kleist, Lispector, and Tsvetayeva*. Translated by Verena Andermatt Conley. Minneapolis: University of Minnesota Press, 1991.

Critchley, Simon. *Very Little—Almost Nothing*. London: Routledge, 1997.

Dolar, Mladen. *A Voice and Nothing More*. Cambridge: MIT Press, 2006.

Edinger, Edward F. *The Mystery of The Coniuntio: Alchemical Image of Individuation*. Toronto: Inner City Books, 1994.

Foucault, Michel. *Maurice Blanchot: The Thought from Outside* [MB]. In *Foucault/ Blanchot*, translated by Jeffrey Mehlman and Brian Massumi. New York: Zone Books. 1990.

Fynsk, Christopher. *Last Steps: Maurice Blanchot's Exilic Writing*. New York: Fordham University Press, 2013.

Gregg, John. *Maurice Blanchot and the Literature of Transgression*. Princeton: Princeton University Press, 1994.

Haase, Ullrich, and William Large. *Maurice Blanchot*. London: Routledge, 2001.

Hart, Kevin. *The Dark Gaze: Maurice Blanchot and the Sacred*. Chicago: University of Chicago Press, 2004.

———, ed. *Clandestine Encounters: Philosophy in the Narratives of Maurice Blanchot*. Notre Dame: University of Notre Dame Press, 2010.

———, and Geoffrey H. Hartman, eds. *The Power of Contestation: Perspectives on Maurice Blanchot*. Baltimore: The Johns Hopkins University Press, 2004.

Hill, Leslie, *Blanchot: Extreme Contemporary*. London: Routledge, 1997.

———. *Maurice Blanchot and Fragmentary Writing: A Change of Epoch*. New York: Continuum, 2012.

Iyer, Lars. *Blanchot's Vigilance*. London: Palgrave MacMillan, 2005.

———. "The Unbearable Trauma and Witnessing in Blanchot and Levinas." *Janus Head* 6, no. 1 (Pittsburgh: Trivium Publications, 2003): 37–63.

Kofman, Sarah. *Smothered Words*. Translated by Madeleine Dobie. Evanston: Northwestern University Press, 1998.

Lacan, Jacques. *The Four Fundamental Concepts of Psychoanalysis*. Edited by Jacques-Alain Miller. Translated by Alan Sheridan. New York: Norton, 1998.

Lacoue-Labarthe, Philippe. "The Contestation of Death," translated by Philip Anderson. In *The Power of Contestation: Perspectives on Maurice Blanchot*, edited by Kevin Hart and Geoffrey H. Hartman, 141–55. Baltimore: The Johns Hopkins University Press, 2004.

Lavelle, Louis. *The Dilemma of Narcissus*. Translated by William Gairdner. Burdett, NY: Larson, 1993.

Lawlor, Leonard. *Thinking Through French Philosophy: The Being of the Question*. Bloomington: Indiana University Press, 2003.

Leclaire, Serge. *A Child Is Being Killed* [AC]. Translated by Marie-Claude Hays. Stanford: Stanford University Press, 1998.

Marder, Michael. *The Event of the Thing: Derrida's Post-Deconstructive Realism*. Toronto: University of Toronto Press, 2011.

Merleau-Ponty, Maurice. *The Visible and the Invisible*. Translated by Alphonso Lingis. Evanston: Northwestern University Press, 1968.

Nancy, Jean-Luc. *The Inoperative Community* [TIC]. Translated by Peter Connor, Lisa Barbus, Michael Holland, and Simona Sawhney. Minneapolis: University of Minnesota Press, 1991.

Pepper, Thomas, ed. *The Place of Maurice Blanchot: Yale French Studies 93*. New Haven: Yale University Press, 1998.

Robbins, Jill. *Altered Reading: Levinas and Literature*. Chicago: University of Chicago Press, 1999.

Wall, Thomas Carl. *Radical Passivity: Levinas, Blanchot, and Agamben*. Albany: State University of New York Press, 1999.

Index